CEDAR C ⟍ S0-AIM-112 ⟍RARY
ALLE.... .... .u104

Annual Review of Jazz Studies I

CEDAR CREST COLLEGE LIBRARY
ALLENTOWN, PA. 18104

Annual Review of Jazz Studies I

EDITORS
Dan Morgenstern, Charles Nanry, and David A. Cayer

ASSISTANT EDITORS
Edward Berger and Robert M. DeMartino

Transaction Books
New Brunswick (U.S.A.) and London (U.K.)

820216

Copyright © 1982 by Rutgers Institute of Jazz Studies, Rutgers University, Newark, NJ 07102.

All rights reserved under International and Pan-American Copyright Conventions. No part of this book may be reproduced or transmitted in any form or by any means, electronic or mechanical, including photocopy, recording, or any information storage and retrieval system, without prior permission in writing from the publisher. All inquiries should be addressed to Transaction Books, Rutgers—The State University, New Brunswick, New Jersey 08903.

ISBN: 0-87855-896-9 (paper)
Printed in the United States of America

CONTENTS

EDITORIAL BOARD

Richard B. Allen, *Hogan Archive of New Orleans Jazz, Tulane University*

David Nathaniel Baker, *Chairperson of Jazz Studies, Indiana University*

Howard S. Becker, *Sociologist, Northwestern University*

Rudi Blesh, *Author, Lecturer*

D. Russell Connor, *Discographer, Author; Vice President, Federal Reserve Bank of Philadelphia*

R. Serge Denisoff, *Sociologist, Bowling Green State University*

Frank J. Gillis, *Director Emeritus, Archives of Traditional Music, Indiana University*

David Hall, *Head, Rodgers and Hammerstein Archives of Recorded Sound, New York Public Library*

Morris B. Holbrook, *Marketing, Columbia University*

Irving Louis Horowitz, *Sociologist, Rutgers University*

Phillip S. Hughes, *Sociologist, Rutgers University*

Gerald Johoda, *School of Library Science, Florida State University*

Neil Leonard, *Department of American Civilization, University of Pennsylvania*

Don Luck, *Rutgers University Libraries*

Robert J. Menges, *Program Director, Center for the Teaching Professions, Northwestern University*

James Patrick, *Musicologist; Director, Jazz Studies Program, State University of New York at Buffalo*

Richard A. Peterson, *Sociologist, Vanderbilt University*

Larry Ridley, *Contrabassist; Jazz Program, Mason Gross School of the Arts, Rutgers University*

Max Roach, *Percussionist; Music Department, University of Massachusetts*

Gunther Schuller, *Composer, Conductor, Musicologist*

Ernest Smith, *Film Collector, Author*

Edwin A. Steane, *Author*

Robert A. Stebbins, *Head, Department of Sociology, University of Calgary*

William Walling, *English Literature, Rutgers University*

William M. Weinberg, *Advisory Committee, Rutgers Institute of Jazz Studies*

Christopher White, *Contrabassist*

Martin Williams, *Director of Jazz and American Culture Programs, Smithsonian Institution*

Introduction

This is the first volume of *The Annual Review of Jazz Studies,* a venture in scholarship which is new but also part of a tradition. It is a successor publication to the *Journal of Jazz Studies,* which was founded in 1973 and published eleven issues during the decade of the 1970s.

ARJS has succeeded the *Journal* for a number of reasons—reasons of scholarship, broader readership, and, inevitably, economics.

The rapidly growing field of jazz scholarship is producing many studies which are longer than typical journal articles and which sometimes pose special publication problems. The greater length of an annual publication will give *ARJS* the flexibility to publish pieces which would have had to be broken into two or three installments in the *Journal,* and to give each article accepted upon recommendation of our Editorial Board the fullest possible attention. John Edward Hasse's interview with Gunther Schuller in this volume is an example of the greater scope provided by the *Annual Review of Jazz Studies.* Kelso B. Morris's reminiscences of black college jazz bands of a half-century ago has an illustrative photograph, which the *Journal* could not have published.

We hope and believe that an annual paperback volume will bring jazz scholarship to a wider readership. Libraries and individual readers may continue to receive annual volumes of *ARJS,* but we will have the additional potential to reach an enormously broader audience through the book distribution system of our publisher, Transaction Books. In particular, we believe that annual book distribution will make this scholarship available to the enthusiastic audience for jazz outside the United States of America; for many of these potential readers, a serial publication will be far more readily available through book dealers than a scholarly periodical published in the U.S.A.

And the annual schedule will provide economies of scale in production—printing, binding, and mailing—and in promotion. In an era of inflation, these savings are doubly valuable.

We want to express our gratitude to longtime subscribers to the *Journal of Jazz Studies* for their constant support, and we welcome new readers who have purchased this inaugural volume of *ARJS.*

Our hopeful beginning is clouded by one sad note. With the death of Morroe Berger, this publication and the world of jazz scholarship have lost a friend, colleague, and inspiration. Professor Berger's contributions are described elsewhere in this volume in a brief memorial by Dan Morgenstern. Without these contributions, the entire field of jazz scholarship would have been much poorer and publications like this one might well have been impossible.

Dan Morgenstern
Charles Nanry
David A. Cayer

MILTON L. STEWART

GRID NOTATION:
A NOTATION SYSTEM FOR JAZZ TRANSCRIPTION

Jazz is a music in which rhythmic displacement is the rule rather than the exception. The ability to leave and return to the beat without losing contact with it is perhaps the characteristic that gives jazz its swing. Until the advent of free jazz, this swing was an essential element of jazz.

The problem for jazz transcribers has been that the standard (European) notation system was not designed to capture the amount of rhythmic displacement that usually occurs in jazz. Consequently, most transcribers of jazz solos adjust the sounds played by the musicians to fit the regular subdivisions of the European notation system. These adjustments usually result in the interpretation of rhythm to the nearest eighth or sixteenth-note subdivision. The products are often strings of evenly divided notes which are easy to read but represent an omission of some of the most important features of the music—often the features that make the music jazz!

When attempts have been made to indicate the placement of notes before or after the beat, the result has usually been multi-flagged notes and rests, elaborate ties, and other potentially misleading means of rewriting.

A notation system designed properly to represent the rhythmic displacement and other commonly overlooked features of a jazz solo has been developed by this author and University of Michigan Professor Richmond Browne. The new notation system is based on the traditional European one but includes certain alterations and additions intended to make the new system somewhat more flexible and precise.

The new system utilizes various special devices designed to represent graphically some of the means and resources which the jazz musician uses; it is written with the simple note values, but shows, visually, how they occur slightly before or after their normal temporal position. I refer to the new system as grid notation.

THE GRID SYSTEM

The most prominent of these special devices is a grid system which represents the time value of each beat as the distance between any two adjacent, vertical lines on the grid. This system permits a spatial representation of any displacements from, or strict adherence to, the takt (or "stroke") of the performance by the jazz soloist. The solid lines represent the first beat of each measure and the dotted lines represent each successive beat.

Milton Stewart is assistant professor of music at the University of Washington, where he teaches the history of jazz and baroque chamber music, and directs jazz combos. He has a Ph.D. in Musicology (Ethnomusicology) from the University of Michigan. He plays the French horn and jazz piano. © 1978, Milton L. Stewart. All rights reserved.

Ex. 1.

Short, vertical, dotted lines which appear between two full-length vertical lines are used to indicate the mid-point of a beat. These short lines are useful for indicating rhythmic displacement at submetrical levels, e.g., the upbeat of the takt.

The late trumpet artist, Clifford Brown, made considerable use of rhythmic displacement during his solos. Consequently, his recordings provide good examples to test the effectiveness of grid notation.

One such example can be found in measures 1-9 of Brown's second take of "I Can Dream, Can't I?" on Prestige 7761. Brown uses rhythmic displacement in these measures for at least three purposes:

1. To create the aesthetic sensation known as "swing."
2. To draw attention to his *melodic and rhythmic patterns.*
3. To set off *important structural notes.*

Grid notation enables the researcher readily to identify these usages and purposes.

The following example represents a transcription of a portion of this solo using grid notation.

Ex. 2. Clifford Brown, "I Can Dream, Can't I?"

Ex. 2. (cont.)

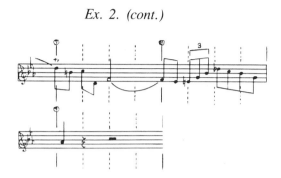

THE CREATION OF SWING

Clifford Brown creates swing in these measures by leaving the takt and returning to it without losing contact with it. This is accomplished by creating alternating areas of rhythmic displacement and conformity with the underlying takt. These areas are never more than two measures apart and are connected by smooth transitions.

The areas of rhythmic displacement and conformity can also be referred to as areas of clash and resolution, respectively. The tendency for each clash to resolve creates a propelling motion forward as well as a swing back and forth when each area of conformity leads to an area of clash.

For example, Brown's notes in measure 1 are all rhythmically displaced behind the takt (see Example 2). With the exception of the first note, all of the notes of measure 2 conform with the underlying takt. The uniform, behind-the-beat, displacement of notes in measure 1 and the smooth return to the takt in measure 2 indicate that Clifford Brown is well aware of where the beat is at all times.

Grid notation is very useful here because it enables the transcriber to show, spatially, where and how far (relatively) notes are displaced from the takt. This system also enables the transcriber to show, visually, when and where areas of rhythmic displacement resolve to areas of rhythmic conformity.

The traditional European notation system, while very useful, offers two possible procedures for transcribing the above mentioned music:

1. To ignore Clifford Brown's rhythmic displacement and place all notes on the nearest beat or after beat.
2. To interpret Clifford Brown's rhythmic displacement as subdivisions of the takt and place dots behind rests and add flags to notes.

The first procedure completely omits an aspect of the music that is perhaps essential for its being jazz. While the second procedure captures Brown's actual rhythmic placement of the notes, it makes a determination of the relative spatial distance between notes and beats difficult to ascertain quickly. Also, the second procedure implies that Brown adheres strictly to the takt at all times and is playing areas of greater and lesser subdivisions rather than areas of clash and resolution.

Grid notation eliminates this latter implication; it simply presents the notes at their relative distances to the beats and afterbeats and leaves it up to the researcher to decide whether Brown was displacing the underlying takt or subdividing it.

The practice of rhythmic displacement being followed by rhythmic conformity continues throughout measures 1-9. For example, after the return to conformity in measure 2, rhythmic displacement takes place in measures 3-4. This is followed by conformity in measure 5, displacement in measure 6, conformity in measures 7-8, and displacement in measure 9.

The rhythmic displacement and conformity in measures 1-9 can be diagramed as follows:

Diagram 1

D = rhythmic displacement
C = rhythmic conformity

measure(s):   1 2 3-4 5 6 7-8 9
              D C D C D C D

The alternation of displacement with conformity during these measures creates swing and propels the music forward to the end of the phrase. Diagram 1 demonstrates how grid notation can enable the researcher to identify displacement or swing patterns that the musician may be using during his performance.

Grid notation can also enable the researcher to identify different *levels* of swing. For example, measures 3-4 in Example 2 represent a D section at the surface level of the entire nine measures. These measures also contain areas of rhythmic conformity and displacement which represent swing at a level below the surface. In measure 3, for example, the a^{b1}-b^{b1}-a^{b1} progression is played in conformity with the takt. The f', however, begins slightly behind the second half of the second beat before it resolves to conformity during the third beat. The following is a displacement diagram of measures 3-4:

Diagram 2

D
C D   C D   C

Combining Diagrams 1 and 2, here is a diagram showing rhythmic displacement and conformity or swing operating, simultaneously, at different levels:

Diagram 3

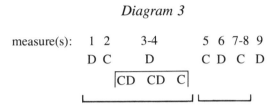

MELODIC AND RHYTHMIC PATTERNS

Grid notation enables the researcher to make a quick observation of how Brown uses rhythmic displacement to draw attention to the repeated pattern found in measures 3-4. He does so by reducing the time between the areas of rhythmic displacement and conformity from one measure to one or two beats.

The repeated pattern which is emphasized by means of rhythmic displacement, in turn, emphasizes a^{b1} or $\hat{4}$ in measures 3-4. [The superscript initial "b" represents the symbol for "flat."] This is the neighbornote prolonging g^1 or $\hat{3}$.

Grid notation enables the researcher to observe how Brown uses rhythmic displacement to emphasize a^{b1} or $\hat{4}$ at measure 9. Here Brown plays a^{b1} as a rhythmically displaced note following an area of rhythmic conformity. Attention is drawn to this note because it comes after the completion of a symmetrical pattern of areas of rhythmic displacement and conformity. The a^{b1} in measure 9 is necessary to complete the phrases but its rhythmic displacement makes it anticlimactic to the completed symmetry which precedes it (see Diagram 3).

OTHER TRANSCRIPTION METHODS

Other transcription methods which would enable the jazz researcher clearly to indicate rhythmic displacement on paper would include the hand graph[1] (Example 3) and electronic devices such as Charles Seeger's Melograph.[2]

Hand-graphing, using lines and squares, enables the researcher clearly to transcribe rhythmic displacement; however, it may make reading and communication to musicians and scholars trained in traditional notation difficult to achieve.

The use of an electronic machine such as the melograph produces graphs which, while more precise than grid notation, pose similar reading and interpretation problems to those of the hand graph.[3] In addition, there is the problem of the availability of such a machine.[4]

Grid notation takes what is perhaps the most important characteristic of the latter two methods—regularity of spacing—and combines it with the familiar Western notation. This combination produces a system which is more effective for jazz transcription than the traditional one and more practical than the hand graph or electronic methods.

The following example is a hand graph of measures 1-2 of Example 2.

Ex. 3.
1 square = 1 eighth note

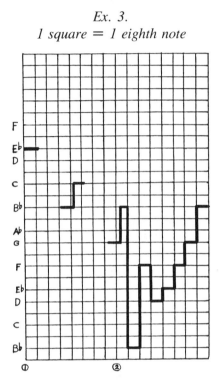

ARTICULATION DEFINITIONS

Other commonly overlooked features, such as those found in a jazz horn solo, include different definitions of articulation. These definitions are often combined to form patterns which are used in the prolongation of steps of the fundamental melodic line of the piece.

The following is a sampling of symbols used to represent articulation definitions in the music of Clifford Brown:

> d—This symbol represents the emphatic, slap-tongue style frequently used by Clifford Brown. Brown used at least five different definitions of the slap-tongue style which can be represented by the superscript symbols: d^1, d^2, d^3, d^4, d^5. These symbols represent increasing levels of intensity for the slap and they range from a legato caress, d^1, to a violent slap, d^5.
>
> s—This symbol is the basis for superscript symbols used to indicate four different kinds of slurring which Brown uses. These symbols are as follows: s^1, s^2, s^3, s^4.

Based on the intensity of the increase in air pressure, there are three levels of accent used by Clifford Brown: $\wedge^1$, a light accent; $\wedge^2$, a medium accent; $\wedge^3$, a heavy accent.

A system of such superscript symbols can be used in conjunction with the grid system to give a clear, visual representation of articulation patterns and the resultant structures. For example, in the chorus shown in Example 2, Clifford Brown combines two definitions of his slap-tonguing into a d^2-d^3 pattern, which is used in the prolongation of $\hat{3}$, the third scale step of the fundamental melodic line. This pattern, which will be labeled tonguing pattern 1, is introduced on b^{b1} and c^2 of measure 1.

Ex. 4. (Tonguing Pattern 1)

Tonguing pattern 1 was no doubt inspired by the d^3- $\wedge$ d^3_i progression in the preceding, measure 32 of chorus one. Brown uses either tonguing pattern 1 or variations of it for each of the next two-note groupings: d^2-d^3 on g^1-b^{b1}, d^2- $\frac{4}{\wedge}^1$ on b^b-f^1, d^1-d^2 on d^1-e^{b1}. When he arrives at the f^1-g^1 or f^1-$\hat{3}$ grouping, however, he reverses pattern 1 to a d^3-d^2 progression. This pattern-reversal structure thwarts the expectation established by the repetitions of tonguing pattern 1 and its variations and draws attention to the unfolding or anstieg of $\hat{3}$ (see appendix).[5]

When a d^3 tonguing is applied to the b^{b1} which follows g^1 in measure 2, it becomes apparent that Brown has actually continued tonguing pattern 1 but has displaced it metrically so that the more intensely tongued note falls on the afterbeat (see appendix).

A study of further uses of tonguing pattern 1 reveals that, in general, when it is applied to descending groupings, the more intensely tongued note falls on the afterbeat (see appendix).

This established practice is thwarted at measure 10 when a d^5 tonguing is applied to g^2 which falls near the second half of the first beat (See appendix). As a result, additional attention is drawn to this note and to the prolongation of $\hat{3}$.

ADDITIONAL APPLICATIONS OF GRID NOTATION

Additional areas where grid notation is likely to be beneficial include the study of rhythmic relationships between a soloist and his accompanying rhythm section or between various instruments involved in collective improvisation. Grid notation should permit the researcher to study what effect, if any, certain accompanying musicians have upon a particular soloist. This author looks forward to these and many other discoveries.

APPENDIX

Reductive Analysis of Chorus 2:
Clifford Brown, "I Can Dream, Can't I?"

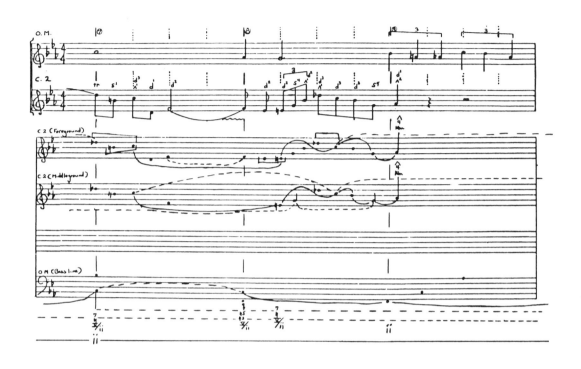

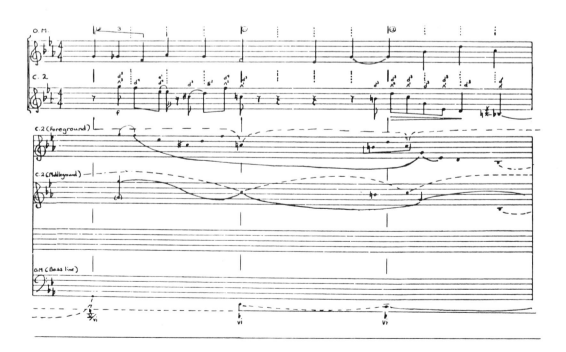

NOTES

1. Bruno Nettl, *Theory and Methodology in Ethnomusicology* (London: The Free Press of Glencoe, Collier-Macmillan Ltd., 1964), p. 121.

2. Ibid., p. 123.

3. Charles Seeger, "Prescriptive and Descriptive Music Writing," *The Musical Quarterly,* 44 (April 1958), Plate III.

4. Charles Seeger, "Toward a Universal Music Sound-Writing for Musicology," *Journal of the International Folk Music Council* 9 (1957): 65-66.

5. The reductive analysis of chorus two is arranged so that corresponding measures of the original melody (O.M.) and the Clifford Brown Chorus (C. 2) are in direct vertical alignment.

ROYAL FAMILY U.S.A.

I. THE KING

Papa Joe.   Joe Oliver.   The King
of New Orleans horn men. Young Louis Armstrong
was proud to carry Papa Joe's horn in parades
so all the winded King had to do was walk
and sweat and miss the piles of horse manure.
Besides parades, Papa Joe played honky-tonks
in Storyville. Pete Lala's. Funky Butt Hall.
Got so good he made it to Chicago.
Played the Plantation. Pretty soon sent for Louis.
(He'd given the kid his first real horn, a York.)

Was royalty also by right of temperament.
Knew all about that stuff called *noblesse oblige:*
The obligation of Papa Joe's nobility
was to be so generous of audience
that he would keep on playing long past the time
his teeth went numb, pressed too long to the mouthpiece;
his lips, held too long in embouchure, split and bled.
(A horn man's life hangs on his lips and teeth.)
But His Royal Highness never counted the choruses.
In "Dippermouth Blues," say, he went the whole gutbucket.
"Play that thing!" His Majesty's sole command.
(Your genuine monarch is no bookkeeper,
doesn't dribble out choruses for profit
nor bank exuberance to buy self-preservation.)
King Oliver was not sensibly frugal with glory.

So the grief began. Used up when he hit New York.
Lip half-shot. Teeth loosened by pyorrhea.
(A horn man's life hangs on his lips and teeth.)
Drifted back South. Small bands with smaller musicians.
Vegetable stand outside Savannah, Georgia.
Janitor's job cleaning up a local bar.
And one last one-night stand, backstage with Louis,
one happy night among his loyal subjects:
Old Lear in high button shoes and box-back coat;
Old Richard Two, still the king of his griefs.
After that, he died. A heart attack . . .?
Depends entirely what you mean by heart.
"Couldn't go no further with grief," Louis said.

II. THE DUKE: A PORTRAIT, CIRCA 1940

The Duke makes his aristocratic entrance . . .
    (ducal coronet a Stetson hat
    creamy café au lait in color, nobly wide of brim,
    doublet a soft-as-silky-flannel shirt
    also café au lait, like the cashmere cape
    draped carelessly from his titled shoulders.
    They say he puts a fortune on his back. What Duke does not?)
        He has this night presided over
        has, indeed, provided
        a musical entertainment
        a masque   a revelry
        sometimes called a University
        Spring Prom
    (he has his own orchestra, of course;
    no princely court should ever be without one.
    Beethoven had Lichnowsky's; Haydn, Esterhazy's.
    Poor Mozart, having none,
    starved and died too soon.)
Time now for midnight supper in the banquet hall . . .
        Before His Grace condescends to sup
        he jots down a musical idea or two:
        something for tomorrow's entertainment?
        some courtly folderol or fiddledeedee?
            Apparently.
        Milord writes music   lightly, swiftly, fluently,
        the way other people write letters.
        Something new for horns in "Echoes of Harlem"?
        New bridge between sections of "Black and Tan Fantasy"?
        He stuffs the score in his pocket carelessly.
        Lots more where that came from.
    (lots more will include "In the Beginning God";
    jazz bursting with worship, performed in churches.
    Also a mystery Pulitzer—why not given?—
    and a seventieth birthday party at the White House)
So let the banquet begin . . .
        The Duke of Ellington lowers his noble person
        to the broken stool
                      in front of the grimy counter
        under the fly-specked lights
                      that reveal the dirty floor
    of the only place in town where he will be served:
        the dingy railroad station restaurant
            in Urbana, Illinois.

III. THE COUNT

The Count sits, gravely happy
  at his black and white keyboard,
grinning with his lips but somber about the eyes.
  His phallic fingers quest among the keys.
  They tinkle merrily, merrily in the treble
And dire away   DOOM DOOM DOOM   : the doom's in the bass.
    (O it's gather ye gather ye roses in the treble
        And KYRIE ELEISON in the bass)
    His musicians cradle in arms,
    crooning or tonguing into
    twisted brass and hollowed wood
caressing or whaling the daylights out of
    hoops of tautened hide
while he himself hovers tenderly, fatherly,
over ivory and ebony in a harp-shaped coffin,
a grin on his face as wide as the eighty-eight,
    and sorrow in his eyes.
    (Yes, it's gather ye, gather ye roses in the treble
        And CHRISTE ELEISON in the doom-doom bass)
    There's no place he'd rather be—
    That's clear as a new-born tear—
  than in this recording studio gaunt as cathedral
    and empty of rosiness as any tomb,
tinkling and dooming his way through "How Long Blues"
grinning and questing his way through "One O'Clock Jump"
    (with its gather ye gather ye roses in the treble
        And KYRIE ELEISON in the bass)
    William, Count Basie, at his piano sits
    Squaring the ancient circle of opposites:
    His treble grin makes merry, nor denies
    The doomsday sadness bass-grieving in his eyes.

Annemarie Ewing is a poet who learned about jazz musicians during her years with the Press Department of the Columbia Broadcasting System in New York. Her novel, *Little Gate,* is about jazz musicians. She later taught English and creative writing at Los Angeles Harbor College.

KELSO MORRIS and his 14 – COLLEGIATE HARLEM ACES

"THE SOUTH'S GREATEST COLLEGIATE DANCE ORCHESTRA"

WILEY COLLEGE, (MARSHALL, TEXAS.

1934 – 1935

Seated in front row, left to right: Walter Duncan, Tanny Busby, E.W. Perry, Kelso Morris, Sheridan Rosborough, LeMon Thompson, Fleming Huff, and Lemuel Talley. *Rear, left to right:* Bert Adams, Joseph McLewis, Edgar Graves, Duke Groner (with baton), Edwin Griffin, Thomas Pratt.

KELSO B. MORRIS

THE WILEY COLLEGIANS: REMINISCENCES OF A BLACK COLLEGE BANDLEADER, 1925-35

Jazz historians continue to make a commendable effort to find individuals still living who can contribute authentic material from their own memories. Relatively little has been done to document college dance orchestras, although some attention has been given to performers whose collegiate origins led to lengthy professional careers in popular music, such as Fred Waring and his Pennsylvanians or Rudy Vallee and his Connecticut Yankees.

This article is the first known to the writer which seeks to give attention, based on personal acquaintances and recollections, to a few of the outstanding jazz and dance bands at the black colleges in the decade 1925-35, with emphasis on the jazz scene at Wiley College in Marshall, Texas, where I was a part of that scene as student, teacher, and, of course, musician.

Wiley was by no means unique in having a fine dance orchestra during that period. From personal experience, I know of fine organizations at other Negro institutions, including Alabama State College, Montgomery, Alabama; Fisk University, Nashville, Tennessee; Morehouse College, Atlanta, Georgia; Prairie View College, Prairie View, Texas; and Wilberforce University, Wilberforce, Ohio. A number of other colleges and universities no doubt had equivalent bands.

OTHER COLLEGE DANCE BANDS

Alabama State College had two dance orchestras during at least part of the 1925-35 decade, the Alabama State Collegians and the Alabama State Revelers. The best known individual musician to emerge from that school was Erskine Hawkins, who led the Alabama State Collegians at the end of that decade. Hawkins, a trumpeter, became a successful bandleader by the end of the 1930s; his version of "Tuxedo Junction" was a hit recording and became his theme.

My own connection with Hawkins was based on a joint venture, which unfortunately did not materialize but which did illustrate the optimism and enthusiasm that characterized the musical life in the black colleges of that era. We tried to arrange a joint tour by the two Collegian bands of Wiley and Alabama State, offering public dances with a "Battle of Music" theme in a series of one-night stands. There was to be a postseason intersectional football game between Wiley and Tuskegee Institute at Tuskegee, and Hawkins and I hoped that a number of cities in the region would know about our orchestras and support such a tour, possibly culminating in a performance linked to the game. The cities we hoped to play included Shreveport, Alexandria, and New Orleans in Louisiana; Little Rock, Arkansas; Mobile and Birmingham in Alabama; and several others.

The project was bigger than we had anticipated. We hoped to take large groups, requiring two buses for at least 60 persons. The bus companies insisted on contracts, and this basic commitment, combined with the need to provide food and lodging for so many performers,

Kelso B. Morris is professor emeritus of chemistry at Howard University in Washington, D.C.

made us hesitate. At least some events would be outdoors, and rain would mean what we then called a "turkey"—a non-paying cancellation due to inclement weather.

Other notable musicians emerged from these black institutions, although, as noted above, their full history has not been adequately studied. Horace Henderson, for example, studied at Atlanta University (as did his brother Fletcher) and then at Wilberforce, where he was graduated in 1926. At Wilberforce he formed and led a band, Horace Henderson's Collegians, which toured in the summers and included Rex Stewart and Benny Carter (neither of whom were Wilberforce students). This group briefly used the campus as a base of operations and then turned professional under the same name after Henderson's graduation. Another example is Ray Nance, who briefly attended Lane College in Jackson, Tennessee, and played and recorded with the College's band, the Rhythm Rascals.

Further research into the period would provide more detail than we now have about other college-educated black musicians of the period and their involvement in student bands (for example, Coleman Hawkins attended Washburn College in Topeka, Kansas). Jimmy Lunceford, who received his bachelor of music degree in 1926 from Fisk, became a high school teacher in Memphis, where he formed a student band. In 1929, three recent Fisk graduates joined him—Willie Smith, Henry Wells, and Edwin Wilcox—who became mainstays of Lunceford's professional band. (Lunceford's own high school experience in Denver is of interest to jazz historians, for his teachers included Wilberforce J. Whiteman, Paul Whiteman's father and an important figure in American musical education.)

For many young musicians of the period, music provided a secondary but important interest en route to other careers. My only personal acquaintance with the Southern Ramblers of Morehouse College in Atlanta, Georgia, was Harold "Dick" Finley. Finley described to me a trip which took the Southern Ramblers to New York to appear at the Savoy Ballroom and the Cotton Club. Years later, he received his doctorate in zoology at the University of Wisconsin and was my colleague at Howard, serving as head of the Zoology Department until just before his death. Similarly, Dr. Walter Booker, retired head of the Department of Pharmacology at Howard's Medical School, was a member of dance orchestras at Prairie View College in Texas. His son, Walter, Jr., is a well-known jazz bassist.

JAZZ AT WILEY COLLEGE

My own experience at Wiley College spanned the 1925-35 period, first as a student and later as a teacher of mathematics and chemistry. During the 1925-30 period, groups were led at various times by LeRoy Taylor (percussion) and Sheridan "Bubba" Rosborough (alto sax). I was a pianist with both men. Then, around 1932, I taught myself to play the trumpet and soon received some featured solos on that instrument, largely to emulate the style of Louis Armstrong, while continuing to concentrate on the piano.

Another student with several instruments was M. J. "Curk" Barrett, a drummer who also excelled on two more "rural" instruments—the musical saw, held between the knees and played with a violin bow, and the old-fashioned whiskey jug used as a wind instrument.

Other performers at Wiley between 1925 and 1930 included Xenophon Brooks, banjo;

Bobbie Carpenter, banjo; Allison "Linx" Jackson, trumpet; Roz Gaines, trombone; Paul Prince, tenor sax; Leon "Isky" Dillard, trumpet; Edwin Griffith, vocalist; Howard Wallace, B-flat tuba; M.B. Buchanan, alto sax; James Williams, trumpet; Jerome "Little Mex" Collins, trumpet; and Nolan H. Anderson, E-flat sousaphone.

The students of that period were well aware of the professional scene, particularly in the Midwest and South. I was conscious, for example, of groups like Walter Page's Blue Devils and the Benny Moten band and of associated performers such as Jimmy Rushing and Count Basie. A more direct contact was with the George E. Lee band from Kansas City, which came to our area in the late 1920s or early 1930s, with the drummer Baby Lovett (originally from Shreveport) and the arranger Jesse Stone. Our drummer-leader, LeRoy Taylor, purchased an arrangement of "Sweet Georgia Brown" from Stone for our orchestra, and Stone personally rehearsed us in that number.

For the two years 1933-35, I led the Wiley Collegians, all excellent readers both of familiar stock tunes (such as "Love in Bloom," "Vilia," and "Stay As Sweet As You Are") and special arrangements (such as "Tiger Rag," "Rose Room," "Wrapp'd in Ermine," "Club Rendezvous," "Hazel Eyes," and "Glory"). In addition, it was fashionable to imitate famous professional bands, and we gained popularity with renditions of Duke Ellington's "Sophisticated Lady" and "Rockin' in Rhythm," Cab Calloway's "Minnie the Moocher," and Earl Hines's theme, "Deep Forest."

The accompanying photograph shows some of the players of that period, with this writer (white suit) as leader, pianist, and sometime trumpeter. Others seated in the front row (left to right) are Walter "Man from Harlem" Duncan, Tanny O. Busby, and E.W. "Don" Perry, trumpets; Sheridan "Bubba" Rosborough, LeMon Thompson, and Fleming "Snooks" Huff, alto saxes (the latter par excellence); and Lemuel Talley, tenor sax. In the back row (left to right) are Bert Adams and Joseph McLewis, trombones; Edgar Graves, percussion; Duke Groner (with baton), vocalist; Edwin C. Griffin, guitar; and Thomas Pratt, bass. Not pictured, but also active in this general period, were George Monroe, percussion, and Nolan H. Anderson, E-flat sousaphone.

In June 1935, the 14-piece group disbanded. Five or six performers joined the Nat Towles band in Omaha, Nebraska. Later, McLewis played for several years with Earl Hines in Chicago. Duke Groner still plays bass with his own sextet in Chicago. (After our departure, William "Wild Bill" Davis, the organist and arranger, was at Wiley for a year or two in the late 1930s.)

THE PERILS OF TOURING

In recalling this long-past era, one can remember incidents which had both humorous and threatening overtones and which reflected the era and the region. On one such occasion, we were engaged to play a dance sponsored by an exclusive social club in a rather rough oil field town in another state. We arrived early enough to obtain an excellent dinner at little cost by taking advantage of a local church's fish fry. The members of the band prepared for a long evening of performing by gorging themselves on such local favorites as fried catfish and sweet potato pie. The dance went well until intermission, when the club's president announced a waltzing contest with a keg of beer as first prize. He asked me, as leader, to play "Over the Waves." I responded, in my best manner, "I am sorry we don't have that number, but we do have some other very beautiful waltzes." A local police officer heard the exchange, saw the president's disappointed look, and said "The man said 'Over the Waves!' " We noted the two large pistols at his hips. One of our alto saxophonists knew the tune well enough to start, and the rest of us became reluctant improvisors.

Most of our memories, however, were of the music and our fellow musicians. We have occasionally learned that others heard and remembered the Wiley Collegians. When Illinois Jacquet and his sextet played at Blues Alley in Washington in January 1979, he recalled for me and members of his group that he and his brother Russell, a trumpeter, had listened to the Wiley band with admiration whenever we played in Houston in the mid-1930s. From such comments, and from the later professional careers of our players (and those of other black college bands), we can conclude that the student jazz bands and dance bands of the 1920s and 1930s merit further attention from jazz historians.

NEIL LEONARD

SOME RELIGIOUS IMPLICATIONS OF
THE LEGACY OF KING OLIVER

Students of religion tend to draw a sharp distinction between the sacred and profane, relative terms distinguishing the holy, pure, and spiritual from the secular, impure, and material. Yet studies of specific societies often reveal that, despite the attempts of believers to keep the sacred and profane apart, the two are usually woven together or intermixed.

Certainly much in the values and behavior we associate with jazz falls somewhere between the sacred and profane. Many of us, however, are accustomed to thinking of jazz primarily in secular terms, mainly because of its associations with forms of sensuality frowned upon by upholders of orthodox religions. But in linking it chiefly, or sometimes exclusively, with the profane, we tend to ignore its important sacred manifestations and influences—for instance, the significant religious aspects of its background on both sides of the Atlantic or the latter-day religious compositions of Duke Ellington, Mary Lou Williams, and John Coltrane. In doing so we neglect instructive keys to the music and its proponents.

This paper deals with one of these keys, certain cultic aspects of the jazz community. It is no secret by now that jazzmen and their supporters have often acted like brethren in a religion of art. The music has had for them a sacred, or quasi-sacred, quality which gives magic and meaning to their lives. Hence, the communal rites at performances and recording sessions; the priestly role and rhetoric of jazz criticism; the musician's sense of occupational calling; the trials and testing rituals which are sometimes part of initiation practices; the various badges of identity; the disdain for impure outsiders and the veneration for certain saint-like figures, whose mysterious and magical powers become mythical, lending authority and security to the jazz life and legitimacy to the music and its innovations. Let me focus mainly on this last point with reference to King Oliver, for it helps to put the other cultic elements in this paragraph in perspective.

MARTYR, CULTURE-HERO, SHAMAN

Oliver was one of the early saints of jazz. Frederic Ramsey, Jr., cast him as a noble martyr, patient and long suffering.[1] Martin Williams saw him as a culture-hero whose story, more pathetic than tragic, suggests the medieval tale of success undone at the hands of capricious fate—fickle public taste, in this instance.[2] And Whitney Balliett notes that Oliver remains enshrined "mysterious, almost primeval."[3]

Neil Leonard, professor of American civilization at the University of Pennsylvania, is the author of *Jazz and the White Americans* and several articles on jazz. This article is based on a paper delivered at a seminar on "The Legacy of King Oliver" sponsored by the Rutgers Institute of Jazz Studies in June 1978 in cooperation with the Newport-New York Jazz Festival and the New Jersey Jazz Society. The seminar was made possible by a grant from the New Jersey Committee for the Humanities, an affiliate of the National Endowment for the Humanities.

If nothing else, Oliver had what Max Weber called charisma, that much-abused term denoting in this context a magic attraction based on the power to evoke ecstasy.[4] I think we can understand Oliver's prophetic attraction, and that of many another artist and entertainer, by seeing him as a vestigial extension of what we call a shaman in some societies and a wizard, medicine man, or other such name elsewhere. A classic account of a shamanic performance appears in Waldemar Bogoras's description of a seance among the Chuckchee of Siberia,[5] which speaks, among other things, of the shaman, after the evening meal, occupying a special master's space near the back wall of a dark, crowded room; using strong tobacco; rhythmically beating a drum; employing ventriloquism and sleight-of-hand tricks, and singing seemingly repetitious songs, some of which are identified primarily with him or are part of a larger repertoire recognized and reacted to by the audience with vocal or physical response. Other shamans use different musical instruments and not uncommonly ingest drugs, spiced water, or aromatic plants which are presumed to help generate the magic "heat" indicative of ecstatic behavior.[6] Whether manifested in emotional excitement, perspiration, or another form, "getting hot" is often seen as evidence of superhuman power, the shaman's ability to evoke ecstasy, or semi-trance states.[7]

ELEMENTS OF SHAMANISM IN OLIVER

There is a strong suggestion of all of this in the picture we have of King Oliver in 1923 in Lincoln Gardens, one of the shrines of jazz mythology. On the evidence of Louis Armstrong, George Wettling, and others, the image emerges of the imposing Oliver on his altar-like bandstand directing a large chaw into the cuspidor, tapping his foot on it to give the beat, then with overflowing imagination blowing his beautiful, poignant tones, or performing a variety of "magic" tricks, e.g., making his cornet resemble a human voice. Visiting musicians gathered around the bandstand are galvanized, and behind them dancers perform Dionysian gyrations under a large, slowly revolving crystal ball, which scatters specks of light around the dark, closely packed hall. After forty-odd minutes of "High Society" or "Dippermouth Blues," the King looks down at one of the young acolytes before him, winks, and says, "Hotter than a forty-five." Whereupon he seeks refreshment or energy at the bucket of heavily sugared water which he keeps on the bandstand and drinks in large quantities.[8]

Needless to say, much in the presentations of Oliver and the shaman differed, in matters of dress, preparation, bodily movement and so forth, but there were broad similarities in their performances. Both worked in the evening; occupied semi-sacred spots reserved for them in close, crowded rooms; used sleight-of-hand tricks and rhythmic music with the help of stimulants to create the "heat" necessary for transcendent experience. The shaman, as Mircea Eliade points out,[9] creates a magic music permitting ascension to the sky to visit the gods or descent into the underworld to consort with the dead, and certainly something of this is true of Oliver (as well as many another artist). His charismatic playing evoked transports to spiritual realms, heights and depths inaccessible through ordinary experience.

We can sense this charisma and transcendence in the words of two of his young admirers who came to worship at the shrine. One of them, Garvin Bushell, recalled:

> We went on the road with Mamie Smith in 1921. When we got to Chicago, Bubber Miley and I went to hear Oliver at the Dreamland every night. It was the first time I'd heard New Orleans Jazz to any advantage and I studied them every night for the entire week we were in town. I was very much impressed with their blues and their sound. The trumpets and clarinets in the East had a better "legitimate" quality, but *their* sound touched you more. It was less cultivated but more impressive of how the people felt. Bubber and I sat there with our mouths open.[10]

There is also the testimony of George Wettling, who was struck by the band at its later engagement at Lincoln Gardens, especially the imposing figure of Oliver in his prime:

> If anyone ever looked good in front of a band it was Joe Oliver. He had a way of standing in front of Louie, Johnny and Baby Dodds, and the other cats, that was too much. I think one of the greatest thrills I ever got was hearing Joe play *Dippermouth Blues*. He and Louis Armstrong had some breaks they played together that I've never heard played since. I don't know how they knew what was coming up next, but they would play those breaks and never miss. Joe would stand there fingering his horn with his right hand and working his mute with his left, and how he would rock the place. Unless you were lucky enough to hear that band in the flesh you can't imagine how they played and what swing they got.[11]

As this implies, not just Oliver, but the entire band with its unbelievable sounds and mysterious techniques, cast a powerful spell which converted a number of future jazzmen.

ARMSTRONG AS DISCIPLE AND NEOPHYTE

Of course, Oliver's greatest disciple was Louis Armstrong, with whom he had a master-neophyte relationship suggesting a shamanic initiation. Eliade has shown that such initiations are often related to those involving acceptance into adulthood or into secret societies. Such rites are not necessarily public formalities. They sometimes occur in private, even in solitude, but in most instances they involve instruction and certification by a recognized master, who often sponsors the candidate. The prospective shaman learns not only ecstatic knowledge through dreams, visions, and trances, but also traditional lore, which includes secret information and techniques as well as mythology.[12]

In the course of his less formal initiation, the jazzman learns some of these same kinds of things as he undergoes endless hours of instruction, practice, tryouts, road trips, cutting sessions and other tests of musicianship and character which prepare him not just for his role as a performer, but as a man and member of the relatively closed jazz community.

We can see much of this in the initiation of Louis Armstrong. Oliver took over his training while they were both still in New Orleans, steering the young protégé through the initial rites and demands of the profession. Earlier young Armstrong, as a member of the "second line," had reverently carried his idol's horn in street parades; now he invented reasons to hear the King whenever possible and intently pursued the lessons Oliver gave him on the cornet. Oliver kidded the youngster about being his "step-father" and helped him find work before going to Chicago in 1918.[13]

Four years later, when Oliver called him North, Armstrong could barely conceal his pride. "I lived for Papa Joe. So his calling for me was the biggest feeling I ever had musically,"[14] he would later say, indicating something of the sacredness of the master-neophyte relationship and the sense of passing a major milestone in his initiation. But it was not over yet. He would spend two more years under Oliver's tutelage in the Creole Jazz Band. "Sitting by him every night," Armstrong recalled of this period, "I *had* to pick up a lot of little tactics he made. . . . I'll never run out of ideas. All I'll ever have to do is think about Joe and always have something to play off."[15] By 1924 it became clear that it was time for Armstrong to set out on his own, and with some trepidation he ended the semisacred tie with his master and went on to become a musical prophet, or more precisely perhaps a mystagogue, in his own right. The lengthy rites of passage were over.

The unofficial, uncodified process which ushered Armstrong into the status of adult jazz-musician was not nearly as formal as what we would expect in a primitive society, yet his initiation retained clear traces of the pattern described by Eliade with its neophyte-master (or godfather) relationship, its public and private shamanic rites, and its rituals of seclusion, study, trial and certification, involving both ecstatic and traditional knowledge. Once again then we find evidence of religiously rooted early practices surviving, in part at least, in our modern, desacralized society.

OLIVER'S DECLINE AND SUFFERING

Before Armstrong departed from the fold, Oliver was known not only as "The King," but as "The World's Greatest Cornet Player," "The Supreme Sultan of Chicago," who attracted crowds in droves.[16] Shortly, however, he would begin his long, painful decline which ended in an unmarked grave in 1938. The physical and mental suffering which came with these hard times has a strong religious implication. Biographical accounts of Oliver's last years make much of the anguish he went through: agents cheating him, endless travelling between one-night stands, broken-down cars, smashed buses, ruined instruments, cancelled jobs, infighting among musicians, continual debts, brushes with the law and with racial bigotry, ragged clothes, wretched food, bedbugs, no beds, meager pay, and then poor health with its frequent colds, pyorrhea which eventually doomed his teeth, and finally the hypertension and heart disease which killed him. But these accounts also emphasize the dignity, grace, and courage with which he faced these overwhelming hardships.[17]

The connection between suffering and magic is well known to students of religion.[18] In some societies masochistic submission to self-imposed pain is thought to enlist magic powers or provide special strength, and a magico-religious force is sometimes ascribed to one who manfully endures suffering at the hands of a cruel fate. As Durkheim demonstrated, it is by the way that a man endures pain that his greatness is best manifested, setting him apart from ordinary mortals and heightening his charismatic attraction.[19]

Accordingly, the tales of Oliver's suffering seem to have enhanced the magic aura about him, and his powers of patient endurance have a peculiar poignancy. We are peculiarly touched by the tale of the band bus breaking down in winter in the middle of nowhere and the bandsmen in desperation burning one of the tires to keep warm, or by accounts of hopeless sidemen like Paul Barnes who wrote:

> I will never forget that moment when I quit the band because things were just going too bad. King was so sad that he had tears in his eyes. He could stand losing anyone but me. I left the band very sad and that was the last time I saw the great king who had shaken the whole United States with his jazz orchestra.[20]

And we are further touched by Oliver's heart-rending letters to his relations telling with stoic resignation how he faced death virtually alone and penniless in Savannah. Here is part of one:

> Dear Sister:
> I open the pool rooms at 9 A.M. and close at twelve midnite. If the money was only ¼ as much as the hours I'd be all set. But I can thank God for what I'm getting. Which I do night after night. I know you will be glad when the winter say goodbye. Now Vick before I go further with my letter I'm going to tell something but don't be alarmed. I've got high blood pressure. Was taking treatment but had to discontinue. My blood was 85 above normal. Now my blood has started again and I am unable to take treatments because it cost $3.00 per treatment and I don't make enough money to continue my treatments. Now it begins to work on my heart. I am weak in my limbs at times and my breath but I can [sic] not asking for money or anything. . . .
> It's not like New York or Chicago here. You've got to go through a lot of red tape to get any kind of treatment from the city here. I may never see New York again in life. . . .
>   Joe[21]

For many admirers of King Oliver, Louis Armstrong seemed to speak a special truth when he said of his master's death, "Most people said it was a heart attack. I think it was a broken heart. Couldn't go no further with grief."[22]

MYTH AND SUPERNATURAL POWERS

Doubtless the magic connected with King Oliver's suffering helped to nourish the myth which grew up around him. We have already noted how he appears variously as a martyr, culture-hero, and saint, and thus, like other mythical figures, he is a composite of several prototypes. Like many other mythical heroes, too, his background and origins remain fuzzy. He was born in 1885 or earlier[23] in or near New Orleans and grew up in that romantic dreamland during the heyday of Buddy Bolden and other giants in the earth. But our knowledge of his early years is sketchy, and even though we know more about his later life, he remains enigmatic. His image fails to focus very clearly.

This is in part because of stories about his supernatural powers both on and off the bandstand. Like the legendary Charlie Parker after him, he was said to have performed prodigious feats of appetite, eating enough for four ordinary men, or downing twelve pies at one sitting on a bet, to the astonishment of unbelieving onlookers. But his superhuman powers had mainly to do with his music. We have numerous tales about the magic of his horn, the result in part of his pioneering use of mutes, buckets, and other devices which allowed him to create various "freak" effects, some involving an uncanny verisimilitude. Trumpeter Mutt Carey recalled how "Joe could make his horn sound like a holy roller meeting,"[24] and he had a routine in which he preached a sermon on his cornet. Louis Armstrong observed that Oliver seemed to "shout" his tunes.[25] For the most part, however, his spell resulted from his inventive powers and the sheer intensity of his sound. Although his phonograph records do not accurately reflect his in-person performances, we have numerous testimonials to their magic. Pianist Richard M. Jones told of the now-famous incident in New Orleans in which

> Freddie Keppard was playin' in a spot across the street and was drawin' all the crowds. I was sittin' at the piano, and Joe Oliver came over to me and commanded in a nervous harsh voice, "Get in B-flat." He didn't even mention a tune, just said, "Get in B-flat." I did, and Joe walked out on the sidewalk, lifted his horn to his lips, and blew the most beautiful stuff I have ever heard. People started pouring out of the other spots along the street to see who was blowing all that horn. Before long, our place was full and Joe came in, smiling, and said, "Now, that ------ won't bother me no more."
>
> From then on, our place was full every night.[26]

Obviously this is the raw material of mythology. Frederic Ramsey, Jr., found an epiphany in it in his marvelous gospel-like chapter on Oliver in *Jazzmen*. Note the tone and rhetoric.

> Jones says something got into Joe one night as he sat quietly in the corner and listened to the musicians who were praising Keppard and Perez. He was infuriated by their tiresome adulation; didn't they know that Joe Oliver could play a cornet, too? So he set forth from his silence, strode to the piano, and said, "Jones, beat it out in B-flat." Jones began to beat, and Joe began to blow. The notes tore out clear as a bell, crisp and clean. He played as he never had before, filling the little dance hall with low, throbbing tones. Jones backed him with a slow, steady beat. With his rhythm behind him, Joe walked straight through the hall, out onto the sidewalk. There was no mistaking what he meant when he pointed his cornet, first toward Pete Lala's, where Keppard played, then directly across the street, to where Perez was working. A few hot blasts brought crowds out of both joints; they saw Joe Oliver on the sidewalk, playing as if he would blow down every house on the street. Soon every rathole and crib down the line was deserted by its patrons, who came running up to Joe, bewitched by his cornet. When the last joint had poured out its crew, he turned around and led the crowd into Aberdeen's, where he walked to the stand, breathless, excited, and opened his mouth wide to let out the big, important words that were boiling in his head. But all he could say was, "There! that'll show 'em!"
>
> After that night they never called him anything but "King" Oliver.[27]

It is not difficult to see how a myth could spring from such an image, and indeed a comparison of the Jones and Ramsey versions provides an interesting study of one stage in the mythopoetic process.

MYTH, REALITY, AND MYSTERY

Needless to say, the myth did not always conform to reality. It was a mixture of fact and fiction, meeting the emotional needs of Oliver's followers. Although generally good natured and generous, Oliver's behavior at times was scarcely saintly. He could be petty, jealous and suspicious, especially as he got older. He resentfully envied not only the successes of Keppard and Perez but of Bunk Johnson too. Clarinetist Buster Bailey, who played with him in the twenties remembered,

> Joe was a jealous guy. He knew what some of the musicians who came to listen to him were after, and so he wouldn't play certain numbers. But they'd come in and sneak in and steal the riffs. They'd write down the solos, steal like mad, and then those ideas would come out on *their* records. When Joe would see them coming, he'd play something different, but they'd steal everything.[28]

Later, as Martin Williams pointed out, Oliver was hurt by a series of bad business decisions during which he suspiciously shunned proffered managerial counsel and assistance.[29] And he could be extraordinarily tough, a far cry from the gentle, patient giant of the myth. Drummer Fred Moore, with the Oliver band in 1931, recalled how the King enforced promptness at rehearsals:

> The King would walk in with music on his arm and his gun in the bosom of his coat. He would throw everything down on the table and look around to see if everybody was there. Then he would pick up his gun and ask "Is everybody here?" Everybody reported yes, we were there, then he would put his gun back on the table, and the rehearsal would go on.[30]

Quite understandably, the Oliver myth tends to ignore his shortcomings and to dwell on his seemingly larger-than-life qualities. As Walter C. Allen and Brian Rust point out, "we prefer to pass over these aspersions against an old man soured by adversity and remember the Grand King of the Lincoln Gardens and Plantation Cafe, setting Chicago back on its heels with his powerful 'trumpet of gold.' "[31] We prefer to see him not as an ordinary mortal but as the noble figure who looks from his photographs with Buddhist composure, in proud command of himself and those around him, a strong, primitive figure of stoic resolution, whose head was not turned by early success nor bowed by the misery to follow. Thus we square our ideas of the man with the greatness of his music, making him into a semidivine figure, possessed of the mystical knowledge and magic powers that we find in his work. He emerges as a man of deep and powerful intuition, who knew much of joy and sorrow and thus could evoke feelings of both heaven and hell on his horn.

Eliade demonstrates that one function of the myth of the hero is to tell the sacred story of what a divine, or semidivine, person did in the past, preferably in a time out of mind.[32]

And in a sense we have made Oliver virtually primordial. As Whitney Balliett said, he is "mysterious, almost primeval."[33] If not necessarily paradigmatic, his image, like that of many another mythical character, functions to awaken and maintain an awareness of a larger-than-life, or sacred plane, an absolute realm beyond ordinary experience. As such it contributes a sense of direction and security, reassuring a shaky jazz community which inhabits the unexplored, dark frontiers of creativity without social, economic, or artistic certainty. In King Oliver, then, jazzmen and their followers found, and to some extent continue to find, an ideal model who not only demonstrated what music should be, but provided confidence for a way of life which others frowned upon.

THE RITUALS OF THE JAZZ COMMUNITY

The repeated practices and precise symbolic acts which we call ritual are closely connected to mythology. Myth and ritual tend to emerge at roughly the same time from the same, often religious, sources and although the two are very closely interdependent, it is not clear whether myth emerges to justify ritual, or ritual evolves as enactment of myth.[34]

Either way, the jazz community is rich in ritual in a variety of forms: from the language it speaks, to the clothes it wears, to the jokes it makes, to the music it plays. Specifically at Lincoln Gardens, for instance, we can point to the ritualistic quality of the duet breaks of Armstrong and Oliver and the various slow drags of the dancers out on the floor.

The basic elements of the music take ritual form too. In discussing this point, Harvey Cox reminds us that not all rituals are beneficial. Those that serve the ends of idiosyncrasy or ideology often are not profoundly rooted in our imaginations and become perfunctory or ossified in time, arresting us in static tradition and numbing our creativity. But there are also what he terms "liberating" rituals, which provide a "formal structure within which freedom and fantasy can twist and tumble," formulas which offer access to a wealth of imagination and feeling. Cox feels that a good example of a liberating ritual lies in Dixieland jazz with its repeated rhythmic, melodic, and harmonic patterns which encourage individual and collective improvisation.[35] Of course, some of these patterns in Dixieland have long since hardened into a deadening orthodoxy, but many of them, as used or invented by Oliver in the twenties or earlier, were fresh and liberating (as his records tell us) just as are today's jazz innovations. The point is here that without *some* prescribed rituals there could be no jazz, only cachaphony, whereas with them the individual musicians can tap their creative wellsprings and stimulate one another to explore new realms of sound.

The rituals of the jazz community, then, both on and off the bandstand, provide limits and expectations which are honored and practiced by both musicians and audience and which, like myth, encourage solidarity and integration within the cult—sometimes long after their original functions have ceased to exist. Thus, the rituals we associate with King Oliver, repeated over and over again by himself and others (e.g., his celebrated solo on "Dippermouth Blues"), had a buoying and unifying effect on jazz enthusiasts of the twenties and afterward, and at the same time contributed to Oliver's mythic stature.

JAZZ AND QUASI-RELIGIOUS FESTIVITY

Finally, a word about religiously rooted festivity, which is often marked by the kinds of rituals we have been discussing. Cox points out that festivity not only provides opportunities for creativity and expression, but can also enlarge the range of our relationships to one another and to the past.[36] At its best, festivity raises our sense of personal worth by involving us in a larger history than our awareness usually encompasses. Along with myth and ritual, festivity heightens our consciousness of earlier heroes, concepts, or feelings which are in a sense out of time and yet, paradoxically, have stood its test. In commemorating a time out of mind, we celebrate in the present but take a holiday from our usual duties and reach out for something eternal which lends an enlarged sense of personal meaning and of community with our fellow celebrants.

Where it is a part of festivity, music has a significant place in all of this. We can see the festive role of jazz in the funerals, Mardi Gras, and other religiously related celebrations which abounded in New Orleans during King Oliver's youth and later. We can see how the down-home music of the Creole Jazz Band evoked earlier times in the Crescent City to the merrymakers at Lincoln Gardens. And we can see elements of religiously implicit festivity in the events which provided the occasion for the first version of this paper, read at a seminar on "The Legacy of King Oliver" sponsored by the Institute of Jazz Studies at the part of the Newport-New York Jazz Festival held at Waterloo Village, New Jersey in June 1978. Following the seminar, there was an evening concert of the music of King Oliver and Louis Armstrong, some of which had been transcribed note for note in written arrangements, played by the New York Jazz Repertory Company with a running commentary incorporating fact and fiction about Oliver's career. The enthusiastic crowd responded warmly to all of this, especially the familiar ritualistic and mythical parts, and applauded appreciatively when some of Oliver's relations were introduced in the audience.

The day had its antiquarian aspects, but it did more than simply resurrect something of the past. In its own way it exemplified the kind of festivity we have been talking about, with elements of myth, ritual, and audience participation, but more importantly it heightened our awareness of present meanings. It was not just a celebration of the sounds, practices, and events of earlier times, but it also involved us (however unconsciously) in a larger religious and esthetic dimension implying not simply the past but something universal. In a sense, we were both in and out of time, or at a point of their intersection, immersed in an ongoing tradition which enhanced our awareness of ourselves, our heritage, and something which seemed to transcend them.

NOTES

1. Frederic Ramsey, Jr., and Charles Edward Smith, eds., *Jazzmen* (New York: Harcourt, Brace, 1939; Harvest paperback, 1967), pp. 59-91.

2. Martin Williams, *King Oliver* (New York: A.S. Barnes & Co., 1960), pp. 2, 34.

3. Whitney Balliett, *Improvising* (New York: Oxford University Press, 1977), p. 23.

4. Max Weber, *The Sociology of Religion,* Ephraim Fischoff, ed. (Boston: Beacon Press, 1964), pp. 2-4.

5. Waldemar Bogoras, "Shamanistic Performance in the Inner Room," in William A. Lessa and Evon Z. Vogt, eds. *Reader in Comparative Religion: An Anthropological Approach,* Third Edition (New York: Harper & Row, 1972), pp. 382-87.

6. See Mircea Eliade, *Shamanism: Archaic Techniques of Ecstasy,* Willard Trask, trans. (New York: Pantheon Books, 1964), pp. 446-7; Eliade, *The Myth of Eternal Return,* Willard Trask, trans. (New York: Pantheon, 1954), pp. 92-94, 146-48.

7. Mircea Eliade, *Rites and Symbols of Initiation,* Willard Trask, trans. (New York: Harper & Row, 1958), pp. 85-87.

8. Nat Shapiro and Nat Hentoff, eds., *Hear Me Talkin' to Ya* (New York: Dover, 1955), pp. 99-102; *Louis Armstrong—A Self-Portrait,* interviewed by Richard Meryman (New York: Eakins Press, 1970), p. 29.

9. Eliade, *Shamanism,* p. 180.

10. Williams, *Oliver,* pp. 21-2.

11. Shapiro and Hentoff, *Hear Me Talkin',* p. 100.

12. Eliade, *Rites and Symbols,* pp. 87, 123-4; see also Eliade, *The Quest: History and Meaning of Religion* (Chicago: University of Chicago Press, 1969), pp. 114-6; Arnold van Gennep, *The Rites of Passage,* Monika B. Vizedom and Gabrielle L. Caffee, trans. (Chicago: University of Chicago Press, 1960), passim; and Emile Durkheim, *The Elementary Forms of the Religious Life,* Joseph W. Swain, trans., (London: George Allen & Unwin, 1915; Free Press paperback, 1965), pp. 348-51.

13. See Meryman, *Armstrong,* pp. 13, 17; Louis Armstrong, *Satchmo* (New York: Prentice Hall, 1954; Signet Edition, 1955), pp. 17, 27.

14. Meryman, *Armstrong,* p. 27.

15. Ibid., p. 29.

16. Ramsey and Smith, *Jazzmen,* p. 81.

17. The best account is in the biographical part of Walter C. Allen and Brian A. L. Rust, *King Joe Oliver* (London: Sedgwick & Jackson, Ltd., 1958); see also Ramsey and Smith, *Jazzmen,* pp. 76-91; and the first part of Williams, *King Oliver.*

18. See, for instance, Durkheim, *Elementary Forms of Religious Life,* pp. 351-5.

19. Ibid., p. 355.

20. Allen and Rust, *Oliver,* p. 40.

21. Ramsey and Smith, *Jazzmen,* pp. 90-1.

22. Meryman, *Armstrong,* pp. 49-50.

23. See Balliett, *Improvising,* p. 29.

24. Shapiro and Hentoff, *Hear Me Talkin',* p. 42.

25. Ibid., p. 43.

26. Ibid., pp. 45-6.

27. Ramsey and Smith, *Jazzmen,* pp. 62-3.

28. Shapiro and Hentoff, *Hear Me Talkin',* p. 96.

29. Martin Williams, *Jazz Masters of New Orleans* (New York: Macmillan, 1967), p. 80.

30. Ibid.

31. Allen and Rust, *Oliver,* p. 46.

32. My ideas about myth in religion have borrowed heavily from Mircea Eliade, *The Sacred and Profane,* Willard Trask, trans. (New York: Harcourt, Brace & World, 1959), pp. 68-115; and Eliade, *Myth and Reality,* Willard Trask, trans. (New York: Harper & Row, 1963), pp. 8, 18-20, 139-41. See also Claude Lévi-Straus, *Structural Anthropology,* C. Jacobson and B. G. Schoepf, trans. (New York: Basic Books, 1963), esp. Ch. 11 which is a version of his well-known, controversial essay, "The Structure of Myth"; and Lévi-Straus, *The Raw and the Cooked,* J. and D. Weightman, trans. (London: Jonathan Cape, 1970). Also of interest is Edmund R. Leach, *Pul Eliya: A Village in Ceylon* (Cambridge: Cambridge University Press, 1961), which applies some of Lévi-Straus's theories about myth to concrete data.

33. Balliett, *Improvising,* p. 23.

34. See Clyde Kluckhohn's well-known essay "Myth and Ritual, A General Theory," *Harvard Theological Review* 35 (January 1942): 45-9.

35. Harvey Cox, *The Feast of Fools* (Cambridge: Harvard University Press, 1969), pp. 70-5.

36. Ibid., p. 18.

TALKING ABOUT KING OLIVER:
AN ORAL HISTORY EXCERPT

Clyde Bernhardt, veteran trombonist and singer, was born in Goldhill, North Carolina, on July 11, 1905, and moved to Harrisburg, Pennsylvania in 1919. He began to play trombone in 1922 and soon went to work with local bands, coming to New York in 1928 and working for several leaders prior to joining King Oliver from March to November 1931. Subsequent affiliations included Marion Hardy's Alabamians, Edgar Hayes (with whom he visited Europe for the first time in 1938), Fats Waller, Jay McShann, Luis Russell, and Claude Hopkins. He has long since led his own groups as well as freelancing in New York, and from the 1970s on has made frequent tours of Europe, mainly in the company of other seasoned players and singers. He recorded with his own groups in the 1940s and 1950s, and again in the 1970s. Gifted with almost total recall, Bernhardt has been a primary resource for scholars and researchers, and is a born raconteur. He makes his home in Newark, New Jersey.

His remarks were part of a panel presentation at a seminar on ''The Legacy of King Oliver'' in June 1978. Funded in part by a grant from the New Jersey Committee for the Humanities, an affiliate of the National Endowment for the Humanities, this seminar was co-sponsored by the Rutgers Institute of Jazz Studies, the Newport-New York Jazz Festival, and the New Jersey Jazz Society. The transcription of these reminiscences was completed under the auspices of the Jazz Oral History Project, a program of the Institute of Jazz Studies funded by the National Endowment for the Arts.

I started to work with King Oliver, and the first job I played with him was in February 1931. At that time I was playing with Ray Parker at the Shadowland Ballroom in New York City, located at 44th Street and Eighth Avenue.

I knew King Oliver; I'd met him in 1926 in Chicago. I was playing with a little band in Battle Creek, Michigan, and I heard his band one night at the Plantation. I was just talking with him; I said, ''I like your band, I hope some day I will be good enough to play in your band.'' He said ''I don't know how good you play now, but you must be able to play something or else you wouldn't come up and talk to me like that. I think some day you might be able to play in my band.'' That made me feel good. That was in 1926.

Five years later, in March 1931—the first part of March—I decided to join his band. I had played about six jobs with him. I got a leave of absence from Ray Parker to play these jobs. I didn't tell him what I was going to do; I just told him I wasn't feeling well and I wanted to get off. I wanted to see how I liked the band. To tell you the truth, I didn't like the band as good as I did Ray Parker's band, because we had more of a modern New York beat and we had a very nice eight-piece band. And so my uncles (I had five uncles in New York, and my mother and father)—all of them told me; ''You're crazy if you don't go with King Oliver. That man has got a name; if you go with his band, your name will go down in history. He don't have to play as good as Ray Parker. He's got a name. He can just stand and blow two notes and the people say, 'That's King Oliver.' ''

Well, you know I was young, I just couldn't see it that way. But anyhow, I always was a person who would listen. I never did think I knew everything. I would always listen to see how things would work out. So I decided to join King Oliver.

He told me, "I like your trombone playing very much." He was very outspoken. If he told you anything, you could believe that was what he meant. He said I tried to imitate him. He said, "I like your trombone playing very much but Jimmy Archey is my favorite trombone player. After him, I'll take you, because you play a damn nice trombone. You have a bright future in front of you, and I hope you will like my band as well as you like the band you've been playing with downtown."

PLAYING THE WHITE BALLROOMS

We left New York in the latter part of March; we went on a tour all out through the Midwest. The Frederick Brothers out in Wichita, Kansas (they also had an office in Kansas City, Missouri) were booking the band. All the jobs we played were big-time white ballrooms. I don't think we played a colored job the whole time I was a member of his band, from the 1st of March to November 10, 1931—that's when I left the band. We played some of the finest white ballrooms in the Midwest. We were the first colored band to ever play the Coliseum in Tulsa, Oklahoma, and there's no ballroom in New York— including the Roseland and the Arcadia, and I played in both of them—they didn't touch the Coliseum, no kind of way. They weren't as large and they weren't as fine. The Coliseum had microphones; there were very few ballrooms that had microphones in 1931. . . . That was the first time I'd seen a microphone. I didn't know what the thing was; the thing scared me. It was such a loud tone.

I enjoyed the tour. It was really better than I thought it would be. We were playing at Spring Lake Park in Oklahoma City. That was one of the finest white ballrooms in Oklahoma City. They had a white band, I can't remember the name, but it was a very good band. And as far as I'm concerned, they were a better band than King Oliver was, but the people didn't think so. However, we played there and it went over very good there the first time, and we played there a few more times; that was proof that we were liked. One time, we were leaving; we were going to Fort Worth, Texas. We had a little bus which carried about 20 passengers, it was large enough for us. So, when we got ready to ball, we would go into the back of the bus (what I mean by "ball" is we would drink our corn and talk loud and play our record players, they called that the "red light district," in the back of the bus).

BIRTH OF A SINGER

So, we stopped at a little old restaurant there with home cooked meals and they had this corn—real corn whiskey—and I tell you the truth, I won't lie, I even like real corn whiskey to this day. The only thing is, I just can't get any! And they were selling this stuff in coffee cups. If you wanted to take it out, they had fruit jars. They had pint jars and half gallons, I think a half gallon jar at that time would cost you two dollars, a pint jar of corn would cost you one dollar, and a coffee cup, that would cost you fifty cents. After I went in there and drank two coffee cups of that stuff, I got on the bus, and I was feeling real good. We had to go about, I guess, between 150 to 200 miles from Oklahoma City to Fort Worth. There were a lot of boys who could sing. I didn't go in for singing. I liked to listen to other people. I liked to play, and that's what I did.

That corn made me think I could sing. So I got up, and they said, "What are you going to sing, man?" I said, "I ain't singing nothing." Everybody else said come on, sing something. So I got up there and started singing the "St. Louis Blues." Old Pop Joe sitting up front, said, "Who in the hell is singing them blues?" So one of the boys said, "That's Clyde back there," "I thought that was Jimmy Rushing," he said. "Tomorrow night, don't you forget you're going to sing." He said, "Don't tell me; you're going to *sing* tomorrow night." So the next night, we were playing at the Lake Worth Casino in Fort Worth, and I thought he had forgotten all about it. This was just an instrumental number. So some young white couple came up and said, "Hey, King, we want to hear you play the 'St. Louis Blues'. We want to hear you do that wa-wa chorus in there." He said, "Okay. We'll play the 'St. Louis Blues'." So he said to me: "Hey, after I play this intro and the vamp, you come in and you sing." I said, "I can't sing nothing." He said, "The hell you can't; you were singing last night. You're working tonight. You're in my band; you have to do what I say. I'm not going to fire you, but I know one thing—I'll whip the hell out of you if you don't sing." So I got up there, and I figured I'd do the best I could. They had good microphones in there. I got up there and did the number. It went over very well. All the guys in the band liked it. It sounded better then than it did when I was singing without a microphone.

So from then on, King Oliver started me singing other numbers, like "St. James Infirmary," you know, different numbers like that. He told me one time—this is at night when we finished playing—"Boy, I want you to keep up that singing, because one of these days, if you keep it up and listen to me and put that with your trombone playing," he said, "you're going to make a name for yourself, like Jack Teagarden and Jimmy Rushing." He said, "You sound very good. But the thing is this about you. You don't have any confidence about yourself. Everybody has confidence in you but yourself. You play much better trombone than you give yourself credit for; did you ever stop to think, when people like me hire you, I can get any trombone player, practically, for the price I'm paying you. If you couldn't play good, play what I want, you sure in hell wouldn't be in my band." And he meant that. So that started giving me a little confidence. I tell you one thing, I never did get to the place where I thought I was great, not to this day, I never thought it. I could always see room for an improvement.

OLIVER'S "INFERIORITY COMPLEX"

So I want to tell you more about King Oliver. He was a man who had an inferiority complex. A lot of people thought he was evil a lot of times. He had the feeling that a lot of younger people didn't want to be around him. I was taught to always have respect for older people, regardless of race, creed, or color, or whatever they were. He liked that about me. He would talk to me and sit down at the table and eat with me, where he wouldn't do it with the other guys—not even Paul Barnes. Paul was one of his favorites in the band. But Paul would snatch biscuits and put them on the side and do things like that, and King obviously didn't like this. . . . I played with the band until the tenth of November, and gave him a two-weeks notice and it was about four weeks before I left. He asked me would I stay 'til he got another trombone player; he tried out about three or four. He didn't like them; he just didn't like a lot of good musicians. He just didn't like their style of playing, so he didn't take these guys. So I stayed there until we got into Topeka, Kansas; myself and Freddie Moore left at the same time.

Well, I had a job waiting for me in New York, that was one reason why I wanted to get back 'cause I hate that part of the country. It's extremely hot in the summer and extremely cold in the winter, and it began to get cold out there, and I didn't want to be caught out there, so I left and came back to New York. But before I was in New York a week, King Oliver sent me a telegram telling me that if I came back, he was going to pay me ten dollars more salary. Well, I loved the band, I liked all the fellows in the band but I didn't have no eyes for going back out there; not in the wintertime . . . all my people were living in New York and New Jersey, and I was homesick and I came back to New York.

OLIVER'S FABULOUS APPETITE

Is there anything else you would like to know about King Oliver? There is so much I could tell you. I tell you one thing, he was one of the biggest eaters that I ever saw.

I played with Fats Waller, and Fats was a big eater, but King Oliver could eat one roast chicken, five or six pound roast chicken, he could eat all that chicken by himself. And I know he could eat a whole apple pie, because I saw him do it, and he wouldn't give nobody a crumb! One of the guys say, "Hey, pop, can you just give me a little piece of that?" and he said, "Oh hell no; *you* pay somebody to make you a pie. I paid the lady fifty cents to make me this pie." You know, fifty cents was good money back in those days. So he would eat a whole pie, and he would drink one of these coffee pots that hold around 10 cups of coffee, he would drink all of that.

I took him to a lady's house where I would eat in Beaumont, Texas. You know, those people down there at that time, they would never say King Oliver; they'd give him a new name, so when he came to town—all the boys were making a little money; we add dressed nice—they said, "That must be one of them with King Solomon; he looks just like one of them on the poster." The posters had all of our pictures on them. So they thought I was playing with "King Solomon"—that was his new name. And this lady where I stopped at said to me, "Are there any more of the boys who have no place to eat? I fix some good home cooked meals; I charge 25 cents for breakfast and 35 cents for dinner. Son, I put the food on the table and you can eat all you want."

So I told her that the leader of the band didn't have a place to eat, and she said, "Who? Mr. King Solomon? Oh, bring him here, honey, bring him here. I'd just love to have him in my house." I brought him, and he ate two meals; he ate everything but the plate on the table. She told me, "Mister, I made a mistake when I told you to bring that King Solomon here. That is the *eatingest* man I've ever seen. I took that man six eggs and he asked me did I have any more. I can't feed that man for no 35 cents!''

When I told King Oliver what she'd said, he said, "I know I'm not the smallest eater in town, but I like to enjoy what little I eat. If she wants some more money, I'll pay her more money. How much do you think I should pay her?" I said, "You should give at least a dollar." He said, "Well, I'll give her a dollar." So I told the lady; "He said he'd pay you a dollar if you feed him; a dollar for breakfast and a dollar-and-a-quarter for dinner." She said, "Well, since he's away from home, and don't have nobody to cook for him . . . I feel sorry for you boys. I know you all got money. I don't mean to rob him. I think I can break even if I charge him a dollar for breakfast and a dollar-and-a-quarter for dinner. I think I will come out just right, because you don't eat too much yourself, and so I can shave a little bit off there, you know. You tell him he can eat here."

He liked me for looking out for him. The rest of the boys never really did that for him. As you know, a musician, if he is working for a man that has a big name, is not particular about getting too close with him, because he has an inferiority complex, and the fellows in the band had it towards him, too. So you know, that is an awful feeling. He felt that they felt themselves better than him, and they thought that he thought himself better than them. I knew him pretty good, you know; I'm kind of psychic to things, and some people think I'm a fortune teller because I have this on me. But I'm not a fortune teller; I just can kind of dig people right off from the start. So by being around him for a short time, I could understand his attitude. He used to say I could dig his attitude, man; so I got along with him very well, but he had his strong likes and dislikes about people, and there is so much I could say about him that I wouldn't want to say. The man is dead and gone and is not able to talk for himself, so I would rather say something good that is the truth about him than to say some of the bad points I know about him. None of us are perfect, so I don't think it would be right for me just to say a lot of evil things they have said about him. A lot of times people can make you evil, but I loved to work with the man and think he was a wonderful man to work with when you put it all together. I don't look for nobody to be perfect, because I'm not perfect myself. But I am honest, I will say that. Thank you one and all!

RESPONSES TO QUESTIONS

After Clyde Bernhardt's remarks at the seminar on "The Legacy of King Oliver," other panelists addressed questions to him. The following are transcribed from the tape of the seminar, with questioners identified when possible.

Question (Richard Sudhalter): Was he a pressure player—a high-pressure player?

Yes, he was. For a certain thing, I tell you why, because he had plates—denture plates, upper and lower—and I say for an hour, an hour-and-a-half he'd sound like King Oliver— he could hit a high note; hit it on the head, and play a tune. He said that those plates would bother him after that time, but what he would do, he wouldn't mess up, he said; "Boys,

I'm getting off the stand; you boys go ahead and play,'' and he'd stand alongside the bandstand. He wouldn't play no more, maybe, until it was time to close; then he would come back and play again.

Question: When he was rested, in other words?

I tell you, he really did sound good; he sounded like himself. I have never heard no trumpet player—give all the credit to Clyde McCoy—I have never heard *no* trumpet player take a wah-wah mute, and a plunger and play ''Sugar Blues'' like I heard King Oliver play. I mean, he really put something in there, he put a feeling, he put one of those feelings there and his tone—like he was crying, moaning, and so on. I never heard no other trumpet player play like that. When he'd be on a job, sometimes just for devilment he just make that trumpet almost talk. He would laugh, or say, ''There's so and so . . .'' He'd just worry me to death sometimes. He just had something about his playing that was magnetic.

He didn't play that well all the time, only when he felt like himself. That was 1931, now; I don't know about those later years after I left, but he could still play then. He idolized Louis Metcalfe. Louis Metcalfe was one of his favorite trumpet players. He liked Louis Metcalfe—and this is something unusual for a New Orleans person, to like a person from some other place. But King Oliver was a person, if he liked what you played he didn't care where you were from. A lot of people said, when I was in the band, that I was from Kansas City. A lot of them in New York still think that; they say I had that Kansas City style on my trombone. Well, I had gone to Kansas City with the late Whitman Sisters' show, and I heard some of the bands while I was there, but I wasn't a Kansas City musician long enough to change my style. I was born in North Carolina, and I made up my style from this one to this one trombone player. Sometimes I heard something I'd like, and sometimes I'd hear a riff from some trumpet player, and I would try to play it where it fit. I didn't have no set way of playing the same thing the same way all the time. I just played the way I felt, and that's one think King Oliver liked about me. . . . If I played a solo a little different tonight from the way I played last night, he would say, ''That sounds mighty damn good''; he'd say, ''Now, I bet you can't play it that same way tomorrow night,'' and I couldn't. I couldn't play it the same way, and I'm that way today. I don't know—there's just different ideas that run in my mind in playing, the harder I try to do a job as well as I can.

Question (Lawrence Gushee:) What kind of open tone did he have? Was it a very full sound?

You mean, when he was playing open horn? Yes he had a real vibrato. Lip vibrato. He didn't have to shake his horn.

Question: Strong attack as well. Was Dave Nelson in the band at the time you were there?

No, not at that time. He had another trumpet player named Herman Elkins. Dave Nelson was a good friend of mine and gave me a lot of jobs, and I liked Dave Nelson, but Herman Elkins was a better trumpet player than Dave Nelson—far better than him—and he had a style similar to the New Orleans type of playing. He wasn't from New Orleans; a lot of people thought he was from there, but some thought *I* was from there, and when I would get down in Mississippi—you see, we were playing for white people all the time— they'd come up there and say, you play good trombone, say, where are you from, and I'd say I'm from New Orleans. I wasn't about to tell them I was from New York. You know all the jobs we played were big-time white ballrooms. I don't think we played a dozen colored dances. When we did play them it'd usually be on a Monday night, our weekly off night. When we did play a colored dance, we had a tremendous crowd, because all the places we played had a radio wire, and they were broadcasting, and the people heard the band before we had played in that city.

Question: One other thing about King. On a night-to-night basis, did he show a lot of inconsistency, where one night he was very strong and the next night he wouldn't be able to get it moving?

Yes, he did. Not only him, all of us. Of course the public didn't recognize it, but we did among one another. That happens, I don't think any musicians have any control over it because if your system is run-down and you are tired, I don't care how much you want to play, you just can't play your best. I know that from experience. The people may think you are playing very good, but you just don't feel like yourself, because if your system is tired, you cannot get everything out of that instrument. That's the way it seems to me, and to a lot of other musicians.

JOHN EDWARD HASSE

AN INTERVIEW WITH GUNTHER SCHULLER

Gunther Schuller is a unique figure. He pioneered in fusing "classical" music with jazz, even coining a new term for such fusions. He authored a land-mark history of jazz and headed one of the world's best-known music conservatories. He is a major American composer and a well-known conductor. He champions neglected American musics. As are few others, he is equally at home in the world of Bix, Basie, Blakey, and Braxton as he is in the realm of Schubert, Strauss, Stravinsky, and Stockhausen.

The son of a violinist who played in the New York Philharmonic, Schuller was born in New York City on November 22, 1925. During the 1940s and 1950s, he performed as horn soloist with the Cincinnati Symphony and the Metropolitan Opera. Schuller taught horn at the Manhattan School of Music and composition at Yale University, and from 1967 to 1977 was president of the prestigious New England Conservatory of Music.

Since about 1950 he has been actively involved in various fusions of jazz and classical music, and in 1957 coined the term "third stream" to denote such blends. Schuller has composed more than 85 works, including several operas and numerous chamber and symphonic works, a number of which include jazz elements. He is also one of the foremost scholars of jazz; his 1968 book Early Jazz: Its Roots and Musical Development *set new standards for musical histories of jazz.*

Schuller has been a leading figure in the revival of ragtime. In 1972 he founded the New England Conservatory Ragtime Ensemble, and, through its zestful performances and recordings (on Angel and Golden Crest records), brought orchestrated ragtime a new popularity and status. He and his ensemble played concerts across the country, appeared several times on public television, made a four-week tour of the Soviet Union in May and June, 1978, and were heard worldwide via shortwave radio on the Voice of America.

I interviewed Schuller as part of my research for a book on ragtime. Since he keeps a hectic schedule which includes frequent trips to Europe, I was unable to arrange a face-to-face meeting. We therefore conducted our interview by telephone between his home in Newton Center, Massachusetts, and mine in Bloomington, Indiana, on October 1, 1978. I tape recorded our conversation for deposit in the Indiana University Archives of Traditional Music, and Karen L. Gatz transcribed the interview. Schuller later made minor corrections in the transcript and has had the opportunity to make further revisions in the version printed here. Portions of this introduction and interview will appear as part of the chapter "Rudi Blesh and the Ragtime Revivalists" in my book Ragtime: Its History, Composers, and Music *(New York: Schirmer Books, forthcoming).*

In the first part of the interview, we discuss Schuller's attraction to and involvement with ragtime, the origins and nature of the style, the genius of Scott Joplin, and Schuller's

John Edward Hasse, a Ph.D. from Indiana University, is editor of *Ragtime: Its History, Composers, and Music* (forthcoming), co-editor of *Discourse in Ethnomusicology* (1978), co-producer of *Indiana Ragtime: A Documentary Album* (1981), and recording artist on a solo piano album, *ExtraOrdinary Ragtime* (Sunflower 501).

activities in other vernacular American musics. The second part of the interview focuses on Schuller's 1978 tour of the Soviet cities of Donetsk, Odessa, Tiblisi, Tashkent, Moscow, and Novosibirsk. He reveals fascinating, little-known details of jazz in the Soviet Union: the remarkable jazz scene of the 1920s, the serious attitude accorded jazz today, the speed at which the music passes through what I would term a "jazz underground," and the talents of Vladimir Feiertag and other native jazz experts. For many in the Soviet Union, Schuller relates, jazz represents a philosophy of freedom and democracy— fundamentally, spiritual survival.

HASSE: Mr. Schuller, when and how did you first become interested in ragtime?

SCHULLER: My interest in ragtime coincides and starts with my interest in jazz, which, of course, goes way back into my own teen years, although I must admit that in those earlier years—I'm speaking about the 1940s—I was much more intensely involved with the jazz of the then new music called bebop and the music of Duke Ellington and people like that. At first my interest in ragtime was somewhat peripheral, but later I began to study the subject more, read and listen more. I also came under the influence of Martin Williams. I think he was the first one to really make me aware of the unusual qualities, especially the structural qualities of ragtime. In the middle and late fifties Martin had been writing occasionally on ragtime and doing interesting structural and formal analyses of some of the rags of Joplin. We were working together on the *Jazz Review,* a very good magazine of that period. We saw a lot of each other and, of course, exchanged ideas a lot. So from him I got a deeper and better understanding of ragtime. And this coincided with my reading Rudi Blesh's book *They All Played Ragtime,* a book that has been a revelatory experience for lots of people, I imagine, in regard to ragtime. So, those two things together—Martin's somewhat more analytical approach to the actual music and Rudi Blesh's opening up that whole world to me—made me very keenly interested in the music.

But I am a French horn player, and with a French horn there isn't a lot you can do with ragtime. If you're a pianist, you can play it. But I'm no pianist at all, and so there was always this gap between what I *knew* about the music on the one hand, and what I might do about that as a performer on the other hand. My first chance actually to do something with ragtime occurred when, through Vera [Brodsky] Lawrence, I got some copies of the legendary "The Red Back Book," which I had heard about through all those years. But I had always understood that all copies of "The Red Back Book" had disappeared off the face of the earth, and that it was pointless to look for it. But when these arrangements came into my hands through Vera Lawrence, I then seized the opportunity to get personally involved with ragtime as a performer. And I guess the rest is history. The formation of the New England Conservatory Ragtime Ensemble and the concert that we gave at the Smithsonian—again, Martin Williams was the instigator of that—and then Angel [Records] recording us, and then the Grammy [Awards], and that led to *The Sting,* and so on. So, to answer your question in a summary way, I had always been interested in ragtime. It wasn't something that I suddenly discovered in 1972. It had been an abiding interest, about which, however, I couldn't do anything as a performer, until a vehicle in the form of "The Red Back Book" came along.

A SIMPLE BUT PERFECT MUSIC

HASSE: Would you say that the first thing that attracted you to it was the musical sound of it? Or was it the study of it?

SCHULLER: It was a combination of both. I don't think I can ever separate those aspects in my own studies of anything. I'm a composer, a creative person, and I tend also to be quite analytical. But I'm also a performer; and I'm always making the translation from the one realm, the creative, to the other, the recreative.

But what attracted me when I was merely studying and enjoying the music as a listener (of the old piano rolls, for example) was the perfection of the materials, even though the means used were very simple. The forms were very simple, closely related to the march form; also the simple melodic and harmonic ideas, and essentially a very uncomplicated structural approach—but perfect! I think I always appreciated in ragtime this kind of "perfection in miniature"—the small form carried to a very high level of skill and beauty, as high as one finds in certain classical composers, like Chopin or Delius, who also worked very well in small forms and were often not as successful in the large extended forms. This kind of miniaturized perfection is something that I appreciated, particularly since I'd already been for many years a very keen student and performer of Anton Webern, who is probably the greatest small-form composer of the twentieth century.

But then when I performed the music, I learned to love and appreciate another aspect of it, which really had more to do with its inner essence: and that was that whole fantastic combination of a consistently *joyous* and positive music, perfectly put together; in other words a music which one can appreciate on the most analytical intellectual level, if one wants to, but which one can also enjoy purely as an enjoyable *entertainment* music. And this is, I think, the reason that ragtime enjoys now, in this revival, such an enormous success. It really speaks to both types of listeners—those of a more intellectual or culturally experienced background and those who just simply turn to music—whether it's jazz or rock, or a Strauss waltz or a Beethoven symphony—as consumers and as enjoyers and listeners. They can enjoy it on a sort of surface level, without even being particularly conscious of the compositional and technical niceties of the music. And that is a rare, almost unique, combination. Among most musics that I know in the world—the entire spectrum from popular to ethnic musics and art musics—there are very few that combine those two levels of perception in such a brilliant way. And that was really a revelation to me, when I began to perform the music. And, of course, when I saw the audiences' reactions and the reactions of my musicians, I knew that this was a unique music.

I think the most startling thing about ragtime is that it is the *only* music—and I really want to emphasize this—the *only* music that I know of (and I know almost every kind of music; I enjoy a wide-ranging catholicity of taste and have studied everything from the Ars Nova to the most advanced combinatorial serialism and all kinds of Third World musics, African, Japanese, you name it), I know of no music other than ragtime that I could perform *so consistently* over *so many years* and *so many times* the same pieces—I mean the "Maple Leaf Rag," "The Entertainer," or "Pineapple Rag," or whatever—and *never once* fail to enjoy. Never once! I really don't fully understand that. After all, I have played and conducted so much music in my life. For example, I played for fifteen years in the Metropolitan Opera, and I must have played works like *La Traviata* or *La Bohème* three hundred times. I played with the New York Philharmonic and the Cincinnati Symphony, where I played Tchaikovsky symphonies, Mendelssohn, Beethoven, Brahms, or whatever many times. But I must say that even in those very high realms of music—the great classical masterpieces—there is a limit to how many times you can play or hear those works. I remember specifically a tour with the Cincinnati Symphony when I was seventeen years old and playing first horn. We did the Tchaikovsky Fifth Symphony more than a dozen times. Although I loved the piece—the Fifth Symphony is a treat for a horn player because it features that great horn solo in the second movement—after about the eighth performance, I almost couldn't stand certain parts of the piece any more. And I could cite hundreds of examples of music that I've performed a great deal where, after a certain amount of time, they begin to bore a little, to pale, or at least to lose some of that original captivation.

Now I can say truthfully that in these countless ragtime performances that I've done with our ensemble, this has *never* happened, even for one fleeting moment. In fact, the contrary. I can come to a ragtime concert totally exhausted from an impossible day—everything's gone wrong, and I'm tired, and I haven't had any sleep—and after three seconds of the "Maple Leaf Rag" I feel refreshed and alive. It's like a tonic. It's the most amazing thing! And I think it's attributable—I don't pretend to fully understand it—to that rare combination of a kind of technical perfection *and* this other mysterious quality, this irresistible and genuine joy of the music.

HASSE: That is remarkable. Have you noticed this same effect on any other people?

SCHULLER: The players in my ensemble virtually all feel the same way. And, of course, everything I'm saying is also borne out by our audiences everywhere over the years. We leave our audiences supremely happy, not because we're so great but because the music is so irresistibly infectious and positive.

HASSE: This has been my experience, too. It is very interesting to hear you say this. I play piano in a supper club on weekends, and the same people show up week after week asking for the "Maple Leaf Rag," and "The Entertainer." They just don't get tired of it. It's just such a fine music.

SCHULLER: Yes. There's a human quality in it which is beyond explanation.

HASSE: Can we go back a little way? I'd like to ask how you would define ragtime if you were pressed.

SCHULLER: Well, from a somewhat surface point of view, one could say that it is a music which in its pure form—in the classic Midwestern, Saint Louis, ragtime tradition—combined the African or Afro-American feeling of syncopation and rhythmic swing with certain European structural formal elements, most particularly the march form as it had been developed and perfected by John Philip Sousa. And many of the formal and stylistic elements of the march are, of course, maintained in ragtime, including the oom-pah "left hand" accompaniment, which provides the rhythm, the harmony, and the bass lines all at once; and then the cross-accented, "syncopated," melodies and rhythms, which were the *new* element—the really *new* contribution of these mostly black composers. That's the essential element that differentiated ragtime from the musics that came before it. Its fascination lies in the combination of the steadiness of the beat, the left hand in a piano rag, and the *un*steadiness and irregularity of the right hand. It's the classic combination and contrast of the predictable with the unpredictable. And this has an effect upon people of which they never tire.

JOPLIN'S STROKE OF GENIUS

HASSE: You have written that the evidence points overwhelmingly to the march as the primary progenitor of ragtime. Do you have any ideas on how specifically ragtime originated from the march?

SCHULLER: Well, I think it was a stroke of genius on Joplin's part, because I think it was clearly he who most especially put that particular formal stamp on ragtime. When Joplin was, so to speak, shopping around for a formal mold into which to pour his music, he discovered that there already existed one in perfected form, and that was Sousa's march form. After that it was mainly a matter of overlaying the Afro-American elements that he heard in his head on that form. One has to remember that by the 1880s, which is when Joplin became active as a musician, the march as perfected by Sousa and many others—Reeves, for example, was a great march composer of that time—was *the* ruling popular music of the country, this in a time when there were, of course, no radios, no televisions, no records—no nothing.

The one consistent musical entertainment in the entire country—not just in New York, but in Colorado, in the mining camps or wherever, in Connecticut, or Maine, or New Orleans—was the band concert, a well-established tradition which was brought and developed here mostly by German band masters. There was a period of several decades—from the 1880s well into the twentieth century—when the band concert was almost the only form of musical entertainment that the average American could enjoy. Charles Ives comes out of that tradition to some extent, too. So Joplin—whether it was fully conscious or half-conscious or subconscious hardly matters—simply latched on to this popular march form and gave it a new twist which, of course, Sousa *didn't* have: the African sense of rhythm and syncopation.

It is interesting to note, by the way, that by 1900 Sousa himself had become ragtime's greatest booster and proselytizer. And it was Sousa who brought ragtime music to Europe on his famous European tour of 1900, in addition to bringing it to all corners of this land on his extensive transcontinental tours.

THE MINSTREL TRADITION

HASSE: Do you think that "ragging," that is, playing an existing piece in a ragged rhythm, preceded or followed the development of the piano rag, per se?

SCHULLER: I think it followed. I think that this all connects up to some extent with the earlier minstrel music tradition, particularly the black minstrel music. There's no question that musicians in minstrel shows did a certain amount of "ragging" of previously existing music which hadn't been originally intended to be "ragged." That probably was not a fully conscious thing, but more likely the result of musicians not formally trained playing the music a bit loosely. Also, at first this pre-ragtime music did not have such a very pervasive influence. But I think after ragtime, especially after the great successes with Joplin and James Scott (and unfortunately many of the lesser ragtime composers, many of whom became even more popular than Joplin in commercial terms) took hold, then everybody began to "rag" everything. That was also the period when you could write any piece of junk, but as long as you put the word "rag" on it, it would sell. I mean this was when Tin Pan Alley got a hold of ragtime. So, I think the popular idea of "ragging" something came after the first explosion of ragtime; and I think the term "ragging" came into being more because a new music which *had* that "raggedy" effect had come into being rather than because somebody was "ragging" the Dvorak "Humoresque" or the "William Tell Overture". I think that kind of playing came a little later, when you get into James Europe and people like Eubie Blake, and even Jelly Roll Morton, who ragged a lot of classics.

Now, there's another very important and interesting aspect to all of this, and this is also why I put the main emphasis for the creation of this music on Joplin. There were other stylistic elements which at first vied for priority in ragtime; a whole range of then popular musics in the middle and the latter part of the nineteenth century. And you can still see this in some of the rags that were written and published *before* Scott Joplin's "Maple Leaf Rag," rags in which the style elements are not yet fully assimilated. For instance, you can hear that clearly in some of Tom Turpin's rags, which are very eclectic and contain large doses of what one would have to call fiddle music—country fiddle music, especially the black fiddle music of that time. We have to remember that besides the banjo the most prominent instrument among the slaves and later the emancipated blacks was the fiddle, which they often made out of cigar boxes and cat gut strings, anything they could find around the house. They were ingenious at making their own fiddles because they sure couldn't afford to buy one. The fiddle was not something you bought in a store—you didn't get a Stradivarius—you just made it yourself and in that way the homemade fiddle was to be found all over, in Oklahoma, Arkansas, New Orleans, or Alabama or wherever. And so one of the main forms of entertainment, and to some extent employment, for blacks at that time was through fiddling.

And that fiddle music was a very important element in the very early and prehistoric days of ragtime. But it eventually got pushed aside by Joplin, who developed a less eclectic, more cohesive, and I would say purer strain of ragtime by mating the march with *his* particular kind of melodic and rhythmic ideas. So the whole range of black musics—from fiddle to minstrel and even the ballads and to some extent the blues and spirituals—all of these were vying for a place in their music in the days before ragtime, when it wasn't yet called ragtime. I'm speaking about 1885 to about 1895. In those ten years I'm quite certain that a lot of these different popular and dance musics competed for a priority role in the formation of what eventually became ragtime. Then Joplin, with one stroke of genius in the "Maple Leaf Rag", really put things in order and in effect eliminated certain elements and emphasized certain others—which is, by the way, exactly comparable to what composers like Mozart or Monteverdi did in their time. This type of innovative genius not only invents something new, but also at one and the same time eliminates certain things which he considers to be not germane, or second rate, or whatever.

HASSE: In your definition of ragtime, do you allow for ragtime songs?

SCHULLER: Oh, yes. Of course, but the ragtime song tradition again comes more out of the vaudeville and minstrel tradition. It wasn't long before people wanted to sing these pieces. So words were put to them, and there developed a whole ragtime-song tradition. My definition of ragtime certainly is large enough to include that. I would say, however, that the pianistic tradition was the primary one, and the one that produced the best works, and the one that constantly generated the continuity of that style.

SIMILARITIES AND DIFFERENCES

HASSE: Besides classical music, Third Stream, and modern jazz, you have been involved as a performer and a conductor in a number of other and sometimes older American musics—of course ragtime, the opera *Treemonisha,* Sousa and march music, country fiddle band music, the musics of Paul Whiteman and Jelly Roll Morton. That's quite a variety. In the course of your work with these musics, how have you come to perceive their similarities?

SCHULLER: Well, it's like anything else--there are similarities and there are dissimilarities. One could argue it either way. One could find certain common threads through many of those musics that you just enumerated. On the other hand, I think what is probably more important is not so much the similarities, but the things that make them distinctive. Because it is those distinctive qualities which made those musics survive in their time and beyond, into our own time. So it is the distinctive qualities of an Ellington or a Whiteman or Jelly Roll Morton or Joplin or Ives that make us talk about them still in 1978. Interestingly, the *similarities* are often the same elements that to a large extent exist also in all kinds of second-rate and mediocre music, so those are not as interesting per se.

What all these musics do have in common, except that they present it in different and personal ways, is an enormous rhythmic vitality, which we now regard as a particularly or peculiarly American contribution. And indeed, it is a contribution which, again, comes to a large extent from the black people, and which is not common to the European classical tradition—at least not to that extent. To this very day, most Europeans have great trouble performing American music of any kind—classical, popular, or whatever—with that true rhythmic vitality, not because they're not musically skilled or because they're incompetent, but because that kind of rhythmic vitality is just not in their bones. So that is one particularly American element which one could say is common to all these composers, to all these musicians. But then there's a vast difference between the harmonies and melodies of a Duke Ellington, let's say, and the arrangers who worked for Paul Whiteman: Grofé and Challis. And yet, in my view, they are of almost equal *quality* as styles—just different.

Of course, there's a whole other segment of earlier American music which I've also dealt with extensively, and that is the whole nineteenth century classical tradition; the music of all those composers who began composing in the mid-to-late nineteenth century—John Knowles Paine, George Chadwick, [Frederick S.] Converse, Arthur Foote, and Arthur Bird, and dozens of others—all of whom were the first practitioners of what one then used to call the "serious" art of composing. But they were strictly, or at least primarily, influenced by the prevailing European trends—the Romantic music of Beethoven, Schumann, and Mendelssohn, and later Wagner. But some of these composers began to realize that by working strictly out of the European, mostly Germanic, concepts and traditions, they were never going to be particularly "American" composers. And a few of them, especially at the instigation of Dvorak, who came here in 1892 to head the New York Conservatory of Music, began to realize that there was in American native musics, particularly that of the blacks and the Indians, a whole other indigenous musical tradition to which they ought to pay some attention. And eventually they did. And it's interesting to note that that awareness occurred precisely at the same time that ragtime and jazz also developed.

NEGLECTED AMERICAN MUSICS

HASSE: Do you see yourself in part as a champion of neglected American musics?
SCHULLER: Yes, I do. I don't wish to make a whole career of it or do *only* that, but among the many things that I do, I definitely do see myself as a champion of that music because (a) I find much of the music to be of great merit and value and beauty, and therefore it deserves to be performed and heard; and (b) because I know from studying the whole history of the development of the arts in the United States that we have suffered for a long time (and still do to some extent) from a tremendous inferiority complex about our own music. That's understandable when one realizes that we are a very young country and we had to import our musical traditions primarily from Europe in order to have any; and that that whole development is bound to take a long time—several centuries, perhaps. Before one can establish one's own tradition, there's a lot of acquiring and imitating and borrowing that has to be done. But during that period one tends to be sort of aware of that and so one tends to develop a sense of inferiority about that. But I think those days are long gone now, and it's high time that America be proud of its musical traditions—past and present, classical and popular—in its best forms, of course. Needless to say, there's a lot of junk which is produced in all periods, in all generations, and in all styles; and perhaps more today than ever before, so one can't be proud of *everything*. But one can be proud of the best things, and I think one should be. In recognition of that, I certainly would champion all good music without going so far as to claim that our older music is better than the Europeans'. It's just a question of putting our music in its proper perspective vis-à-vis the rest of the tradition.

I maintain that there are any number of very fine "classical" pieces by American composers of the nineteenth century which are just as good as some of the minor pieces by a Mendelssohn or a Schumann that are constantly played just because they have German names attached to them. We just don't appreciate the best of our home-grown products, and we certainly don't appreciate something that is perhaps less than the best; also, we don't seem to recognize the important fact that every musical tradition has to begin some-where. And so, if the first fifty pieces by classical composers in the nineteenth century in America were not all of the caliber of the *Eroica,* so what? I mean, we had to start somewhere. The fact that those earlier composers did it at all, and did it so well, that's what's important, not whether it finally measures up to the *Missa Solemnis.*

HASSE: Some individuals see a conflict between creating art and analyzing it in a schol-arly fashion. Have you felt any tension between these disparate activities in your many endeavors?

SCHULLER: Not one iota. I totally reject that notion. I know that creativity of any kind—in music, painting, literature, whatever—is at least fifty percent analytical and criti-cal. That other notion represents a complete misunderstanding of the creative process, as if being analytical somehow subverts one's creative impulses. One simply has to know how to *use* these things side by side. And of course there is the possibility of a kind of pedantic, academic analysis, which is certainly anti-creative. But on the other hand, un-controlled uncritical permissive creativity is not such a great thing either. And there is no such thing as a composer—whether it's Schubert or Joplin or Stravinsky or Charlie Parker—who isn't at one and the same time, when he is creating, both creative and analyt-ical, because the creative function is that which generates and produces something, and the analytical function is the part that assesses whether that which is being created is valid.

HASSE: The feedback.

SCHULLER: Yes, if you wish—as if you have a sort of third ear listening out there all the time. After all, you could just turn out the most ridiculous drivel in the euphoric white heat of "inspiration" and not know that it's quite mediocre, or that it's something that someone else has already written, and better. If the analytical or critical faculty is not functioning, I don't see how you can be any kind of a creative person. You just have to know how to balance these things. It's a little bit like that other equation of creativity I am fond of citing, which is that in its highest form it consists of fifty percent emotion and fifty percent intellect or intelligence. And to the extent that *that* balance is perfectly maintained—to that extent, as I look at all the great masterpieces of all cultures through the centuries—those are the great monuments of our cultural heritage.

SCHULLER'S RUSSIAN TRIP

HASSE: Can we talk about your trip to Russia? How did this trip come about?

SCHULLER: Well, the State Department receives from the Congress a very tiny budget to send American cultural presentations to various parts of the world. Ever since the Cold War, the State Department has concentrated what little money and effort it has primarily on the Communist bloc countries, and to some extent Africa and Asia. As a result there is a regular exchange of cultural organizations and groups between the Soviet Union and the United States, which is based on an agreement which, I believe, is renegotiated every five years, and in which it is specified how many groups from each country will go to the other country. So in effect our trip was sponsored jointly by the State Department as an American cultural presentation *and* by the Soviet Union through *Goskonserts,* which is the Russian state-controlled organization which screens and invites all foreign groups. You cannot perform in Russia without going through the screening of *Goskonserts.* It is a kind of gigantic Sol Hurok-style management office which controls all of the musical life in Russia, both for outsiders and for Russians.

The third part of the exchange process is the American Embassy, which gets to work and figures out *where* they want a group to appear—whether it's just in Moscow or whether they want a group to travel all over the Soviet Union. That depends, of course, on available funds and time, and similar factors. So there were really three entities involved in planning and financing our trip and in discussions and negotiations, which took nearly two years.

HASSE: And you took the entire New England Conservatory of Ragtime Ensemble?

SCHULLER: Right.

HASSE: How many people?

SCHULLER: There were sixteen players plus myself; and two managerial or stage crew persons to set up the concerts.

HASSE: And you were in Russia from May 26 through June 23 [1978]?

SCHULLER: I think that's right.

HASSE: And you went to Donetsk, Odessa, Tiblisi, Tashkent, Moscow, and Novosibirsk?

RAGTIME UNKNOWN

SCHULLER: Novosibirsk, yes. Novosibirsk is a city of four million on the western border of Siberia. . . . I think the surprise for all of us was that they knew nothing about ragtime in the Soviet Union. One or two intellectuals or one or two jazz musicians were sort of dimly aware of ragtime, but one can really say that virtually nothing was known about the music. This was combined with the fact that the average person in the Soviet Union—I would guess 98 percent—think that when an American comes to Russia to perform music, it must be either jazz or rock. They have virtually no notion of our doing anything other than that. Some people know, I'm sure, that the Cleveland Orchestra has played there, or the New York Philharmonic, or an American classical chamber ensemble—but when it comes to the more popular musics, that's strictly jazz and rock for them. And ragtime, which is a music they didn't know how to place historically or stylistically at all, just doesn't even exist for them. They really expected us to play jazz— Dixieland jazz or even modern jazz. And in many places they were very disappointed. Indeed, in some places we were *sold* as a "jazz band," which I resented very much. And so in every concert and in every city that we came to, we first had to educate the audience and the whole population to the fact that we were not going to play jazz (although we always play a few Jelly Roll Morton pieces in our programs and some others which would qualify as early jazz), but *ragtime.* Once that was understood, our concerts were a tremendous success. The same pattern happened everywhere. We always played at least two concerts, in some places as many as five.

Here is the exact pattern of how things went. First concert: Within fifteen minutes, out of an audience of maybe 5,000, three or four hundred would walk out, because they had really expected rock or jazz. We didn't get to ask them, but it was obvious that we were not playing what they had expected, what they had been *told* we were going to play. So they walked out. The other people stayed, and by the end of the concert we had standing ovations, or at least ovations. And then, in each successive second and third concert the word got around—everything there is by word of mouth—that, "Hey, this is great stuff. We don't know what it is, and they call it ragtime, but it's terrific. You should go hear it." And then those people who did not want to hear that ragtime would not come. You could always see them in front of the hall selling their tickets to those who *wanted* to hear the music. And so, this crescendo pattern developed in every concert and in every town, consistently, including even Moscow.

HASSE: And you ended your tour in Moscow?

SCHULLER: Yes.

A SOVIET EXPERT

HASSE: You had an interpreter, then, at the beginning of each concert to explain?

SCHULLER: Well, not an interpreter, strictly speaking. In America or in Europe, I always narrate our concerts. We don't just play the music. I envelop the entire concert in a narration which introduces each piece and each composer. But, of course, I don't speak Russian. So I was very fortunate that I had two people in Russia who did exactly that same sort of thing in Russian. They narrated it, based on my notes and my suggestions to them. One of these was a man named Vladimir Feiertag, who lives in Leningrad and who is one of the most knowledgeable people in jazz and ragtime that I have ever met anywhere. I mean an absolutely encyclopedic knowledge, mind you, in a country where it is darn hard to get hold of this information. You cannot buy American records, you cannot buy American books; and yet, this man knows everything I know and all of us—Leonard Feather and Martin Williams and so on—put together. It's absolutely incredible.

After we had consulted for maybe twenty minutes on a few points, he narrated extemporaneously—little introductions which were anywhere from twenty seconds to maybe three or four minutes. And while doing that, he very cleverly was explaining to the audience what they should and should not expect. It was absolutely ingenious. And there were moments when maybe, had he not been there, many more of the audience would have walked out. But he had a way of holding them and saying, "Wait a minute. Just hang on. Wait until you hear the rest of this." Whatever he said—as I say, I don't speak Russian—he was absolutely fantastic. He is not exactly a *persona grata* in Russia. On the other hand, he's not exactly a dissident. He sort of ekes out a precarious living, because the field that he's interested in—jazz—is, although it's now very accepted and popular and all that, still not by any means a way of making a living in the Soviet Union.

HASSE: What does he do for a living?

SCHULLER: He lectures and teaches. He speaks several languages. He sort of puts together a living out of various kinds of lectures in various cultural fields, but his own primary interest is in jazz. And to some extent he does make part of his living from jazz. He is the premier narrator and M.C., for example, for all the jazz festivals in the Soviet Union, of which there are now many, in Riga, in Tiblisi, in Donetsk, wherever; and he is always the sort of George Wein or Willis Conover who does all the introducing and presenting. We just loved that man, and we cried bitter tears when we left him.

HASSE: Has he published in the country or outside of it on jazz?

SCHULLER: Yes, in the Soviet Union he has published articles and also books. I think he wrote the first history of jazz in Russia many years ago. I forget exactly when. But in any case it wouldn't be available to us except in smuggled copies.

HASSE: Is this the man who had some recent scores of your classical works that were only a few years old?

SCHULLER: No, that was another remarkable man, in Georgia, in Tiblisi, who is perhaps even more remarkable because his knowledge is not limited to jazz and ragtime, but extends to all musics. And he knew everything about me, as did many others by the way. I was amazed at what they knew about me, and how much they revered and respected what I did. I was treated like a god by these people and not only because of the multiplicity of the things that I do. For some I was an important man who had invented "the third stream idea"; to others I was the guy who had worked with Miles Davis in the *Birth of the Cool;* to others I was the guy who had worked with Ornette Coleman and Eric Dolphy; to still others I was the one who had made Duke Ellington reconstructions; to others—a few—I was the one who got involved with early jazz and ragtime; and for many of them I was important because I did all these things. And then, of course, for this man in Georgia, it went beyond that. He knew all my contemporary "classical" music, and the fact that I conduct all over the world. It was unbelievable. Nowhere else in the world have I been received quite like that. They appreciate everything so much.

A MUSICAL UNDERGROUND NETWORK

HASSE: How did he get your scores in?

SCHULLER: Everything is done by some underground or unofficial means, because either it's illegal or it's just impossible to get. And so what happens—whether it's jazz or classical music or whatever—somebody gets a copy in somehow and then it is photocopied and duplicated in a sort of private and underground network. Or in the case of many of the jazz records, they simply sit by the radio and copy everything off Willis Conover's program [on the] Voice of America, and from the BBC.

HASSE: With a tape recorder?

SCHULLER: With cassettes, anything. And the minute one cat in Novosibirsk copies it off Willis Conover, then he immediately gets it to the 55 other people there who are interested in jazz. This underground network is critically important, because they simply cannot buy the records.

HASSE: The Soviet record company does not issue American recordings?

SCHULLER: They have just begun to. After all, jazz hasn't been officially allowed for more than ten years now. But just now, let's say within the last year or two, they have begun to issue some major jazz figures on the Melodia label. But the number of records I'm talking about could be counted maybe in a dozen or a couple of dozen.

HASSE: So, it's really the short-wave radio, the BBC, the Voice of America, perhaps Radio Free Europe that—

SCHULLER: Yeah. And you see, since Willis Conover never plays any ragtime, that's one very simple reason why they didn't know anything about ragtime. Everything they know, they know from those sources. And what those programs don't offer, they don't know. Which gives you a sense of the power of the radio, both by omission and commission.

HASSE: Do they listen to Conover in his English language program? He doesn't broadcast in Russian, does he?

SCHULLER: No. They all understand enough English to get what he's saying. He's not giving three-hour lectures on each piece, after all. He's more or less just announcing the pieces and the titles and something about the musicians. These people knew records intimately that I didn't even know the existence of. And I pride myself on knowing quite a bit. But these people just put me to shame. I was embarrassed time and time again.

HASSE: That's really amazing.

SCHULLER: But you see, jazz is not just a music for them, or an entertainment, or something you dance to, or something you mildly like. It is a question of life and death; it's a philosophy, a *way of life.* It represents freedom and democracy to them. It means a thousand times more than it does even to the most avid American. It's associated with a human and political and spiritual survival for them.

HASSE: Especially for, I suppose, the intelligentsia.

SCHULLER: Absolutely. And, you know, there's a lot of intelligentsia there. It's not such a small upper crust as one might think. *These people are all very well educated.*

THE APPEAL OF JAZZ

HASSE: Is that the group that was particularly in attendance at your concerts? I'm wondering to what segments of Soviet society jazz particularly appeals.

SCHULLER: Well, I can't answer it that way, because it is not divided into segments the way it is in our society. I would say that demographically it cuts across all societal levels. Of course, the Soviets claim they have no class system anyway. Nonetheless, at our concerts I saw politicians and members of the Party, always sitting in the front rows, and also further back people whom I guess you would call intellectuals or intelligentsia. But the majority of them were just ordinary folks who work in shops or drive tractors, or God knows what. So there was no intellectual distinction there as correlated to a class of people. Even people whom we would not regard as "intellectuals" or scholars or historians enjoyed the music—our music—and enjoyed jazz, just becaust it's a fine music. They don't have the prejudices about the music that most Americans have.

Another aspect of this is that while for many years the Soviet government was deathly afraid of jazz—because jazz is, of course, the most individualistic music, and they feared that it would lead to revolution and to outbreaks of individualism which they couldn't control—by now they've swung around to the other extreme where, I swear, they seem to appreciate jazz more than we do in this country. I mean as a nation, including even the government officials, the people in Goskonserts, the heads of conservatories, the heads of philharmonic organizations, and so on. And the key there is that they simply make the very same equation that I have made all my life, which led to the whole third stream idea and for which I have often been ridiculed and lambasted: namely that the best of jazz is as good as the best of anything else. And they just take jazz very seriously as a music when it's done well. It's as simple as that. So they listen to Tchaikovsky and then they listen to jazz—Duke Ellington, or whatever—and to them it's more or less the same in quality. Different in style, of course, totally.

I was interviewed dozens of times by government officials and conservatory heads with an eye towards my advising them how they can, now that they've arrived at that juncture in their history, put jazz into the conservatories. They have just about arrived at the point where they want to do that, and they wanted to know from me—since I had put a jazz department into the New England Conservatory the minute I arrived there—how it's done, and what are some of the problems and pitfalls. And, of course, they do have problems, such as insufficient faculty to teach and all of the usual problems relating to the teaching of jazz. But the fact is that there's no longer any ideological argument as to whether they should have jazz, whereas it's still a big ideological question in lots of places in the United States.

HASSE: That's right. Did you find more people who were involved in conservatories and the mainstream of classical music who were hospitable to jazz than you find here in the U.S.?

SCHULLER: Yes. Either hospitable to it or aware of its importance without, perhaps, yet having done anything specifically about it. As I say, they have arrived at a particular juncture where they don't yet have it in the conservatories, where they don't have the faculties and the resources yet. But they *want* very much to do it, and knowing them, I think they will succeed within the next five years in doing just that.

HASSE: Will they import method books, like David Baker's series, thinks like that?

SCHULLER: I imagine they will. They'll be very conscientious and consistent and I might add, critical and selective about this. They'll also create their own textbooks and method books.

HASSE: What do you think their main tack will be? Will it be performance and improvisation, arranging, composition, history—

SCHULLER: *Everything!* They look at all these areas as contributary and complementary. I also heard some remarkable jazz groups and orchestras and musicians. I didn't hear many ragtime musicians, but we heard one fantastic pianist who also played excellent ragtime out in Novosibirsk. His name is Igor Dimitriev. He's an electrical engineer by profession, but he's a *superb* pianist, not just a good amateur.

HASSE: And he had the scores somehow.

SCHULLER: No, he didn't even have any of the sheet music. I think he just took things off piano rolls or records of piano rolls. I really never understood exactly how he learned ragtime. He didn't speak very much German or English, which are the two languages I speak mostly, and I could never really get it completely straight. I was so enamoured of him that I put him on one of our concerts; he was the only Soviet musician with whom I did that. And we had to *lend* him the "Pineapple Rag" sheet music for him to learn it, which, of course, he did very quickly—in one day, as a matter of fact. Now, he didn't know *all* the ragtime literature, but he knew some of the more famous pieces like the "Maple Leaf Rag." But he was the only one. All the other musicians knew modern jazz much more, and particularly avant garde jazz. That's very big right now. There was a *very* good and advanced trombone player in Novosibirsk. His name is Victor Budarin, and he is, I gather, the best in the entire Soviet Union.

HASSE: You mentioned piano rolls. Did the player piano appear in the Soviet Union earlier in the century and was there American music available on rolls? And what about other early jazz?

EARLY SOVIET JAZZ

SCHULLER: I don't know specifically. I mentioned that grabbing at straws. As I say, I don't know how Dimitriev learned ragtime. It's conceivable that amongst the things that these people get hold of they'll occasionally also get a tape of a piano roll—of Joplin playing some rag, or Fats Waller, or whatever. They are very industrious and thorough in all this. But the answer to the other part of your question is yes. There was an enormous invasion of jazz in the Soviet Union in the 1920s, and for a while jazz was *very* popular and *very* successful. And one of the fine black bands of that time—he was a sort of rival of Duke Ellington and went to Berlin and to Warsaw and to Russia in the late twenties—Sam Wooding, who had a big orchestra, a sort of cross between Paul Whiteman and Duke Ellington—spent some time in Moscow in the twenties. And in the wake of that, many Russian orchestras sprang up which played excellent 1920s jazz for that time. I didn't know this before, but these Russian bands recorded, and people gave me these recordings on this trip. There are several orchestras from the late 1920s and early thirties, before Stalin began to forbid jazz, that are absolutely outstanding; comparable to most things produced in the United States, except for the great classics by Armstrong or Morton. But the general level was very high.

HASSE: And these have been reissued on LP?

SCHULLER: Yes.

HASSE: Isn't that remarkable. We don't know anything about this whole period.

SCHULLER: No. No.

HASSE: Do you suspect that there was and also is, but especially was, a lot of good jazz elsewhere in the world that Americans are just unaware of?

SCHULLER: Yes, I think there's more than we generally know about. I mean, you and I and jazz writers and aficionados and the big record collectors and a few other people, we know that there was a jazz band in Calcutta and in Berlin and in Stockholm and in Barcelona and all that. But the average jazz fan, let alone anyone else, knows nothing about that. But it is a fact that jazz, once it took hold, spread like wildfire. Both live and in recordings, it just suddenly existed in all parts of the world. Even in Johannesburg, South

Africa, or distant places like that. I mean *everywhere*. A lot of this was imitative, of course. But this band that I heard from the late twenties or early thirties in Russia impressed me immensely.

HASSE: That's fascinating.

SCHULLER: I mean, they were technically as good as any of the best bands of Ellington or Henderson or Whiteman, and even musically very sharp, at times in small ways even original, but of course imitators overall. This is one area they haven't claimed to have been the first to do.

HASSE: Do you remember the names of these bands?

SCHULLER: One of them was Alexander Varlamov, who I think recorded in the early thirties.

HASSE: And were they performing American compositions?

SCHULLER: Of course. They were doing all the repertory that they had heard from the American records of that time, tunes like "Sweet Sue" and "Blue Moon," often with the lyrics sung in Russian!

THE RAPID SPREAD OF CURRENT MUSIC

HASSE: You mentioned that there were many people in Russia interested in modern jazz. Is there a time gap of a few years in what they're aware of that's going on here?

SCHULLER: No.

HASSE: No? They're up to date?

SCHULLER: Absolutely. I mean, if something happened in the loft scene in New York two weeks ago, I assure you some of them know about it. It is quite incredible, and it is, again, the same phenomenon: they are so desperate to know about this music, because it represents something much more than music to them. It is freedom and a way of life.

HASSE: How much does the prominence of black in American jazz have to do with their attitudes towards it?

SCHULLER: Surprisingly little. One would have thought that both the government and other pro-Soviet thinking people would exploit that factor. It appeared not to be a factor at all as far as I could tell. It was never mentioned or intimated. Now, whether some of them think that but just didn't happen to talk about it, or whether in deference to me they didn't mention it, I don't know. But I would have thought that if it were really a cause with most of them, it would have shown itself somehow, somewhere, sometime. It never came up once. In fact, the one time that *I* brought it up, it was sort of denied, and genuinely, with no semblance of a false denial. They said, "Look, we're interested in this as music, so we don't care who plays it, whether they're black or green, or what."

POLITICAL AND RACIAL ASPECTS

HASSE: So they were denying the protest aspects of jazz.

SCHULLER: No. I wouldn't go *that* far. They were fully aware of the fact that it is black people who have created this music, jazz. But they weren't making a political ideological issue out of it, the way Paul Robeson tried to generate that in Russia, for example. I mean, they weren't making the blackness of the music a political issue. For them it's music first, of high quality, and while they know that it was created by oppressed black people and that there are all kinds of sociological, political, and economic factors that came into the formation of the music, it is not something that they exploit politically, and say, "We are going to support this music because it is by the black people, the downtrodden black people of America." Not at all!

HASSE: Well, on the other hand, you say that for the jazz aficionado, it represents a music of freedom.

SCHULLER: Yes, that's true.

HASSE: So, what I'm wondering is, if for many black American jazz aficionados, if not just in general, jazz is a music of a certain kind of personal freedom, might it not be the same thing in Russia?

SCHULLER: Yes, and that is the bridge, the connecting link which I tried to establish a couple of times. And they did not accept that. While they saw it as the music of individualism and freedom, they wanted not to make that the primary point of their involvement with it, other than in the most personal way for themselves, but not related to the blackness in America. You understand? For them, it's a very subtle point. For themselves, yes, it is a terribly important music because it represents America and freedom and all of that. But if you then say, "Well, is that the main reason why you like this music, or is it the only reason you like it?", then they right away will turn around and say, "No, no. Wait a minute. This is *great* music. I love the harmony, I like the melody, or the rhythm" or whatever it is they like. So, it's not as political and simplistic as we might tend to think or wish to impose on them.

ROCK IN RUSSIA

HASSE: I see. What about rock? Are they as aware of American rock as they are of American jazz?

HASSE: Almost. Not quite, because there the Soviet authorities still are controlling it with a rather heavy hand. In fact, while I was there two major rock groups were scheduled to appear in Leningrad, and there had been negotiations for months and months between the governments and between various concert agencies and what not. And it was on and off, and on again and so on. Finally, one and a half days before the scheduled appearance, the Russian authorities abruptly cancelled. I understand they had a real problem. Not a riot, but all these kids came to this big square in Leningrad, expecting to see this group, which never showed up. That *would* cause a riot in this country. So, they're a little afraid of rock, and of course, maybe we all are a little. I think there are parts of this whole rock development which are truly distasteful and ridiculous and even dangerous, but then there are other aspects of it that are marvelous. I think the government in Russia does not feel that it has the control to sort that out properly. And neither can they deal with it as freely as we can. We, in the fabric of our society, can sort of let things happen. It gets absorbed one way or another. Over there, they're a little worried about it. Nevertheless, they certainly are aware of the rock culture and you see quite a bit of it on television and other influences of it. And you certainly hear a lot of bad rock music in the hotels and on the radio.

HASSE: Oh, on the radio, too?

SCHULLER: The worst kind. The worst manifestations of American popular music are, of course, the ones that really travel the easiest. To sit in these hotels to which we were always, as foreigners, relegated, the so-called Intourist hotels, and to be forced to listen to this absolute *worst* music that you can imagine, knowing that it was a result of an American influence, was very unpleasant to contemplate.

HASSE: American rock music?

SCHULLER: Well, not exactly. It was the worst of a kind of Soviet imitation of American rock music, with Russian lyrics. But I mean *the worst!*

HASSE: And that's for domestic consumption as well as for the tourists, who are mostly from Iron Curtain countries.

SCHULLER: It's mostly for domestic consumption, and they dance to it—very polite dancing, not disco.

HASSE: Did you find that your book *Early Jazz* was available in the Soviet Union?

SCHULLER: No, but they certainly knew about it. All these people who knew these sorts of things, they knew about my book. That was another thing: I was treated like a god *because* of that book. And they all had either read it or borrowed it or duplicated copies of it, or something. And, of course, I distributed some copies and it was like gold to them!

FAVORITE JAZZ PERFORMERS

HASSE: Who were the most popular American jazz musicians over there, in general?

SCHULLER: Well, the same ones, sort of, as here—[John] Coltrane, McCoy Tyner, Chick Corea, Herbie Hancock, Miles Davis—and Richard Davis is very fondly remembered there from his trip six or seven years ago with the Mel Lewis-Thad Jones band.

HASSE: Oscar Peterson?

SCHULLER: Yes. Perhaps a little less. It tends to be more in the post-Coltrane-Coleman-Dolphy 1960s modern style.

HASSE: Did you find good pianos?

SCHULLER: Oh, yes. Beautiful.

HASSE: What brands?

SCHULLER: They were mostly German. They were Bösendorfers and Bechsteins, and then there *are* some very good Russian pianos—I forgot their name.

RUSSIAN JAZZ FESTIVALS

HASSE: You mentioned jazz festivals. Are those comprised mostly of domestic musicians?

SCHULLER: Yes. It's kind of sad and funny and ironic all at once. They call them "international jazz festivals," and, of course, they're not strictly speaking international at all, because their interpretation of the word "international" extends only to the Soviet Communist Bloc countries. So, it will be "international" in that it will have Czechs and Romanians and Bulgarians and Russians and what not, but it's really not "free world" international. So in that sense it's still kind of closed off.

HASSE: And are there a lot of these festivals?

SCHULLER: Oh, yes. Many of them have now become annual affairs, just like Monterey, or Montreux, and there are new ones springing up all the time.

HASSE: About a year ago I was listening to my short-wave radio and I heard a Voice of America program with you. It was an interview, interspersed with, I believe, your *Red Back Book* recording. It was in English, but I haven't heard much other ragtime on Voice of America. Had anybody heard this program in the Soviet Union that you came across?

SCHULLER: Yes, a few had. I don't recall too many and exactly who. But now that you mention it, I recall this man in Tiblisi, Georgia—again, he was one who definitely had heard it. He hears everything. That man is amazing.

HASSE: He must sleep with a short-wave radio on.

SCHULLER: Well, he's got incredible energy. He seems never to sleep. He just teaches all day, and he's a television producer, and he writes books, and he is at every concert. He's unbelievable. And he can drink like a fish and never feel a thing.

HASSE: What was his name?

SCHULLER: Well, his name is Eugene (Yevgeny in Russian) Machavariani. Georgian names are quite complex. That's a relatively simple one.

HASSE: This has been a fascinating interview for me. Is there anything else you'd like to say while we have the recorder on?

SCHULLER: I guess in respect to the trip there are two things I should say. One is that everything I've said in this interview sounds so wonderful and positive. I must counterbalance this by saying that there were all kinds of other experiences in those four weeks in the Soviet Union which were awful and unpleasant, enough to make you want to leave instantly. Everything from idiotic things like horrendous hotel service, and elevators not working, the food being mediocre, and all kinds of "officialese" things that as an American you just cannot accept at all or even understand. I don't want to give the impression that this was *all* some glorious and wonderful and euphoric trip. We were treated very well—as official visiting artists usually are—but you cannot get away from the Soviet system, with all its stupidities, restrictions, bureaucratic and authoritarian absurdities. I feel that when I was with the jazz people, I was with the best people in the land. There were many other things, however, that I could recount for another two hours, which would counterbalance that picture. So, finally, what I came away with was a quite unbelievable mixture of irreconcilables and inexplicables and unpredictables that makes up the total picture of that trip. That's important to say, lest somebody think, "Well, this guy is just a raving pro-Soviet; thinks everything's great over there." By no means.

The other thing I wanted to say was that I felt that this trip was of enormous importance, not only because we went to places where American musical groups rarely go—Tashkent and Novosibirsk, for example—and where they normally don't hear live American music of any kind, but also because we were doing pioneer work in so far as we were presenting them with a venerable, older American music which they knew nothing about, and which they related to their own very important folk traditions, particularly in the Central Asian countries we visited, like Uzbekistan, which is where Tashkent is. They related to our ragtime music as a folk and native music very much analogous to their own traditions, which, of course, they uphold vigorously *against* the official Soviet line which comes down from Moscow. They see their own folk and national traditions as symbols of freedom to be upheld against the yoke of Soviet oppression. So the pioneer aspect of this was tremendous. And it was more important for them to hear ragtime, I believe, than it was for them to hear yet another modern jazz group—something they've already heard more frequently and which they know about.

LAWRENCE O. KOCH

HARMONIC APPROACHES TO THE
TWELVE-BAR BLUES FORM

The blues, that durable form that has been at the core of jazz from the beginning, has been thoroughly explored by musicians of all eras, but is rarely analyzed in print. The analyses that do exist usually deal with the "blues scale" and its melodic implications, leaving the harmonic function dangling in space. In truth, the harmonic characteristics seem to be derived *from* the melodic approaches—the opposite of most musical truths. This is understandable, however, if one realizes that the form was *vocally* derived and later transferred to instruments; the "blue" notes of the scale were the result of vocal "bending," and instruments merely copied this bit of vocalise.

The "blues scale," as mentioned before, has often been analyzed, but an example is necessary to the understanding of this article. (All examples are in the key of F for ease of examination.)

Ex. 1. Blues scale

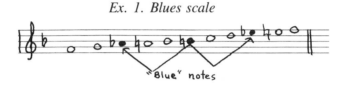

EARLY HARMONIZATIONS

The earliest blues harmonizations were probably formulated from the placing of the *important* blue notes: the flat seventh in measure 4 (I^7) and the flat third in measures 5 and 6 (IV^7).

Ex. 2.

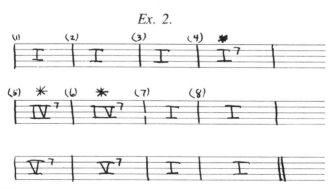

Lawrence O. Koch is director of the Braun School in Pottsville, Pennsylvania. He has combined a teaching career with jazz performing, composing, and arranging. His book on Charlie Parker will shortly be published by Bowling Green Press.

The flat seventh of the scale is the *seventh* (dominant-type) of the tonic chord and the flat third of the scale is the *seventh* of the subdominant chord.

Ex. 3.

It is easy to see that the blue notes were thought of as having a *seventh* quality, and that the harmonic function was so used.

The early improvisors (notably Armstrong) had a predilection for using the flat third in measure 2, and substitute chords were formulated by harmonic players (piano, banjo, guitar) to fit more readily with the usage:

Ex. 4.

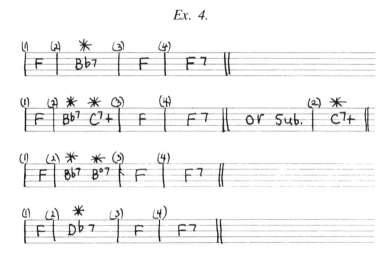

Beside the obvious moving of the IV[7] to the second measure, preserving the seventh function, the players found that the flat third (scale) "blue" note could be used as the raised fifth of a dominant chord (A), the seventh of *both* a IV[7] and a #IV°[7] with upward movement in the bass (B), and *occasionally* as the fifth of a [b]VI[7] (C).

Ex. 5 (A) (B) (C).

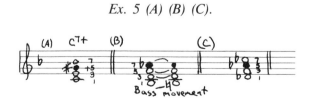

The progression at (B) can be moved to measure 6 also, and the plain IV^7 can be moved to measure 10 (the final dominant measure). In the first case, the second four measures form sequential-sounding harmonic progressions with the first four measures, and in the latter case the progression forms the most frequent retrogression (backward harmonic motion) in jazz. Our blues structure now looks like this:

Ex. 6.

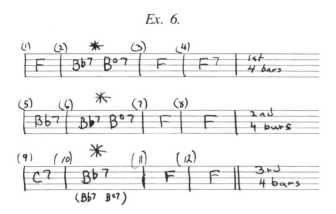

Notice that the IV^7-#IV^{o7} progression can be used also in measure 10, completing the sequence, if desired. These substitutions were also the result of the blue third (7th of IV) being used melodically near the end of the form.

The next substitution comes in measure 8 and involves the VI^7 chord; first used by itself (A), then preceded by a chord containing the blue scale seventh (B) and (C).

Ex. 7(A) (B) (C).

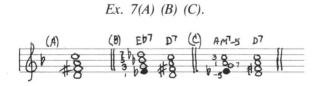

The chromatic progression at (B) above contains the blue scale seventh as the root of the first chord, and at (C) the secondary dominant (D^7) is preceded by its related secondary supertonic with the blue scale seventh becoming the flatted fifth of the secondary supertonic (Am$^{7-5}$). Melodic phrases are often employed which use the blue scale seventh resolving to the scale sixth.

Ex. 8.

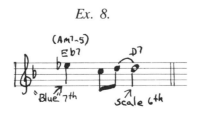

The resolution of the VI^7 is to ii or ii^7 or even II^7 in measure 9, which in turn go to the dominant in measure 10. The ii or ii^7 merely precedes the V^7 and gives the basic dominant sound a slightly different quality, but the II^7 is used as a *secondary* dominant, and the blue scale third can be used melodically as its lowered ninth.

Ex. 9.

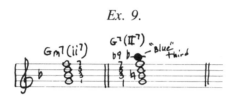

The twelve-bar blues now looks like this:

Ex. 10.

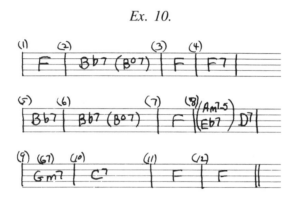

Early treatment of the "turn-around" bars (11-12) involved a series of diminished chords with the ^{b}VI^7 resolving to the dominant at the end, turning the blues around for the next chorus.

Ex. 11.

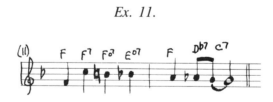

One can see that even with the most basic substitutions, the blues offers a great variety of harmonic possibilities. The possibilities can be explored almost at random by the chord player, depending upon the nature of the blues itself and the character of the improvising soloist.

INNOVATIONS OF THE 1940s AND 1950s

With the coming of bop and cool jazz, the blues harmonizations underwent an intellectualization in an attempt to avoid "bluesy" clichés. Charlie Parker often transferred the opening harmonies of "I Got Rhythm" to the blues, using only major scale tones melodically except for the flat sixth of the scale. This flat-scale sixth was used as the older players used the flat-scale third. It can almost be considered a new blue note. Below is an example from "Barbados" (August 28, 1948—Savoy 12000).

Ex. 12. "Barbados"

Miles Davis can be heard on "Now's the Time" and "Billie's Bounce" (November 26, 1945—Savoy 12079) with Parker. On these two blues, Davis's improvisation's ingeniously use the flat-five *chord-tone* against both the tonic and subdominant harmony. Also notable in this context are Davis's themes to "Weirdo" (March 6, 1954—United Artists 9952) and "Walkin' " (April 29, 1954—Prestige 45-157).

Parker and other musicians of the 1940s often implied the related secondary supertonic before the I[7] in measure 4, and the first four measures often looked like this:

Ex. 13.

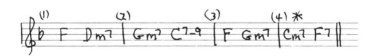

Another favorite progression was in parallel harmony:

Ex. 14.

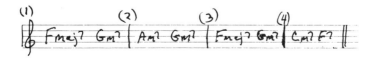

Although it became clichéd, it can be used effectively with tenths in the bass by keyboard players.

An example of an interesting substitute in measure 4 is from Miles Davis's "Sippin' at Bell's" (August 1947—Savoy 12001). Davis uses the flatted fifth substitute (the flatted fifth of one chord is the root of the other) and precedes *it* with its related supertonic.

Ex. 15.

Another transferance used by Parker and by many "west coast" musicians in the fifties was the use of the progression to Parker's "Confirmation" (August 4, 1953—Verve 8005) in the first four bars of the blues:

Ex. 16.

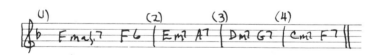

Good examples are Parker's "Laird Baird" (December 30, 1952—Verve 8005) and Frank Rosolino's "Let's Make It" (June, 1957—Interlude MO 500). Shorty Rogers also used this progression in some of his big-band blues harmonizations during the late fifties.

Measures 5 and 6 were sometimes treated as IVmaj^7 resolving to iv^7-^{b}VII^7 progression. This obliterated the blue scale third from bar 5 and created a major-minor relationship between the two measures. An example is again from Davis's "Sippin' at Bell's":

Ex. 17.

The progression in measure 6 can still be used if the normal subdominant (IV⁷) is used in measure 5. This retains the quality of the blue scale third, while still allowing a chord change underneath.

In measures 7 and 8 the main harmonizations involved chromatic parallelism during the 1940s and 1950s:

Ex. 18.

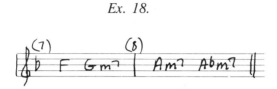

The following are other choices in the same place:

Ex. 19.

The Davis blues, ''Sippin' at Bell's,'' offers a melodic example:

Ex. 20.

All of the above progressions for bars 7 and 8 move smoothly to the ii[7] which in turn moves to the dominant. Bars 9 and 10 were generally treated with the ii[7] to V[7] progression, usually with the V[7] being altered (+9, −9, −5). This led to the "turn-around" bars, which were often treated like the "turn-around" bars in standard tunes:

Ex. 21.

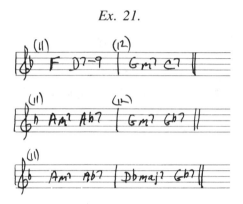

Looking at the blues after the bop revolution, one can construct many interesting harmonic patterns. The beauty is that most of the elements are interchangeable, both within themselves and with older harmonic developments.

Ex. 22. Blues I

Ex. 23. Blues II

Ex. 24. Blues III

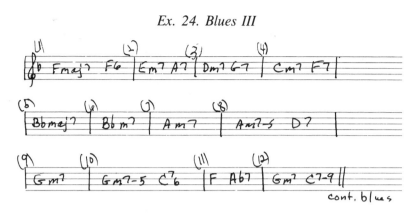

The following is a blues harmonization done by this writer, although he makes no claims to its originality. It involves too many abrupt chord changes for effective improvisation, but is interesting as the harmonization of a blues theme. The author kept the tonic note (F) on top of each chord and used the pattern in a rhythmic form.

Ex. 25.

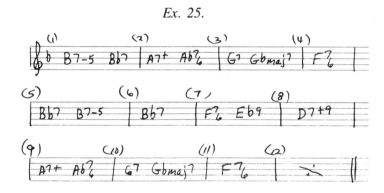

The progression is basically a string of secondary dominants using the flatted-fifth substitution. The tonic melody note (F) serves as a common tone between all chords and is used as the important altered tone in many of the chords (-5 of the B^{7-5}; $+5$ of the A^7+; 6th of the A^{b7}_6; maj 7th of the G^{bmaj7}; the 9th of the E^{b9}; $+9$ of the D^{7+9}). The retrogression going from bar 8 to bar 9 (D^{7+9} to A^{7+}) is unusual in jazz, but here it is necessary in order to use the progression of measures 2 and 3 as a cadence formula to create harmonic unity.

THE MINOR FORM

The minor form of the twelve-bar blues was developed most extensively during the 1950s. The origin is beyond the scope of this work, but it certainly would make interesting research. Charlie Parker did not use this form at all, and little evidence exists in the standard jazz literature and recordings to support any *prevalent* use of the *true* minor form before the 1950s. (Ellington's "KoKo" from 1940 is certainly derived from this form, for instance, but does not hold to it throughout or use it for extended improvisation.)

Because of the basically modal character of the minor, the harmonic treatment is necessarily more simple than the major form. In fact, it is this writer's opinion that it is this form which gave rise to the modal character of much of the music of the 1960s. Before continuing with its evolution, however, let us examine the basic form.

Ex. 26.

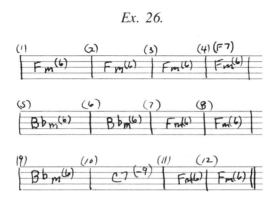

A good example to hear in this form is Dave Brubeck's "Audrey" (October 1954—Harmony HS 11253). This particular blues contains extended improvisations by altoist Paul Desmond in the minor and a lovely closing theme in the parallel major using many of the harmonic changes discussed earlier.

The compositions of Horace Silver contain two excellent examples of creative chord substitution in the minor form. "Señor Blues" (1956—Blue Note 1539) uses $^{\flat}$VI^7 as a replacement for iv and has the retrogression V^7-IV^7 (characteristic of the *major* blues) at the cadence. "Doin' the Thing" (1961—Blue Note 4076) stays on the tonic through bar 6, and then uses a $^{\flat}$V^7 (a iv substitute). This has the effect of inverting the usual function. Using algebraic symbols for easy explanation of this inversion shows the following: What is normally X (4 bars) Y (2 bars) X (2 bars), Silver has transformed to X (4 bars) X (2 bars) Y (2 bars).

The addition of the natural scale sixth to the minor triad (see Example 26) increases the implied modality. It then more definitely implies a Dorian scale (this is a scale like the natural minor but with a natural scale sixth—in other words, D Dorian would consist of the white notes on the piano keyboard, using D as the "final," or tonal, center). This natural sixth makes the structure a rootless B$^{\flat 9}$, and when approached in this manner a dual modality results. Below is a typical modal piano voicing with dual implications.

Ex. 27.

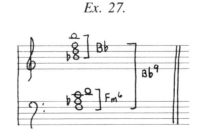

The Fm⁶ implies a Dorian scale on F for improvisation, while considering the structure a Bᵇ⁹ implies a Mixolydian scale (like major with lowered seventh) on Bᵇ. The improviser and the bass player can choose either scale with freedom. Notice that the relationship is a fifth away and that the Aᵇ acts interchangeably as either the flat third or flat seventh, depending on the mode chosen. It seems that here again, even in modal jazz, the "seventh-sound" has dictated the harmony.

Each chord dictates a different set of tonal centers, and we see clearly that the *harmony* governs the *scales* used. In other words the Fm⁶ in Ex. 26 implies the duality of F Dorian or Bᵇ Mixolydian, while the Bᵇm⁶ implies Bᵇ Dorian or Eᵇ Mixolydian. It should be pointed out that, in the dual relationships, the scale notes are exactly the same; it is the "final," or tonal center, that is different. In fact, there are seven possible finals within every major scale (a mode can be explained easiest by thinking of each major scale rearranged with every note of the scale a possible starting note or "final"), and a resourceful improviser can suggest many modes over a given chord.

John Coltrane's "Village Blues" (October 1960—Atlantic SD 1354) uses chord structures such as Ex. 27, and Miles Davis's "All Blues" (April 1959—Columbia CL 1355) offers an excellent example of dual modality, in this case D Dorian and G Mixolydian. The melody is based on the skip of D to B-natural, implying D Dorian (B-natural is the natural sixth), and the piano trills a G against this.

The earlier minor blues (those of the 1950s) were, of course, basically in the true minor as we know it. The use of the I⁷ at bar 4 instead of plain i (Ex. 26) gives an interesting relief from the minor tonality and also acts as a secondary dominant going to iv. Most of the substitutions involved the addition of the natural sixth, the ninth (or both), and sometimes the major seventh to the minor triad. This implies the melodic minor scale and allows an interesting polytonality between F-minor and C-major. A later modal structure might look like this:

Ex. 28.

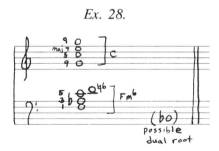

This again *can* be used to imply the major key a fifth down, but seems to be most effective in a blues sense when the tonality is left dangling between the two.

Below are examples of scales mentioned:

Ex. 29.

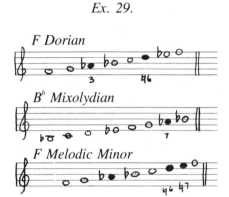

It is interesting to note that the F melodic minor when used in its IV mode can be arranged in thirds from its final to form a B^{b13+11}.

Ex. 30.

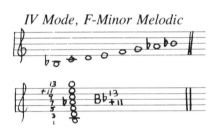

From the above examples, it is easy to relate the roots of modal jazz back to the minor blues of the fifties.

MUTANT FORMS AND OTHER USAGES

The blues as part of a larger form offers a wide range of possibilities that have not been explored. The "blues-with-a-bridge" has been occasionally used and is worth a mention. Sir Charles Thompson's "20th Century Blues" (September 1944—Vogue [French] LDAP 769) and Stu Williamson's "Sapphire" (January 18, 1955—Bethlehem BCP-31) are excellent listening examples. The blues is generally used as the "A" section of an AABA pattern, although certainly other forms are possible. A rondo, for instance ABACA, could be considered and would be improvisationally very interesting.

The Williamson example above is notable also for the fact that a set of substitute chords in the first four bars (see Ex. 16) is used *only* during altoist Charlie Mariano's choruses;

the rest of the time a more traditional treatment is used. It is this type of thinking, which started with Jelly Roll Morton's interesting but free formats, that makes the familiar forms of jazz fresh to the listener's ear.

A 1962 Brew Moore album, Fantasy 6013, contains some interesting devices. "The Monster" has the blues form alternating with a free section and "Piger" is a 12-bar blues with a two-bar rhythmic tag on each chorus. Both tunes are by altoist Sahib Shihab.

John Carisi's "Israel" (March 9, 1950—Capitol M-11026), played by Miles Davis's "Birth of the Cool" group, is an excellent example of wild harmonic approaches and should not be overlooked in an investigation of blues harmonizations; the originality is astounding. The piece is basically in the minor with melodic counter-melody outlining the harmony, but at bar 7 it suddenly states the tonic major as the beginning of a series of three major-seventh chords.

The theme of George Gershwin's Second Piano Prelude (*Three Preludes* [1926]—Nonesuch H-71284) has a beautiful use of the blues form, and an interesting jazz performance of this theme is by a Shelley Manne big band in an arrangement by Johnny Williams (February 25, 1965—Capitol ST-2313).

A device which relies chiefly on the effect of the blue notes is that of using a I^7 or I^9 throughout the first four bars and in all subsequent returns to the tonic. This is very "bluesy" sounding and works well with the theory of dual modality (Ex. 27—B^{b9}) in minor. Many rock and soul groups use this device with a raised ninth on the tonic, allowing the blue third to be heard throughout the harmony.

Ex. 31.

Although this article has only hinted at the many and varied approaches that can be applied to the blues form, the writer hopes that it will stimulate new and original usages and will demonstrate that the blues, far from exhausted, remains a vital and extremely malleable form that is unique to jazz.

IRVING LOUIS HOROWITZ

ON SEEING AND HEARING MUSIC:
NINE PROPOSITIONS IN SEARCH OF EXPLANATION

> *The mass is a matrix from which all traditional behavior to-*
> *ward works of art issues today in a new form. Quantity has*
> *been transmuted into quality. The greatly increased mass of*
> *participants has produced a change in the mode of participa-*
> *tion.*
>
> — *Walter Benjamin*

A problem that has long puzzled sociologists and musicologists is why, in an era of astonishingly high quality recordings, people continue to attend live concert performances. This article considers nine elements relating to concert attendance in an effort to seek a solution to this vexing question: (1) the interactional element; (2) extramusical considerations; (3) social verification of status; (4) musician and audience networks; (5) comparison and confirmation of talent; (6) audiences as confirmation of social tastes; (7) cultural exclusivity afforded by attendance; (8) the act of enjoyment apart from "serious" considerations of purchases; and finally (9) the technology of "live" versus "recorded" sounds.

In its simplest, most atomistic form, the incongruity goes as follows: In the age of electronic recording, the sound of music has become astonishingly precise and higher in quality then live performances; why then should anyone go to hear music in person? This has perplexed twentieth century musicologists and sociologists alike. A variety of reasons have been offered. The issue has become considerably magnified in an era of multiple-track recording engineering that is virtually error-free and increasingly larger than life.

When we consider the actual situation in concert halls and other places where live music is heard—from night clubs to dance halls—all available data points to a huge increase in the number of musical ensembles, musical events, and audience attendance. This is true of all kinds of music, from classical to country-western, and from Lincoln Center to the Grand Ole Opry.

The anomaly is that musical attendance has soared at the very time when the quality of recorded sound has dramatically improved. In ethnographic terms, the question may be posed as: Why should someone attend a dimly lit night club, prepared to be irritated by other people's conversation and tinkling glasses, instead of staying home and listening to a nearly perfect recording of Sarah Vaughan's most recent studio session? Similarly, why should anyone attend a concert hall, which is sometimes acoustically obsolete, and pay a heavy premium to do so, rather than listen to a recording of Lazar Berman, which is probably less expensive and less taxing than attendance at the live performance?

This is not to suggest that live performances are uniformly inferior to recorded sound. Debates about musical engineering are not especially pertinent. What is relevant however is that such comparisons can even be entertained. Clearly, the gap between live and

Irving Louis Horowitz is Hannah Arendt Professor of Sociology and Political Science at Rutgers University, and editor-in-chief of *Transaction/Society*. He has written extensively on the sociology of music for *Psychology Today, Commonweal*, and the *Journal of Jazz Studies*.

recorded performances have been reduced to such miniscule dimensions that it is no longer self-evident that in-person performances have any overwhelming edge. Sometimes the risk of error is taken out of live or television musical performances by verbal mimickry of recorded efforts. Hence the issue of why people continue to see and hear music in contrast to simply hearing music has, if anything, increasing relevance for our age. Having set forth the context of this problem, let me now indicate possible resolutions to this apprent anomaly.

THE INTERACTIONAL ELEMENT

Live performances, especially intimate forms of music such as a classical quartet or a jazz quintet, reveal interactions between musicians that produce quite different effects on the listener than the private act of putting on a recording. For example, a simple-to-listen-to Haydn quartet may in fact be a very difficult and intricate work to perform, resting upon precise melodic and harmonic relations which would be destroyed by improper performance. A recorded musical piece which projects a fluid, effortless quality, may in a concert hall performance create a frenzied, vigorous, pulsating effect. The act of creation is ultimately an act of labor. But the hard work involved in performing a piece of music cannot easily be gleaned from listening to the recording. The empathy, the very sweat of the musicians, is an element that the audience can identify with and share with the musicians.

Another side to this interaction relates not to the audience and musician, but rather the exchanges of the musicians with each other: how they relate to one another in the process of musical creation. This becomes a feature of value, a facet of the performance that an audience can identify with in relation to a group of musicians. The glance, the nod, the smile, the unobtrusive gesture—often indicating approval or disapproval—upon entering and leaving a passage, are extramusical elements that lend themselves to an intense musical experience. Such interactions are particularly fascinating at live jazz performances, where improvised solos may be as new to the other musicians as they are to the audience.

EXTRAMUSICAL ELEMENTS

Seeing a performance involves something akin to watching a high wire act: the audience waits for the mistake, for the human foible, the failed note, the flawed passage. The musician's side of this idiosyncrasy is the strategy involved in live musical performance. Vladimir Horowitz noted in an interview that in his 1928 debut with the Philharmonic at Carnegie Hall, he played the Tchaikovsky Piano Concerto rapidly and loudly—entirely out of keeping with the spirit of tranquility that Sir Thomas Beecham, the conductor, was striving for. His motive was simple: he believed that a highly romantic and virtuosic performance—one designed to be highly successful in audience terms—was essential if he were to succeed in America. If he had emulated the conception of Beecham, Horowitz feared, he might have been shipped back to Europe permanently. He felt he could not risk this one big chance, hence the musical ''mistake'' involved in an extramusical dimension.

Live performances often involve extramusical elements that can only be understood and participated in by those who attend.

SOCIAL VERIFICATION OF STATUS

A key element of participating in or attending live musical performances is to verify that a population segment (fellow attendees) has good taste. Audience members confirm both one another's taste and position in a stratification system. Good taste becomes a function not necessarily of listening to good music but of *where* one listens to good music—which in turn determines quality. To be "hip" in jazz terms is to visit select clubs, which are seen as being "in" by the attendees or the musicians—or both. In the world of classical music, one appears *au courant* with the most acceptable performances and performers—to gain social and cultural verification as a music lover—in rough proportion to the number of times that one attends the great symphonic hall or opera house of any great city, or its smaller chamber or recital halls. Attendance serves not simply to verify the musical taste of the music lover, but also to confirm, by one's presence, the place of technique and style in the verification process.

MUSICIAN AND AUDIENCE NETWORKS

Live performances create living relations between the performer and the patron, unlike a recording which permits great distance in space and time between the performer and the listener. In "live" activities, the networking process draws the two constituencies much closer together. A considerable portion of any audience for music is comprised of associates and acquaintances of the musicians and their cohort. This in itself is part of the networking process. No truer illustration has existed than the scene at the Keystone Corner in San Francisco, where Rahsaan Roland Kirk and the Vibration Society held forth for that self-styled constituency of art-worshipers, who applied Kirk's special doctrines to their own aesthetic projects—in music and elsewhere.

The sale of records also creates a relationship of high expectations between the performer and the audience. Live performances confirm and verify what is on the disc, making clear the authenticity of the recorded sound by permitting comparison with the living performer. The recording, like sheet music in the nineteenth century, assures accuracy and authenticity in performance; and it does so for a much larger audience incapable of reading musical scores. The recording is a secondary confirmation of a presumed primary relationship.

COMPARING FRAMEWORKS

What the above suggests is that recordings function not to replace but to reinforce audience expectations. These expectations provide a framework for measuring and confirming what the recording "says" in regard to quality, innovation, and musical imagination. In the world of jazz this is especially important because the live performance, to be truly successful, must sound like the recorded performance; but at the same time—unlike pop performance—it must not imitate the record. A solo jazz performance must be rich, but not identical; otherwise the listener to a live show may feel "cheated." What the live performance does is verify the quality of the musicians involved. One of the key dilemmas of rock music is that live concerts are often far more imitative of the recorded performance than is the jazz performance.

It is worth pointing out that jazz musicians have been far less prone to use synthesizers, pre-recorded tapes, or signal delay equipment than other types of performers. The commitment of jazz musicians to instrumental no less than artistic purity make them less likely than others to bridge any presumed or actual gap between recorded and live performances. Jazz is the one music where perfect replication is not only considered less than ideal, but a down-right negation of the innovative aspects of solo and ensemble performance. In the jazz world, the recording is but one form of presenting a musical idea; it is not *the* correct way, any more than the live performance is an incorrect way. In this sense, it is only fair to note as a caveat that listeners to live jazz are not measuring the correctness of interpretation, or how well the recording is simulated, but simply searching for variations on a musical theme. In this, the jazz musician shares with the jazz audience a special relationship that guarantees a commitment both to see and to hear a musical performance or a specific musical artist.

Given the importance of engineering capabilities in recording rock music and other forms of music that rely heavily on overdubbing, echo effects, etc., many musicians cannot readily duplicate the sound of their recordings in live performance. As a result, some rock groups and vocalists in particular never venture forth from the studio, or do so only at their own peril. The disastrous comparison of "live" performances with carefully engineered studio performances of such groups as Crosby, Stills, Nash and Young was certainly a contributing factor to their demise. To the contrary, the Carnegie Hall dates of performers like Miles Davis and Benny Goodman enhanced their respective jazz reputations. As a result, a clearer distinction emerges between artistry and theatricality. Many of the newer rock groups emphasize showmanship—light effects, costumes, makeup, bizarre behavior, and any element that can function as a supplement to the music itself. The mutual confirmability of the recorded sound and the live performance form the groundwork for the total audience of any musician or group of musicians.

THE SOCIAL STATUS OF THE AUDIENCE

Social standing is particularly determined by the act of attending a live musical performance. But attendance does more; it also confirms social standing in the larger nonmusical community. This is much more true of the classical musical audience than the jazz musical audience, given the higher socioeconomic status of classical musical audiences. But in all forms, musical participation at concerts confirms social standing in the community generally. There is a veritable pecking order of power in relation to the musical performance. Whether at Lincoln Center or Monterey, the highest status is conferred by such special recognition as listing in the program notes as a special individual or institutional donor to a performing group or special event, followed by whether a persons sits in the orchestra or in the balcony, followed by where in the orchestra or balcony one sits, followed (in some cases) by what one wears to a musical outing. The world of music is a world of fashion, not simply a musical fashion but also fashion in the broad stylistic sense of that term. If the musicians tend to be uniformly dressed, for example, the audience takes on the role of the performer in terms of this and of other extramusical activities. Hence, the question of musical participation or attending the musical performance is also in its cultural model a matter of being seen, rather than of listening.

CULTURAL EXCLUSIVITY

Going to a place called a concert hall, night club, or dance hall, represents a mechanism for class diversification and cultural differentiation. In this specifically sociological sense, attendance at musical functions serves two seemingly disparate functions: first it distinguishes attendees from non-attendees. But it also fuses the people in attendance as an exclusive body unto itself. There is a strong implication that a temporary cluster of people going to a night club to see Miles Davis or Stan Getz, in that very activity, distinguish themselves from all other passing "communities." At the same time, attendance unites those who go to observe the musical performance. The presumption of such commonalities provides for an elitism quite characteristic of class diversification and cultural differentiation in general.

The presumption that such commonalities form the backbone of lasting human relationships is itself probably dubious, but it is nevertheless widely respected. It is an inheritance from an age when music and belief systems were intensely integrated. Anyone broadly familiar with the classical tradition from Bach to Wagner could scarcely doubt this. But in the twentieth century, when music has become bifurcated from theological systems or church attendance, the secularization of culture has led to a desacralization of ritual. And this in turn has led people to view music as such, in itself, apart from other considerations, to provide a basis for cultural fusion and differentiation.

THE SERIOUS AND THE ENJOYABLE

The purchase of recordings by an individual is a serious business. It denotes matters of personalized taste; it involves a statement of preference; and ultimately it commands allegiance to one's own taste, and defense against the criticisms of others. To spend an evening listening to "light" or "pop" music may be enjoyable, even entertaining, but to own a record collection based exclusively upon such music might just as readily be construed as bad taste.

There are elements of risk and of value in assembling a record collection that are not involved in attending concerts or night clubs. New standards of seriousness and of entertainment have come to the fore—above all, the belief that record collections, like book collections, are specialized representations of self, laden with symbolic messages and meanings, for the associates of the collector no less than the individual. Above all, a record is a permanent addition to one's private world, a standard to be measured by, no less than measuring, the artists involved.

In the case of live performances, there is a motion-picture-like atmosphere which builds up, including the right to criticize the performance as well as the music. Attending a concert is a transient event, a happening that leaves few permanent marks or involves few risks. This powerful differential—the serious and permanent nature of a record collection and the transient nature of concert-going—works to maintain high levels of attendance, since this is the best way to insure cultivation without commitment.

MEASURING "LIVE" VERSUS "RECORDED" SOUNDS

The new technology serves as a challenge no less than a threat. Live rock music sound systems, for instance, are now becoming as sophisticated as studio systems although used differently—to amplify volume rather than nuance. Large concert halls, gymnasia, open stadiums, and like places can be filled with as much sound, with as much "separation," as any living room can with a stereo recording. As musicians and ancillary technical personnel become accustomed to the technologies employed in performances before live audiences, their concert dates may more nearly approximate their recording dates. However, this closing of the technical gap only serves to point up special problems of innovation, creativity and authenticity. It does nothing to shake the social bases of audience attachments to live performances. Some groups have even mimed performance, with their recording played through the concert amplification system. In some instances, such groups acquire reputations of being more competent than their recordings would suggest. Some have found that live performances lead to disastrous results, and have lost segments of their audiences, both for live and recorded performances. The use of tape, however, and of signal delay equipment has added new capabilities to simple rock groups. In short, the gap between recordings and live performance is a recognized fact of life that some musical styles and groups have candidly begun to force. The commitment of jazz and classical musicians to instrumental no less than musical purity, make them less likely to bridge this gap between live and recorded performances.

Musical groups, including rock organizations, still opt whenever possible for the intimate club or the smaller, acoustically balanced concert hall. But in a football stadium or a bar on the strip, the hardware is enlarged precisely to simulate a recording studio (and often includes the recorders). It is clear that musical quality is lost in the live performance, no matter how sophisticated the hardware. But whatever the relationship is of the live and recorded performance, whichever is deemed superior by the listener, differences are real and persistent. Thus the mutual confirmability of the recorded sound and the live performance forms the groundwork for the total audience of any musician or group of musicians.

The subject of this essay on seeing and hearing music, while hardly exhausted by this analysis, may open a more intimate dialogue between musicological and sociological forms of analysis. The inherited dichotomies, in which the claims of music and society were perceived as uncomfortable straitjackets on each, may now yield to a closer inspection of the ways in which musical audiences and environments serve to stimulate or retard musical creations. For such an undertaking to be remotely successful, the skills of all concerned will be needed.

TOR MAGNUSSON

FATS WALLER: SOME CONSIDERATIONS ON TWO RECORDING DATES

For more than 50 years Thomas "Fats" Waller has been one of the major figures in jazz and popular music. His life story has been told in no less than three books[1,2,3] and his phonograph recordings have been included in a large number of general jazz discographies, starting in 1936 with *Rhythm on Record*[4] and continuing into the present with the 1978 edition of *Jazz Records 1897-1942*.[5] The recordings have also been listed in greater detail in specialized Waller discographies such as those appearing in the Kirkeby and Waller-Calabrese biographies cited, as well as in other publications.[6,7,8,9] Despite the apparently complete covering of Waller's recordings, there are questions concerning the accuracy of some of the discographical notes. Two recording sessions will be discussed here: one from 1928 and another from 1939.

THE 1928 SESSION

This was not really one session; the recordings were in fact made on two consecutive days: on March 2 and 3, 1928. The titles were "Chlo-E" and "When You're With Somebody Else," and the recordings were issued on Victor 21298 under the name of "Shilkret's Rhyth-Melodists."

The first time any of these recordings were mentioned in connection with Waller was when the second title appeared in the 1953 edition of the discography cited above, *The Music of Thomas "Fats" Waller*. Under the heading "Doubtful items" a note reads:

> Fats may play pipe-organ on this (and other) titles, as it sounds very like him, and Nat Shilkret is reported to have said that Fats was the only coloured artist to record with him.

FIGURE 1

```
SHILKRET'S RHYTH-MELODISTS                    Camden, N.J., 2 Mar, 1928
Lou Raderman(vln), Fats Waller(pipe organ), Milton Rettenberg(pno)
42529-2   Chloe                       Vic 21298

Chuck Campbell(tbn), Francis J. Lapitino(harp) added.  Camden, N.J., 2 Mar, 1928
42532-2   When you're with somebody else    Vic 21298
```

The following note from Brian Rust provides some interesting 'background' to the above;
  On the evening of March 2, 1928, in Trinity Church on Fifth Street, Camden, N.J.,
Lambert Murphy was recording with Sigmund Krumgold at the organ, Lou Raderman on violin
and Nat Shilkret and Milton Rettenberg on pianos. Things hadn't gone too well, and the
boys were thinking of calling it a day when Fats Waller came in, and started playing
CHLOE softly on the organ. Nat Shilkret thought that a non-vocal version of this, by
Raderman, Rettenberg and Waller might be a commercial proposition, so he sketched out a
rough arrangement and they made a few takes. Then they called it a day, returning the
next morning with Chuck Campbell on trombone and Francis J. Lapitino - the harp soloist
of the Boston Symphony, to make WHEN YOU'RE WITH SOMEBODY ELSE. Nat Shilkret himself
volunteered this story to me at his home in Massapequa, N.J., on October 14, 1963, without
any kind of prompting. The record bears it out in every detail.

Tor Magnusson is docent (associate professor) in the Department of Pharmacology at the University of Göteborg in Sweden. His interest in American jazz and popular music extends back to the early 1940s. His discography of Gene Austin was serialized in the British periodical *Matrix* during 1971-1975, and an earlier article on Fats Waller and Gene Austin appeared in The *Journal of Jazz Studies*, vol. 4, no. 1.

In the 1966 edition of that discography, both titles are included, followed by an interesting note. The whole paragraph appears here as Figure 1. It contains a few obvious mistakes: the date for the second title, being recorded "next morning," should of course be March 3; also there is no violinist on this second title. Probably as a consequence of this discographical note, these two recordings have been included in a number of Waller reissue LPs, e.g. the Fats Waller Complete Recordings Vol. 3 (1927-1929).[10]

Despite the story told by Nat Shilkret to Brian Rust, we were, however, not completely convinced that Waller was the organist on these recordings, and so when we published a small discography of the "Shilkret's Rhyth-Melodists,"[11] we listed the organ player as being either Sigmund Krumgold or Thomas Waller.

On May 16, 1976, in a telephone conversation with Milton Rettenberg, the pianist on these recordings, we brought up the "Rhyth-Melodists" recordings, mentioning Waller's name. Rettenberg's answer was very determined: "No, Fats Waller never recorded with us in Camden. That was Krumgold on organ." We later wrote a letter to Rettenberg, enclosing a copy of material shown here as Figure 1. In his reply, dated July 17, 1976, Rettenberg wrote:

> First, I wish to attack the published fantasy concerning the recording of Chloe in Camden. Fats Waller, on that day, was not much nearer Camden than you are now. Krumgold was the organist who played in the old Church at 5th & Federal Streets in Camden, after Victor took it over (not yet RCA) in the late 20's . . . . As to Waller, I knew him well — we *never* were together on a recording date. He used to come up to Gene's apartment, where a few of us played poker. Fats didn't join the game; he just sat at the piano and played half the night, with intermissions to guzzle a bottle of Austin's supply of bootleg gin . . . .

On October 18, 1978, we checked the Victor recording ledgers for these two recordings. They are found on pages 6530 and 6532, and they were listed as performed by "Shilkret's Organ Combination." In contrast to the story for which Nat Shilkret is given credit, the ledgers show that: (1) "Chlo-E" was the first title recorded, followed by two titles by Lambert Murphy, "Little Log Cabin of Dreams" and "Where My Caravan Has Rested;" (2) the time used for the Murphy recordings was 35 and 60 minutes (cf. above, "Things hadn't gone too well"); (3) the recordings were finished at 4:35 p.m. (cf. above, "On the evening of March 2").

We consider it safe to conclude that Milton Rettenberg is correct in his statement that Sigmund Krumgold, and not Waller, was the organ player on "Chlo-E" as well as on "When You're With Somebody Else." Thus, these two recordings should not be included as Waller items, and the discographical notice — including the two recordings by Lambert Murphy — should read as in Figure 2.

FIGURE 2

Shilkret's Rhyth-Melodists
Pipe Organ, Violin and Piano

Nat Shilkret directing Lou Raderman, violin, Milton Rettenberg, piano, Sigmund Krumgold, pipe organ, and William Reitz, traps.

Church Bldg., Camden, NJ, March 2, 1928

42529 - 1, 2, 3   CHLO - E   (78) Victor 21298 - A
                (Song of the Swamp)   (mg) RI - DISC 2 [German] ,
                (Gus Kahn - Neil Morét)   RCA 741 076 [French]

Lambert Murphy
Tenor with violin, piano and pipe organ

Lambert Murphy, vocal, acc. by Lou Raderman, violin, Nat Shilkret, piano, and Sigmund
Krumgold, pipe organ.   same date

42530 - 1, 2, 3, 4   LITTLE LOG CABIN OF DREAMS   (78) Victrola 4038 - A
                (James F. Hanley - Eddie Dowling)

Lambert Murphy
Tenor with piano and pipe organ

Lambert Murphy, vocal, acc. by Nat Shilkret, piano, and Sigmund Krumgold, pipe organ.
                                  same date

42531 - 1, 2, 3   WHERE MY CARAVAN HAS RESTED   (78) Victrola 4038 - B
                (Edward Teschemacher - Herman Löhr)

Shilkret's Rhyth-Melodists
Pipe Organ, Piano, Trombone and Harp

Nat Shilkret directing Chuck Campbell, trombone, Francis J. Lapitino, harp, Milton Rettenberg, piano, and Sigmund Krumgold, pipe organ.
                     Church Bldg., Camden, NJ,   March 3, 1928

42532 - 1, 2, 3   WHEN YOU'RE WITH SOMEBODY ELSE   (78) Victor 21298 - B
                (Gilbert - Etting - Baer)   (mg) RI - DISC 2 [German] ,
                                        RCA 741 076 [French]

Note: the above artist credits are as given on the record labels; for masters 42529 and
42532 the recording sheets show "Shilkret's Organ Combination".

THE 1939 SESSION

The second recording date to be discussed is a 1939 session with Gene Austin. These recordings were discussed in some detail in an earlier article in this journal,[12] but are here brought up again because some new pieces of information have come to hand.

These recordings were mentioned for the first time in a newspaper article[13] by Jim Walsh, written less than two months after the recordings were made. In this article the author writes:

> Of recent years he [Gene Austin] has made a number of Decca records and now has ready for release a Victor of "I Can't Give You Anything But Love" and another old-time hit, in which he is assisted by Candy and Coco, who appear with him tonight. . . .

The recordings have since then been listed in a number of articles and discographies, as reviewed in our earlier article. The recording date has constantly been given as February 27, 1939, and the artist credit has been either "FATS" WALLER AND HIS RHYTHM or simply GENE AUSTIN. In our previous article on these two recordings, we stated:

> They were made in connection with a Thesaurus radio transcription session that Gene Austin made with Candy & Coco in the Victor studios, but the recordings were never issued as 78 rpm records.

On September 25, 1978, we talked with "Candy" Russell Hall about these recordings.

He confirmed that he was the string bass player on that date, and that Otto "Coco" Heimel
was the guitarist. Hall could not remember making Thesaurus transcriptions or any other
transcription records in New York City. The recordings they had made with Fats Waller
were made at 10 o'clock in the morning and certainly not in connection with any transcription recordings, he added.

On October 18, 1978, we were able to locate the recording sheet for this session in the
Victor files; this sheet was filed in a separate folder labelled "FATS" WALLER & GENE
AUSTIN, which is also the artist credit on the recording sheet and which gives the
information shown, rather dimly, in Figure 3, which gives the recording date as "March
6th," not February 27 as previously listed. The recording sheet indicates that two takes were
made of "Sweet Sue;" in earlier listings, only one take of each title is given.[14] Also, note
the agreement between the recording time as given on the recording sheet (9:15 to 10:30)
and the time recalled by Russell Hall (10 o'clock in the morning) nearly 40 years after the
recordings were made. The correct discographical notice is shown in Figure 4.

FIGURE 3

FIGURE 4

"FATS" WALLER & GENE AUSTIN

Thomas 'Fats' Waller, vocal remarks and Hammond organ, Otto 'Coco' Heimel, guitar, 'Candy' Russell Hall, string bass,
and Gene Austin, vocal   Studio No. 3, New York, NY, March 6, 1939

BS 033993 - 1, 1A, 2, 2A   SWEET SUE   (78) Bluebird unissued
                            (Victor Young - Will J. Harris)   (mg) The Rarest Fats Waller Volume I RFW-1,
                                                                      Swaggie S 1243 [Australian],
                                                                      RCA FXM1 7198 [French]

BS 033994 - 1, 1A   I CAN'T GIVE YOU ANYTHING BUT LOVE   (78) Bluebird unissued
                            (Dorothy Fields - Jimmy McHugh)   (mg) The Rarest Fats Waller Volume II RFW-2,
                                                                      Swaggie S 1243 [Australian],
                                                                      RCA FXM1 7198 [French]

This information is relevant to the LP record RCA FXM1 7198,[15] which was issued after
the writing of our previous article in this journal. The album notes (in French by Pierre-
François Cangardel and in English by Roy Cooke) are incorrect on at least two points. First,
the recording date is incorrectly given as February 27, 1939. Second, the personnel for the
session is incorrectly stated as Al Casey on guitar and Cedric Wallace on string bass. The

two writers are also commenting upon the two recordings. Pierre-François Cangardel writes:

> Gene Austin, vieille conaissance, avait enregistré avec son ami en 1929: *"My fate is in your hands"* (cf. RCA 741 094). Le 27 Février 1939, "Fats" l'accompagne à l'orgue lors d'une séance semi-privée: seuls Al Casey et Cedric Wallace soutiennent leur chef. C'est un régal d'entendre le fantastique travail de "Fats" à l'orgue hammond, et de Albert à la guitare! tant en accompagnement qu'en solo. Pour cela, *"Sweet Sue"* et *"I can't give you anything but love"* font figure de petits joyaux. . . .

In translation: "Gene Austin, an old acquaintance, had recorded with his friend [Fats Waller] in 1929: *'My fate is in your hands'* (cf. RCA 741 094). On February 27, 1939, "Fats" accompanies at the organ in a semi-private session: only Al Casey and Cedric Wallace support their leader. It is a joy to listen to the fantastic work of Fats at the hammond organ, and of Albert [Casey] on the guitar, in accompaniment as well as in solo. Therefore, *'Sweet Sue'* and *'I can't give you anything but love'* are like small pieces of jewelry."

Roy Cooke writes:

> The next two titles were made under Gene Austin's name, but "Fats" the accompanist outshines Gene the singer. In *Sweet Sue* "Fats" exclaims: — "Gene—You got your boots on?" Gene answers:—"Yes, Fats—Send Me . . ." "Fats" is excellent, but the majority will find Gene Austin's vocal rather too much on the sugary side. Albert Casey can be heard on guitar in the background. *I can't give you anything but love, baby* is much the better side of the two. "Fats" is excellent on Hammond Organ, and Gene Austin's vocal is much better here, also. . . .

Otto "Coco" Heimel was a guitar player of great merit; he used a four-string guitar throughout his career. We find it somewhat hard to understand how his guitar work can be mistaken for that of Al Casey.

NOTES

Acknowledgment: The author gratefully acknowledges the generosity of RCA Records, New York, for access to their recording files and also the kind assistance of Miss Louise Fox. Sincere thanks also go to Milton Rettenberg, New York, and to Russell Hall, Reno, Nevada, for their kind cooperation and great patience. For stylistic correction of the manuscript he is indebted to Dr. Roger Brown, Bethesda, Maryland.

1. W.T. Ed Kirkeby, in collaboration with Duncan P. Schiedt and Sinclair Traill, *Ain't Misbehavin'—The Story of Fats Waller* (London: Peter Davies, 1966).

2. Joel Vance, *Fats Waller: His Life and Times* (Chicago: Contemporary Books, 1977).

3. Maurice Waller and Anthony Calabrese, *Fats Waller* (New York: Schirmer, 1978).

4. Hilton R. Schleman, *Rhythm on Record* (London: Odhams Press, 1936).

5. Brian Rust, *Jazz Records 1897-1942* (New Rochelle, New York: Arlington House, 1978).

6. John R. T. Davies, *The Music of Thomas "Fats" Waller* (London: J. J. Publications, 1950).

7. John R. T. Daives, revised by R. M. Cooke, *The Music of Thomas "Fats" Waller* (London: "Friends of Fats"—The Thomas "Fats" Waller Appreciation Society, 1953).
8. John R. T. Davies, revised by Bob Kumm and the "Storyville Team," "The Music of Thomas 'Fats' Waller," *Storyville* 1, no. 2 (December 1965) through no. 12 (August-September 1967).

9. Tor Magnusson, *An Almost Complete Thomas "Fats" Waller Discography* (Göteborg: issued by the author, 1964).

10. RCA 741 076 [French], *Fats Waller, Complete Recordings, Vol. 3 (1927-1929)*.

11. Tor Magnusson, "The Shilkret's Rhyth-Melodists Sessions," *Matrix,* no. 90 (December 1970): 3.

12. Tor Magnusson, "Fats Waller with Gene Austin on the Record," *Journal of Jazz Studies* 4, no. 1 (Fall 1976): 75.

13. Jim Walsh, "Singer and Record 'Fiend' Find Much to Talk About," *Johnson City Press* (Johnson City, Tennessee), Thursday, April 27, 1939, p. 10.

14. See, for example, Rust, *Jazz Records 1897-1942,* or Tor Magnusson, "The Gene Austin Recordings," *Matrix* 101 (August 1973): 23.

15. RCA FXM1 7198 [French], *Fats Waller, Complete Recordings, Vol. 16 (1939)*.

ELI H. NEWBERGER

REFINEMENT OF MELODY AND ACCOMPANIMENT IN THE EVOLUTION OF SWING PIANO STYLE

Before the end of the Storyville era in New Orleans, Chicago attracted and produced many distinctive blues pianists. Some, such as Jimmy Yancey, Albert Ammons, and Pine Top Smith, were strictly boogie-woogie players; but others, notably Cow Cow Davenport and Jimmy Blythe, showed in their improvisations many features derived from ragtime.[1] And an unusual number of New Orleans musicians migrated to the Windy City with improvising ensembles in the middle and late teens and early twenties. Brown's Dixieland Band, a white group, opened at the Lambs' Cafe in 1915.[2] By early 1917, the Original Dixieland Jazz Band, also a white group and the first jazz ensemble to record (in February 1917; King Oliver's was the first Negro band to commit jazz to wax in 1923) had left Chicago for New York to begin its successful stint at Reisenweber's.[3] In the same year Oliver, later to be joined by Louis Armstrong, came to the Lincoln Gardens; and the Friars' Society Orchestra, later the New Orleans Rhythm Kings, opened in 1921 at the Friars' Inn.

Chicago, then, was the site of a great and diverse amount of musical activity. Accordingly, the contemporary presence of "blues" and "New Orleans" music, the large numbers of improvising ensembles—and, by 1920, bands which played more extensive written arrangements—, the increasing use of jazz orchestras for dancing, and the advent of recordings and radio, brought about by the late 1920s new approaches to the jazz piano.

EARL HINES

Earl Hines is certainly the most important figure to have derived a new musical style from the panoply of Chicago jazz. Born in Duquesne, Pennsylvania, he studied piano with the intent of becoming a concert soloist. In 1922, however, he was working full time in Chicago as a jazz player. With Jimmy Noone and Louis Armstrong, among others, Hines appears in such a solo as his later recording of "St. Louis Blues" (Example 1)[4] to have discarded much of the decorative rhetoric of New Orleans piano playing. His "trumpet style" became one of the focal styles in jazz history.

Somewhat in the way Louis Armstrong points up the principal lines of a tune in his improvising style, so Hines attenuates his left hand and limits his right to a few pointed statements. Indeed, the interaction of the two men on the Hot Five sides of the late twenties is remarkable; Armstrong was probably a potent force in Hines's evolution.

The influence of the "trumpet style" extends through Teddy Wilson, Billy Kyle, Count Basie, and Nat Cole to virtually every recent pianist, including such diverse musical personalities as Mary Lou Williams, Jess Stacy, Mel Powell, and Bobby Timmons. Even Erroll Garner's unique pianism owes a debt to Hines.

Eli H. Newberger is director of the Family Development Study at Children's Hospital Medical Center in Boston, Massachusetts, and assistant professor of pediatrics at the Harvard Medical School in Boston.

Ex. 1. Earl Hines, "St. Louis Blues"

In the sampling of Hines's right hand in Example 1, Hines uses octaves almost exclusively. There is a single "ragtime pivot note," the F# in measure 12. Single tremolos (measures 2-5) and simple riffs (measures 5-7) form whole phrases.

The economy of notes in the right hand is matched in quality, if not in number of notes, in the left. What was a steady but unimposing stride bass becomes tenths and tenths-plus-chords (the kind of more-nearly-4/4 accompaniment which one hears from Teddy Wilson and the swing players) from measure 7 to the end. Also, many left-hand notes and chords are less played than *suggested*. The effect is to emphasize further the salient lines of the chorus. While with Earl Hines "right-handed" piano playing begins, an important feature of his style is the spontaneous creation of complex rhythms between his left and right hands. Such "exchanges," reminiscent of Jelly Roll Morton's, are often heard in the playing of such Hines followers as Art Hodes, Joe Sullivan, and Billy Kyle.

If it were Hines through whom blues and the ragtime-derived music of New Orleans reached the swing pianists, it was also certainly he who led the band which indirectly yielded a still subsequent idiom, bop. "Fatha" Hines had formed his first "big band" in Chicago in late 1928. The Hines band of the early 1940s, which Leonard Feather justly called "the cradle of bebop," included such innovators as Charlie Parker, Dizzy Gillespie, Benny Harris, Shadow Wilson, Sarah Vaughan, and Billy Eckstine.

ART HODES AND JOE SULLIVAN

Art Hodes and Joe Sullivan share Hines's feeling for four-beat rhythm. The proximity of several different approaches to jazz piano playing, when they were presumably forming their first musical impressions, is evident from their respective solos on "Royal Garden Blues" (Example 2)[5] and "Stuyvesant Blues" (Example 3).[6] Hodes's style is perhaps a less complex resolution of these opposing energies then Sullivan's, but it also reflects the influence of Hines.

In his chorus, Hodes integrates Hines's clean attacks and phrases with some of the outstanding features of the two principal Chicago idioms, the patterns of blues and the decorative improvisation of post-ragtime New Orleans jazz.

The chorus begins with ascending passing harmony, outlined both in right-hand arpeggios and left-hand chords. A final arpeggio at the opening of the second phrase (measure 4) ushers in IV harmony, which is in turn sketched in the right hand by a syncopated "riff." Once more, in the seventh bar, passing harmony is traced in both hands. On this occasion, however, it is supplemented by chords in the right hand and a linear passage in the left. The chorus closes with a bit of left hand-right hand interaction. To Hines can be attributed the simple contours, conservative left hand, and left hand-right hand exchange; to Jimmy Yancey and the blues players, the "riffy" rhythms and a virtual boogie-woogie quote in measures 9 and 10 (cf. Albert Ammons's solo on "Woo Woo"[1]), and to Jelly Roll Morton and the New Orleans pianists, the arpeggiate improvisation style.

Joe Sullivan's mercurial style seems also to attest to the musical if not to the physical presence of the stride players, notably of his friend Fats Waller, whom he appears to quote in measures 10 and 11. Sullivan's savage octaves quickly modulate into civilized thirds at the end of measure 7. In the six beats from the start of that bar, the decline in intensity is

Ex. 2. Art Hodes, "Royal Garden Blues"

Ex. 3. Joe Sullivan, "Stuyvesant Blues"

(cont.)

astonishing, and throughout the chorus Sullivan avails himself of a large vocabulary of dynamic inflections "in the small." These are abetted by a number of pianistic devices, including casually interspersed right-hand chords (measures 5, 6, 10), sliding grace notes (measures 1-4), glisses (measures 8-10), and a spectrum of left-hand chords and single notes. While the phrasing of the solo is simple, really like a *blues,* there is an undeniable richness to the presentation. Sullivan seeks still more color over the span of many choruses through tremolos, left hand-right hand exchanges à la Hines, "double-times" (in which, like Fats Waller, he might improvise two 4/4 bars at twice the tempo in the space of one), variously accented blues "riffs," and long-range crescendos and diminuendos.

DON EWELL AND BILLY KYLE

Joe Sullivan's domineering right hand and Fats Waller's varied accompaniment seem to be melded in Don Ewell's evocative "Blues Improvisation" (Example 4).[7] Ewell is a versatile revivalist who began to play with such artists as Bunk Johnson, Sidney Bechet, Muggsy Spanier, Kid Ory, and Jack Teagarden at the end of World War II. His solo is notable for warm passing harmony, brought about by running thirds, arpeggios, and chords in the right hand and by chromatic lines, full, step-wise tenths and chords in the left; and for rich blues feeling.

Ex. 4. Don Ewell, "Blues Improvisation"

Ex. 5. Billy Kyle, "Royal Garden Blues"

Billy Kyle's incisive octaves, concise phrasing and modest left hand in his attractive chorus of "Royal Garden Blues" (Example 5)[8] tell also of Hines's impact. But his facile single-note line in measures 6 through 8, the hearty set of tritones in measures 9 through 12, and the crafty, shifting rhythm reflect an exposure also to more complex "swing" elements which grew to a great extent from Hines's playing.

An arpeggiate three-bar riff begins the chorus. The octaves "fit the hand" nicely and have a bell-like quality not unlike Hines's and swing pianist Mel Powell's. Following a few additional octaves comes a fascinating single-note passage in which the right hand first descends in an E^b dominant ninth chord (measure 6), then climbs in a reversing "in the hand" B^b sixth (measures 7-8). For a moment it seems as if Kyle has dropped a beat; the B^b - G couplet on the first beat of measure 8 inclines to continue down to F and D.

That he hasn't lost the rhythm is shown by the regular, if implied, left hand and further emphasized by the self-assured "comp" before the fourth beat of measure 8. Once more, in the eleventh bar, rhythm is offset; this time the unexpected syncop on the third beat does the trick. Such brazen, hanging cross-rhythms might be unusual even for Hines, who generally resolves each rhythmic dilemma forthwith. *His* exotic left hand-right hand dialogues never so threaten the rhythmic sense.

Kyle's subtlety has brightened the backgrounds of many bands. A spare accompanist who, like Hines, has recorded some very rewarding music with Louis Armstrong, he forged his reputation as a featured soloist with Lucky Millinder and John Kirby in the late 1930s and early 1940s.

COUNT BASIE

Spare accompaniment and tasteful single-note playing are also the hallmarks of Count Basie's style. Born in Red Bank, New Jersey, he frequently visited Fats Waller when the latter was working as a theater organist in Harlem. Basie played a personal brand of stride piano with several vaudeville companies. Out of work when the Gonzel White show folded in Kansas City, he joined the Walter Page Blue Devils for a two-year stint in 1928. Subsequently playing with the Benny Moten Band, Basie came in contact with several of the musicians who were to become members of his own ensemble after Moten died in 1935. In several respects Basie's early band was modeled after Moten's.

Such blues attributes as four-beat rhythm; simple phrasing; repeated rhythmic patterns or "riffs"; emphasis on (12-bar) blues tunes, "hot" solos, and call-and-response arrangements; and the use of guitar, string bass, and drums in the rhythm section gave the nine-man Basie band a special swinging quality which had never been heard in the East. Due in large part to the efforts of John Hammond, the critic who "rediscovered" Meade Lux Lewis washing cars in Chicago, Basie came to New York's Famous Door with a 15-piece ensemble which included Lester Young, Jimmy Rushing, Hot Lips Page, and the rhythm team of Freddie Green, Walter Page, and Jo Jones. Basie allowed the rest of the members of the rhythm section to provide what would be many another player's "left hand." Limiting his activity in the band to subtle rhythmic backing, "comping" such familiar chords as the treble (Example 6) and the tag (Example 7), he would play solos or introduc-

Ex. 6. Basie treble   *Ex. 7. Basie tag*

tions as the present "Magic" (Example 8)[9] in which guitar, bass, and drums might often show through.

This Basie solo is the second introductory chorus to a D♭ tune, and but for the last two bars, a kind of on-the-spot modulation, the chorus is quite distinctly in the key of C. (We may assume that Basie felt more comfortable in the latter key.) The pickup to the first measure introduces one of Basie's favorite patterns, which is in turn punctuated by a familiar I[7] "comp" (measure 1), then slightly changed to fit IV[7] harmony (measure 2), and incorporated into a series of turns ornamenting a simple C-B-B♭-A passing line (measure 4). More "comps" in measures 2 and 5 enclose the phrase and propel the rhythm.

The elegance of Count Basie's solo style is apparent; we feel that the chorus is at once tightly "organized" and loosely swinging. Basie is, furthermore, a superb accompanist; his graceful understatement and sure sense of what is pianistically proper provides an open, ample backing at every tempo. Features of his solo and accompaniment style seem deeply to have influenced various "bop" and "modern" ensemble pianists.

TEDDY WILSON

Teddy Wilson's style became the widely-imitated archetype of piano playing in the later 1930s and 1940s (the so-called "swing era" whose big bands, like Hines's, spawned the smaller, more flexible, and more musically daring bebop groups). Known to the public for his superb work with Benny Goodman in the four years after they first recorded together in July 1935, Wilson was the first black musician to play with a nationally known white band. Wilson had previously worked in Chicago and New York for several years with Jimmie Noone, Erskine Tate, Louis Armstrong, Benny Carter, and Willie Bryant. Stirring together the octaves and refinement of Earl Hines, the lyricism and phrasing of Fats Waller, and the decorative skill and passing harmony of Art Tatum, Wilson evolved an original style notable for its liquidity and charm.

His facile single-note playing seems most directly to have affected the near-commercial swing styles of John Guarnieri and Joe Bushkin and the fluent jazz playing of Nat Cole and Mel Powell.

We hear in Wilson's present solo on "Pres Returns" (Example 9)[10] several of the Tatum-derived ornamental figures which have come down through Wilson's refined style to the keyboards of commerce. In measures 3, 11, and 12, we observe rapid chromatic runs and "fills" and fleeting, romantic arpeggios. Rubato triplets like those in measure 6 may often be heard providing a moment's relief from the rows of thirty-second notes in the "jazzy" pop styles of Roger Williams and Peter Nero.

Ex. 8. Count Basie, "Magic"

Ex. 9. Teddy Wilson, "Pres Returns"

JOHN GUARNIERI AND JOE BUSHKIN

In the solos of John Guarnieri and Joe Bushkin on "A Bell for Norvo"[11] and "Relaxing at the Touro"[12] (Examples 10 and 11), we note how jazz styles may become "commercialized." Where Guarnieri's gossamer touch and arpeggiate lines reflect glossy and ephemeral derivations of Count Basie and Fats Waller, Bushkin's jazz sentiment is virtually smothered in a blanket of flowery squiggles.

Bushkin's left-hand tenths sound very much like those in Wilson's chorus, and the down-up-down phrase contours are not unpleasant to perceive through the lacework. Yet Bushkin's omnipresent grace notes (measure 6) and washes of formless arpeggios (measures 7 and 8) all but drown such a simple melodic idea and tasteful treble-bass interaction as that in measure 5.

Both Guarnieri and Bushkin played and recorded with notable jazz ensembles, the former with Benny Goodman and Artie Shaw, and the latter with Bunny Berigan, Goodman, and Eddie Condon. And if their work is not representative of all that is good in the evolution of the jazz piano through Teddy Wilson, it would be well to remember that pressures of money, audience, newness, fashionability, and even "soul" never relent on the jazz musician. If those pianists whom we find most gratifying speak to us directly, make music honestly, and without undue ambition, pretentiousness, or ornament, convey something of themselves, we ought to consider that for a jazzman to live a life of purest musical integrity he must often sacrifice much.

Teddy Wilson, on the other hand, is a performer of such high talent and flexibility as to enable him to work with a diversity of bands and vocalists, to teach jazz (if such can be done) at the Juilliard School of Music in New York, and to act and play in the movie "The Benny Goodman Story." His characteristically neither-two-beat-nor-four-beat rhythm, sloping lines, easy accessability, gliding left hand, and sense of integrated structure is amply evident in Example 9.

Measures 1 to 4, 5 to 8, and 9 to 12 form three main parts in the chorus, and the melodic divisions are highlighted by several supportive maneuvers. In the first section two related right-hand patterns (measures 1, 2) give way to a more intense sequence (measures 3, 4). Slow left-hand tenths interdigitated with single notes (measures 1-4) lend added impetus and harmonic information. Right-hand octaves and "walking" left-hand tenths dominate the next passage, which features two parallel melody lines (measures 5, 6-7) and still further increased chromaticism. A chromatically derived pickup ushers in the final statement which consists of many more single notes and much less passing harmony. There, too, is a typical counter-melody in the left hand.

Wilson, as the more than five octaves of piano here attest, is an eminently "pianistic" stylist, and his solo playing, like Tatum's and Waller's, employs still more of the resources of the instrument. Unlike the latter artists, however, he seems less often to conjure the force and variety needed for consistently interesting solo performance. But we forgive the bland vichyssoise of prettiness and ornament which is the occasional result of his solo efforts; for Wilson is primarily an ensemble player, and it was in that context that he made his most important contribution to the development of jazz piano style.

Ex. 10. John Guarnieri, "A Bell for Norvo"

Ex. 11. Joe Bushkin, ''Relaxing at the Touro''

Ex. 12. Jess Stacy, "Carnegie Drag"

JESS STACY AND NAT COLE

Jess Stacy also rose to fame with the Benny Goodman band. His early exposure to riverboat jazz in Missouri in the 1920s may account for some of the simple, "New Orleans" feeling in his playing, but there is little doubt that his real "link to tradition," as with Teddy Wilson and the other swing pianists, is Earl Hines. Stacy's solo on "Carnegie Drag" (Example 12)[13] shows an eclectic style. Yet even his tributes to Fats Waller (measures 10-12)[14], to blues and boogie-woogie (left hand, measure 11), and to Wilson himself (left-hand tenths, right-hand single notes and decorations) are presented among incisive Hinesian octaves in crisp phrases and attacks.

Nat "King" Cole, in his days as a jazzman, was known for his relaxed, lightly swinging piano style. After the late 1940's, when his career as a vocalist burgeoned, he made a name for himself in popular music, singing in much the same conservative "mainstream" way he played.

The tentative, evanescent property of his chorus on "Easy Listening Blues" (Example 13)[15], aptly named, may be ascribed to three basic Cole qualities: subdued dynamic level, lack of major volume and harmonic changes, and short, parenthetical phrases. In the latter and in the two octave passages (measures 6-7, 9) are felt the influences of Earl Hines, said often to be Cole's ideal, and Teddy Wilson. The acute, assertive rhythms and attacks of Hines's "trumpet style" are obviously lacking here, however. Tranquility is the mood in typical Cole playing.

His decorative figures, like Wilson's, are well chosen and elegant: three phrases (measures 2, 3, 4) begin with the brush of an F#-G grace note couplet; one starts and one ends with a gentle gliss (measures 5, 11); and one (measure 8) consists of a "fill" passage somewhat similar to what we heard in measure 3 in Wilson's own solo (Example 9).

MEL POWELL

Mel Powell made his precocious jazz debut at about the same time (1939), playing a highly competent and rhythmic piano reminiscent of Earl Hines and Teddy Wilson.

Ex. 13. Nat Cole, ''Easy Listening Blues''

Ex. 14. Mel Powell, ''Rock Rimmon''

Ex. 15. Erroll Garner, "Red Top"

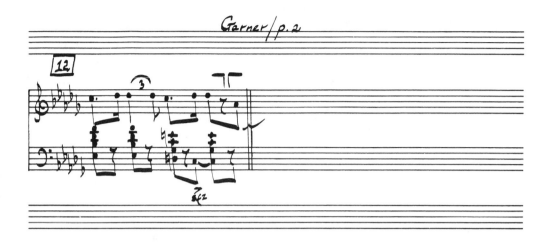

The jagged peaks and startling exchange between right and left hands in the present solo on "Rock Rimmon" (Example 14)[16] recall Powell's early inspiration, Hines. Like Hines, Powell is an impressively "pianistic" player, using the tonal resources of the instrument to express a unique series of sounds. For example, the glittering extended pickup to measure 1 combines left-hand single notes and right-hand octaves; more single note-octave and single note-interval alternations occur in measures 3, 6, 9, 10, and 11; nearly every "comp," octave, and note in the left hand is involved in some kind of interplay with the right; between measure 8 and the end, the chorus spans a five-octave range; and the right-hand chords are so spaced as to give each decided impact.

In that the phrases are clipped, rhythms clear and sure, and vertical rather than horizontal elements predominant, the chorus is relevant to the jazz of the 1930s. At the same time, it is improbable that Teddy Wilson or Jess Stacy would so boldly accent such ninths (measures 1-4, 11) and other dissonant intervals (measures 5, 6, 10), for in a sense Mel Powell's is the most advanced swing style.

ERROLL GARNER

Two idiosyncratic piano styles which are not "swing" ways of playing, but seem in their distinct independence from the broad schools to be closer to this category than to any other, are Erroll Garner's unique approach to solo piano playing, which seems more to have been affected by Earl Hines than by any other pianist; and Duke Ellington, whose fine band won public acclaim and collected its most famous personnel in the 1930s, and who appears to have solidified his "ensemble style" in the time when big bands flourished.

Garner's solo on "Red Top" (Example 15)[17] is the fourth chorus from his D^b-blues theme-song on the memorable "Concert by the Sea" set. Garner was at his crowd-pleasing best for that well-attended session, and he showed many of his jazz capabilities there, too. The present example is set among various quotations from the nursery ("Pop Goes the Weasel"), from the bop era ("Now's the Time"), and from popular music

("Louise," "Alice Blue Gown," and "Pie in the Sky"). In the seventh and eighth bars it has its own pops bit, "Holiday for Strings," amusingly jazzed and integrated into the melody line.

Perhaps Garner's sense of the easily apprehensible accounts for the fact that he has won more public acclaim than any other jazz pianist, including Art Tatum, whose own sense of melody and prodigious mastery of the keyboard brought him a following. Garner's is a more straightforward style than Tatum's. His rhythm is regular and sure; his patterns and phrases generally hew to the beat. Tatum, however, favored the dazzling array of sound, shifting before, ahead of, and on occasion back, to the beat. What chromatics and non-harmonic sounds Garner uses are for the most part contained in his catalogue of thick background chords. Tatum, on the other hand, would sooner mask the fundamental changes of a tune with veils of diaphanous harmony.

A pair of technical devices give Garner's piano much of its characteristic sound. The firm-yet-syncopated feel of his left hand results largely from a rolling motion *into* the beat, either from right to left (measures 2, 4-6) or from left to right (measures 1-10, 12). When the left hand grace or pick-up notes are accented (measures 2, 4, 8, 10, 12), the sense of syncopation is considerably increased.

His other unusual technique, perhaps a consequence of his lack of formal schooling on the instrument, is pointing the notes in the top line with the middle finger of his right hand (measures 5, 7, 9, 10). This gives a kind of xylophone effect, in a way like some of Lionel Hampton's piano playing, which is at once more powerful than simple single-note work and considerably more *dragged*.

Erroll Garner's extraordinary lyrical gift is borne out in the well-fitted phrasing of this solo. The first two phrases form a kind of repeated "A" part. After a typical Garner breather in measure 4, a forcefully syncopated left hand-right hand exchange, "B" begins. The ascending, semichromatic run precedes the above-mentioned "Holiday for Strings" quotation in measures 7 and 8. "C," measures 9 and 10, compresses and reiterates the up-down-up thought contained in "B," and finally the riffy "D" phrases in measures 10 through 12 repeat and recall "A."

DUKE ELLINGTON

Two decades Garner's senior, Duke Ellington's composing and arranging has literally developed along with jazz. While his piano work has been neither technically brilliant nor overly "pianistic," his highly developed sense of harmony, color, and form—those same qualities through which his writing proved able to keep pace with the changing times—lend his style a distinctive clarity. His is a straightforward use of relatively sophisticated structural techniques.

In the present solo on "St. Louis Blues" (Example 16)[18] the lines are simple and clean; the rests and pauses are uncluttered; and the notes in succession describe rich ninths, elevenths, and thirteenths. Even though in his early playing Ellington came under the influence of such New York masters as James P. Johnson and Luckey Roberts (he grew up in Washington, D.C.), it is not obvious from this chorus that he once played a personal stride style.

Ex. 16. Duke Ellington, "St. Louis Blues"

In the third measure occurs the debut of Ellington's unassuming left hand; it buoys down the prime tone of a sparely-outlined dominant seventh chord with minor ninth and thirteenth. After a single-note chromatic descent to IV harmony in measures 4 and 5, a real gem of Ellingtonia begins. G, A, and B^b lead into a sketched IV^7 with minor ninth and thirteenth—a melodic sequence with the passage in measures 3 and 4—which falls chromatically to a third-inversion, arpeggiate I$^{maj.~7}$ (measure 8), itself in rhythmic sequence with the immediately preceding figure.

Ellington's influence as a pianist is modest, although hints of his style can be heard in such diverse modernists as Thelonius Monk, Randy Weston, and Paul Bley. His musical presence, however, is apparent from the course of jazz evolution. Through his skills as leader, composer, and arranger, Duke Ellington was in many ways responsible for the singular and rapid phenomenon of "progression" in the short history of the art.

The refinement of melody and the attenuation of left-hand accompaniment in the swing era presaged the development of bebop and modern piano styles. Such diverse factors as the advent of the big band for dancing and entertainment, the wide promulgation of jazz through discs and radio, and the change in rhythmic emphasis from 2/4 to 4/4 (with a corresponding increase in the use of the string bass in place of the tuba in the "rhythm section") led to new conceptions of jazz pianism. As before, a few visionary stylists took with their two hands the heritage of ragtime and blues and reshaped the special role of the piano.

NOTES

1. E. Newberger, "Archetypes and Antecedents of Piano Blues and Boogie-Woogie Style," *Journal of Jazz Studies 4*, no. 1 (Fall 1976): 84-109. Conceptual and methodologic aspects of the notation of the stylistic examples are discussed in E. Newberger, "The Transition from Ragtime to Improvised Piano Style," *Journal of Jazz Studies 3*, no. 2 (Spring 1976):3-18.

2. M. Stearns, *The Story of Jazz* (New York: Oxford, 1956), p. 117.

3. L. Feather, *The Encyclopedia of Jazz* (New York: Bonanza Books, 1962).

4. Victor LPM-2321.

5. Mercury MG-20185.

6. Jazztone 1258.

7. Good Time Jazz L-12021.

8. Columbia CL-340.

9. American Recording Society ARS-G-402.

10. Jazztone G-417.

11. Continental 160 05.

12. Victor LPM 3043.

13. Jazztone J-1216.

14. This is virtually a quote; see Example 11 in E. Newberger, ''The Development of New Orleans and Stride Piano Style,'' *Journal of Jazz Studies 4,* No. 2 (Spring/Summer 1977):43-71.

15. Capital 1213 2-A (78 rpm).

16. Capitol T-1514.

17. Columbia CL-883.

18. Verve MGV-8317.

MARIE P. GRIFFIN

THE *IJS JAZZ REGISTER* AND *INDEXES:*
JAZZ DISCOGRAPHY IN THE COMPUTER ERA

Jazz is a twentieth century musical genre for which the recorded performance, not the composer's score, the transcription or the arrangement, is the primary source for research and study. This uniquely American music, which is characterized by improvisation and individual interpretation, is preserved for enjoyment and for research because its historical development coincided with the invention and continual improvement of sound recording techniques. The researcher has benefited because the field of discography pioneered by talented amateurs rather than musicologists, developed concurrently with the increasing availability of jazz on phonograph records. However, although advances in electronic techniques '..ave affected the music itself for several decades, it is only recently that computer techniques have been applied to jazz discography. The advantages of this blend of traditional discographical techniques with computer technology are demonstrated in the jazz cataloguing and indexing project, in progress since October 1978, at the Institute of Jazz Studies (IJS), Rutgers University, with grant support from the National Endowment for the Humanities (NEH).[1]

THE IJS PROJECT

In the NEH-supported project major segments of the institute's recorded sound collection are included in the more than 3,000 jazz performances represented in the IJS data base and distributed on the computer-output-microfiche (COM) *IJS Jazz Register* and *Indexes.* The initial project concentrated on jazz recordings of the acoustical recording period, the recording years prior to 1925/1927 when electrical microphones and amplifiers became generally available to recording studies. Early performances of such jazz greats as Louis Armstrong, Fletcher Henderson, Sidney Bechet, and Bessie Smith have been identified. Jazz-related recordings in the general categories of blues and dance music, and other commercial recordings on which important jazz artists played a prominent role as performers or composers, have been included, as well as certain early ragtime, minstrel and vaudeville recordings which influenced later jazz styles.

The institute's acoustical holdings for the following labels have been catalogued: Black Swan, Brunswick, Cameo, Claxtonola, Columbia, Diva, Domino, Emerson, Gennett, Grey Gull, Harmony, OKeh, Oriole, Paramount, Pennington, Perfect, Radiex, Regal, Velvet Tone, Victor, and Vocalion. For the larger producers, such as Columbia, appropriate recordings of both the "race" series (recordings aimed at Black record buyers) and other series were included. This phase of the project not only makes the institute's collections for this period more accessible but also identifies numerous recordings not docu-

Marie P. Griffin, Librarian of the Institute of Jazz Studies, is an associate professor of the Rutgers University Libraries Faculty. She has been involved with this cataloguing-indexing project from the beginning and is now project supervisor.

mented in existing discographical reference sources. Alternate takes, not previously cited in discographies, have now been documented. So prevalent is the possibility of alternate takes existing under the same issue number that, in cases where the institute has multiple copies of a recording, the takes are checked by aural comparison. Because the institute has received more than 10,000 additional recordings, including a sizable acoustical component, since the project began, cataloguing for the acoustical period continues to be added to the data base. Thus, the quarterly cumulations of the COM register and indexes accurately reflect the acoustical holdings of the institute.

The second phase of the project, with support from an NEH continuation grant,[2] is devoted to the cataloguing of long-playing recordings, concentrating on discs recorded between 1962 and 1969 which are not included in the major discographical sources, reissues produced in the 1970s containing important historical performances, and non-studio recordings including airchecks, transcriptions, V-discs, private recordings, and alternate takes of previously issued material. Labels represented include: Alto, Arista Novus, Artists House, Atlantic, Bamboo, Beppo, Blue Note, Bombasi, Chiaroscuro, Collector's Classics, Concord Jazz, Crazed Olaf, ECM Records, Enja, Forsgate Products, Inner City, Jazz Archives, Jazz Connoisseur, New World Records, Opus Musicum (Germany), Pablo, Preservation Hall, Pumpkin, Savoy, Storyville, Unique Jazz (Italy), Warner Brothers, and Xanadu. This cataloguing demonstrates the potential of the project as a supplement to printed discographies. Discrepancies between the information included on the record labels, the liner notes and/or album covers, and the details of the actual recorded performance have been noted and clarified in IJS cataloguing. Numerous errors in existing discographies have been identified. Many broadcast performances not documented in existing discographical reference sources have now been catalogued.

THE CATALOGUING MODEL

The project has developed as a model for archival cataloguing of sound recordings because it combines discographical research with conformance to national cataloguing and automation standards. Cataloguing worksheets are prepared in accordance with *Anglo-American Cataloguing Rules* (AACR)[3] and include data of special interest to archivists formulated in accordance with the *Rules for Archival Cataloging of Sound Recordings,* prepared by the Associated Audio Archives (AAA) of the Association for Recorded Sound Collections (ARSC).[4] The catalogue records are input to OCLC,[5] a national bibliographic network, via computer terminals at the institute using the MARC music format.[6] Each catalogue record is uniquely identified by both a machine-generated OCLC control number and an IJS number.

The IJS number identifies both the physical item and the recorded performance. For example, the IJS number "IJS D000083.02" is determined as follows: the "IJS" symbol indicates that the source of the cataloguing is the Institute of Jazz Studies, Rutgers, the State University; the alphabetical character "D" indicates that the physical object is a disc; the six-digit number preceding the decimal point identifies the particular physical item described in the catalogue record, in this example the eighty-third disc catalogued;

the two-digit number following the decimal point indicates the track or side catalogued, in this example side two of a 78 rpm recording.

Each recorded jazz performance is separately catalogued; normally a performance represents one side of a 78 rpm recording or one track of a long-playing recording. All the essential data elements are coded in machine-retrievable locations in the automated catalogue record: the names of all performers, performing groups, composers, lyricists, arrangers, conductors, and directors; the specific date and place of the performance; the title of the selection, as determined from the first published edition of the music, and variant titles appearing on record labels, liner notes, or album covers; the label name and issue number; the matrix number where applicable; the date of issue and/or reissue; and the physical characteristics of the recording (stereo/mono/acoustical, speed, dimensions, description of label). The process of determining accurate data for all these points of access is the most time-consuming aspect of the project. To facilitate this process a bibliography of basic discographical reference sources was prepared (see fig. 1). Information from these sources is supplemented by the expertise of the institute staff and its director Dan Morgenstern and the specialized resources available at the institute including performer files and topic files, biographical and discographical works on individual performers, extensive holdings of jazz periodicals from all over the world, and manufacturers' catalogues.

The IJS project has been influential in initiating changes in the MARC music format which have expanded the format to include the essential points of access for jazz and other performer-oriented music and which make the format compatible with the second edition of *Anglo-American Cataloguing Rules* (AACR 2).[7] For certain data interim machine-retrievable locations were determined until the newly-described fields were approved by the Library of Congress and the American Library Association interdivisional MARBI Committee,[8] and implemented for the OCLC network. By the use of these specifically tagged field and subfield locations in the machine-record the IJS cataloguing project was able to bridge the gap between the first and second editions of the cataloguing rules.

Conformance with national standards (*AACR, AACR 2,* and the MARC music format)[9] and the inclusion of IJS catalogue-records on the nationwide bibliographic data base OCLC are distinctive features of this project. Accordingly, IJS jazz catalogue-records are available on-line to the more than 2,000 libraries that participate in the OCLC network and can be used by these libraries for reference and cataloguing. The Cleveland Public Library has used IJS cataloguing of acoustical recordings in the cataloguing of its collection. Librarians working on a sheet music cataloguing project at Brown University verify names of composers, lyricists, and performers and titles of selections by consulting IJS catalogue-records on-line.

AUTHORITY CONTROL[10]

For every personal name (for example, Dizzy Gillespie), corporate name (for example, Red Onion Jazz Babies), uniform title (for example, "Just a Closer Walk with Thee"), and name-uniform title combination (for example, "Black, Brown and Beige" by Duke

Ellington) used as a heading, or access point, a unique entry is established. In addition, references are made for alternate forms of names and titles. For example, for the established entry "Ellington, Duke, 1899-1974" a reference is made from "Ellington, Edward Kennedy, 1899-1974." The use of established entries is necessary to ensure consistency of the data. Such consistency is particularly important for the IJS project because the indexed entries are computer-sorted character by character; therefore, a minor difference in spelling, punctuation, or spacing affects the filing sequence. The institute maintains a card file which includes both established entries and all necessary references. This IJS authority file now contains more than 2,000 entries.

Compliance with national cataloguing and automation standards, a distinctive feature of the IJS project, has been complicated by the changes in form of entry mandated by the adoption of *AACR 2,* effective 1 January 1981.[11] Prior to 1 January 1981 the institute used the form of entry previously established by the Library of Congress whenever this was available, for approximately twenty-five percent of the entries in the IJS authority file. Additional entries were established in accordance with Library of Congress practice and, wherever possible, also in compliance with the provisions of *AACR 2.* Since 1 January 1981 all new entries are established in accordance with *AACR 2,* and pre-1981 headings are converted to *AACR 2*-compatible forms as required. References are made connecting the earlier form of entry to the *AACR 2* form.

IJS–Library of Congress Cooperation

The implementation of the project has been characterized by close cooperation with the Library of Congress. Under a special arrangement the Music Section of the Descriptive Cataloging Division provided instruction in Library of Congress authority procedures and the establishment of *AACR 2*-compatible entries to Edward Berger, cataloguer-discographer on the project. Marie Griffin, project supervisor, attended a Library of Congress–supervised workshop on *AACR 2* in April 1980 and conducted a series of seminars, based on the materials presented at this workshop, for the IJS project staff in the fall of 1980. Another aspect of IJS–Library of Congress cooperation is the acceptance by the Music Section of IJS-established entries when these are needed for Library of Congress cataloguing. Entries accepted by the Library of Congress, with appropriate references, are added to the MARC authority file,[12] which is distributed in the United States and Canada to bibliographic utilities and other MARC subscribers.

COMPUTER-OUTPUT-MICROFICHE (COM) REGISTER AND INDEXES

The Rutgers University Library Computer Center receives a magnetic tape from OCLC once a month. This tape contains all the catalogue-records produced and/or updated by the institute during the preceding month.

In the initial stages of the project when certain data, such as the date and place of performance in coded form, were stored in interim locations in the machine-record, catalogue records were "produced" for IJS and then "updated" for the data base with these

IJS-specific fields excluded. As of 1 January 1981 these interim locations are no longer needed; however, certain minor changes in the base record continue to be made until programming changes implemented at Rutgers are synchronized with the programming changes implemented on the OCLC data base. The Rutgers University Center for Computer and Management Services, in cooperation with the Library Computer Center, processes the magnetic tapes received monthly from OCLC, eliminating the "update" transactions and reading the "produce" transactions to an IJS master tape. When a correction is made to a catalogue-record, the corrected catalogue-record replaces the original on the master tape. From the latest IJS master tape the *IJS Jazz Register* and indexes by performer/title; performer/performing group; performing group; composer, arranger, director; title, including variant titles; label name and issue number are produced on computer-output-microfiche (COM) with an effective reduction of 42:1. Vesicular copies are made from silver-halide microfiche originals.

IJS Jazz Register

The *IJS Jazz Register* is cumulated monthly and distributed quarterly. This COM register represents all the entries on the IJS master tape including all corrections and "produce" transactions from the latest magnetic tape received from OCLC. The entries are arranged by IJS number. Each sheet of microfiche has a heading identifying the sequence of IJS numbers included on the sheet, for example, the first sheet of the *IJS Jazz Register* carries the legend:

FR: IJS D000001.01
TO: IJS D000463.02

The register is the source document for the indexes, which are keyed to the register by IJS number. The example (fig. 2) shows the entries on one frame of the 208 frames on each sheet of microfiche.

Indexes

The indexes have been designed to provide direct access to the essential discographical information needed for reference and research. The components of the one-line indexes are fixed-length character strings, each identified in the machine-readable-record by a distinctive field and subfield location. Each index is comparable to a specialized discography giving the researcher very precise data, for example, a chronological listing of the various performing groups with which an artist, both as leader and sideman, was affiliated. Each line of the index includes the IJS number for the corresponding entry on the register. The researcher can, therefore, use the IJS number as the key to the location of additional information on any specific performance.

Performer/Title Index

The Performer/Title Index is arranged alphabetically by the names of individual performers. The brief discography for each performer is arranged by the title of each selection performed and, chronologically, by the date of the performance in coded form (coded year-month-day, for example, May 18, 1920 = 19200518). The performances are identified by the label name and issue number of the recording and the IJS number. In some instances the same selection is listed two or more times on the same date, usually because the original recording was reissued but, occasionally, because more than one take of the selection performed has been issued. This index provides ready reference for queries such as, "How many times did Louis Armstrong record 'St. Louis Blues'?" Moreoever, because all the known performers on each performance are listed, the index provides the same detailed information for lesser-known performers and sidemen (see fig. 3).

Performer/Performing Group Index

The Performer/Performing Group Index is also arranged alphabetically by the names of individual performers. This chronological listing of the various groups with which the individual performer played includes, for each performer, the date of performance in coded form, the name of the group or the featured performer of the group with which the performer played on that date, and the title of the selection performed. In addition, each item is identified by the IJS number so that the remaining members of the group can be ascertained by referring to the complete catalogue-entry on the register (see fig. 4). This index defines each performer's career in terms of his/her associations with other musicians. At the institute the index serves as an adjunct to the authority file.

Performing Group Index

The Performing Group Index is arranged alphabetically by the names of the performing groups. The brief discography for each performing group is arranged chronologically by date of performance and, for each date, by the title of the selection performed. The performances are identified by the label name and issue number of the recording on which the performance is recorded and by the IJS number (see fig. 5). The index serves the researcher who is tracing the history of a performing group. The resources of the institute for any specific performing group of the acoustical era are readily identified using this index.

Title Index

The Title Index lists all titles and variant titles of selections catalogued, as well as album titles, in one alphabetical sequence. Thus, any variation of the title which has been recorded can be easily located. Discographical information for each indexed title includes the date of performance in coded form, which arranges the titles chronologically, the performing group or the featured performer on that performance, and the label name and issue number of the recording on which it appears. Each indexed item is also identified by the IJS number (see fig. 6).

Composer Index

The Composer Index lists, in one alphabetical sequence, composers, lyricists, arrangers, and directors. The brief discography for each individual composer, lyricist, arranger, and director is arranged alphabetically by title and identified by the date of performance, the label name and issue number of the recording on which the performance is recorded, and the IJS number (see fig. 7). Users of the IJS indexes have identified many jazz performers who were also noted composers. The composer index also brings into focus the close relationship between the development of jazz and the emergence of the musical comedy, both distinctively American musical genres. For the young jazz enthusiast, it is interesting to note that Fats Waller's ''Ain't Misbehavin' '' was first featured in *Hot Chocolates* in 1929. The many talents of such famous entertainers as Jimmy Durante, whose career began as a jazz pianist and composer, and Benny Carter, whose extensive composer and arranger credits rival his credits as performer, are documented in this composer index.

Label Name and Issue Number Index

The Label Name and Issue Number Index is comparable to a shelf list of catalogued recordings. The index is arranged alphabetically by label name and alpha-numerically by issue number. Each performance on the recording is identified by the title of the selection, the date of performance, and the performing group or featured performer. Because this index serves as a shelf list, both the OCLC control number and the IJS number are included for each item (see fig. 8).

The COM Register/Indexes Model

The concept of using a COM register and indexes to provide access to bibliographical and discographical information and to distribute cataloguing data is in accord with national and international concepts of bibliographic control.[14] Although computer technology should eventually make it possible for individuals to have bibliographic data bases available on-line on home television screens, the techniques which will make such systems operational are still in the experimental stage.[15] COM is also machine-dependent. However, microfiche readers are relatively inexpensive and portable; it is conceivable that individual researchers could either purchase a reader at a cost of approximately $225.00[16] or use a microfiche reader at a local library.

Paper printouts can be computer-produced at a speed comparable to the production of computer-produced microfiche. COM, however, is less expensive to produce, to reproduce, to mail, and to store than paper products. The current *IJS Jazz Register* and *Indexes* are printed on eleven sheets of microfiche; this represents more than 1,250 pages of computer-printed paper. The Institute of Jazz Studies mails the COM *IJS Jazz Register* and *Indexes* to individuals and institutions all over the world; these two-ounce packages are sent air mail in five-inch by seven-inch envelopes.

The use of an open-ended register, in preference to a listing in which new items must be interfiled, provides for a continuous single-entry file which can be easily updated by add-on supplements. When the register reaches sizable proportions, only the indexes will have to be cumulated each time the file is updated. Because all the data components of a jazz performance are specifically coded in machine-retrievable locations in the catalogue-record and can be assigned fixed-length positions in the indexes, many permutations of the data in a variety of configurations are possible. The initial project did not anticipate a composer index. When the need for this index was suggested in an NEH review of the project in February 1979, this index was added with minimal additional programming. The indexes have been designed so that the various components can be easily rearranged to provide, for example, an index by date of performance. Moreover, additional elements, such as the place of performance or matrix numbers, could be included in the indexes for either specialized research or general reference.

Distribution

Samples of the COM register and indexes are distributed to interested individuals and institutions free of charge. However, because of increased mailing and reproduction costs, the renewal phase of the project, 1980 through 1982, distributes the COM *IJS Jazz Register* and *Indexes* at cost ($15.00 per year). Each annual subscription includes four quarterly cumulations.[17]

THE FUTURE: A UNION CATALOGUE OF JAZZ RECORDINGS

From the inception of the IJS jazz cataloguing-indexing project, the institute has cooperated with other sound archives and has recognized the advantages of developing a union catalogue of jazz recordings. Such cooperation was a consideration in the adoption of national standards, Anglo-American cataloguing rules, and the MARC music format for the project; in using OCLC, a national bibliographic data base, to produce the catalogue-records; in incorporating significant elements of the ARSC *Rules for Archival Cataloging of Sound Recordings* in IJS cataloguing specifications; in outlining the proposed procedures for the project at a seminar for cooperating archives prior to its implementation; and in circulating sample copies of the *IJS Jazz Register* and *Indexes* to a wide variety of individuals and institutions with a request for comments and suggestions. In August of 1980 the institute developed a proposal for a union catalogue of jazz recordings based upon the cataloguing-indexing model, the *IJS Jazz Register* and *Indexes.*[18] This proposal was circulated to the William Ransom Hogan Jazz Archive, Tulane University; the Archives of Traditional Music, Indiana University; the Country Music Foundation, Nashville, Tennessee; the Motion Picture and Recorded Sound Division of the Library of Congress; and the Music Section, Joseph Regenstein Library, University of Chicago. The essential framework has been provided; implementation will require a commitment of resources (time and money) on the part of the various institutions.

SUMMARY

Scholarly research based on recorded performance is coming of age. The theory that the study of performance adds a significant dimension to research in musicology is now generally accepted.[19] The groundwork for such musical analysis was done in the thirties by jazz collectors and amateur discographers who attempted to unravel the mysteries of poorly-documented 78 rpm recordings.[20] Jazz discography, dating from Delaunay's seminal work in 1936,[21] has been the province of many distinguished jazz aficionados; their works are still the basic reference sources for jazz. In 1968 and 1969 speakers at the Conferences on Discographical Research, held at Rutgers University, emphasized the necessity of enhancing this tradition of discographical research with modern technology to produce a more effective and dynamic research tool.[22] The innovative performer-oriented approach to cataloguing and computerization, exemplified by the *IJS Jazz Register* and *Indexes,* is setting the pace for jazz discography in the twenty-first century.

FIGURE 1. Bibliography of Basic Discographical Sources Used in the IJS Cataloguing-Indexing Project

Citation	Code
American Society of Composers, Authors, and Publishers, *The ASCAP Biographical Dictionary of Composers, Authors, and Publishers.* (1966)	Am 66
American Society of Composers, Authors, and Publishers *The ASCAP Index of Performed Compositions.* (1963)	Am 63
Walter Bruyninckx, *50 Years of Recorded Jazz.* 1917-1967. (1967-)	Br 67
Walter Bruyninckx, *60 Years of Recorded Jazz.* (1979-)	Br 79
John Chilton, *Who's Who of Jazz: Storyville to Swingstreet.* (1978)	Ch 78
Charles Eugene Claghorn, *Biographical Dictionary of American Music.* (1973)	Cl 73
Leonard Feather, *New Edition of the Encyclopedia of Jazz.* (1960)	Fe 60
Leonard Feather, *The Encyclopedia of Jazz in the Sixties.* (1966)	Fe 66
Leonard Feather, *The Encyclopedia of Jazz in the Seventies.* (1977)	Fe 77
Patricia Pate Havlice, *Popular Song Index.* (1975)	Ha 75
Jorgen Grunnet Jepsen, *Jazz Records* 1942- (1963-1970)	Jp 42-
Roger D. Kinkle, *The Complete Encyclopedia of Popular Music and Jazz, 1900-1950.* (1974)	Kk 74
Library of Congress, *The National Union Catalog: Music and Phonorecords,* 1953-1972.	LC 53,58,63,68
Library of Congress, *Library of Congress Catalogs: Music, Books on Music and Sound Recordings,* 1973-	LC 73,74,75,76,etc.
Julius Mattfeld, *Variety: Music Cavalcade, 1620-1969.* (1971)	Ma 71
Brian Rust, *The American Dance Band Discography,* 1917-1942. (1975)	Rd 75
Brian Rust, *The Complete Entertainment Discography from the Mid-1890's to 1942.* (1973)	Re 73
Brian Rust, *Jazz Records 1897-1942.* 4th ed. (1978)	Ru 78
Shapiro, Nat, *Popular Music.* 5v. (1964-1969)	Sh 64-69

FIGURE 2. IJS Catalogue-Records Contained on One Frame of Microfiche

IJS D000024.02
Tiger rag [by Nick La Rocca] [Sound recording]   La Rocca, Nick, 1889-1961.   Gennett #968. [1922?] 1183-C.   on side 2
of 1 disc. 78 rpm. mono. 10 in.   With: Tyers, W. H. Panama.   Friars Society Orchestra [later known as New Orleans Rhythm
Kings]; Husk O'Hara, director. [Paul Mares trumpet; George Brunies, trombone; Leon Rappolo, clarinet; Jack Pettis, C-melody or
tenor sax; Elmer Schoebel, piano; Lou Black, banjo; Frank Snyder, drums.]--cf. B. Rust, Jazz records, 1978.
    Recorded in Richmond, Ind., Aug. 30, 1922.--cf.B. Rust, Jazz records, 1978. 19220830 4094. B5.   Acoustic recording.
Gennett 4968 ([Side] B: (4968-B) ; Mx. 11183--C (52 mm.) : label (blue, gold print), shellac (black). IJS).   Jazz octets.
    O'Hara, Husk, 1890-1970, director.   Mares, Paul, 1900-1949, cornet.   Brunis, Georg, 1900- trombone.   Rappolo, Leon,
1902-1943, clarinet.   Pettis, Jack, 1902- C-melody sax or tenor sax.   Schoebel, Elmer, 1896- piano.   Black, Lou,
1901-1965, banjo.   Brown, Steve, 1890-1965, bass.   Snyder, Frank, drums.   New Orleans Rhythm Kings.
oclc4384199

IJS D000025.01
Swanee smiles; fox trot [by] Hager [and] Ring. [Sound recording]   Hager, Fred W.   Gennett 4983, [1922?] 8077-B.   on
side 1 of 1 disc. 78 rpm. mono. 10 in.   With: Snyder, T. You gave me your heart.   Husk O'Hare's Super Orchestra of
Chicago.   Recorded in New York Oct. 19, 1922.--cf. B. Rust, Jazz records, 1978. 19221019 3804. N4.   Acoustic recording.
    Gennett 4983 ([Side] A: (4983--A) ; Mx. 8077--B (66 mm.) : label (blue, gold print), shellac (black). IJS).   Jazz
ensembles.   Dance-orchestra music.   Ring, Justin.   O'Hare, Husk, 1890-1970, director.   Husk O'Hare's Super
Orchestra of Chicago.
oclc4384213

IJS D000025.02
You gave me your heart; fox trot [Sound recording]   Snyder, Ted.   Gennett 4983. [1922?] 8075-B.   on side 2 of 1 disc.
78 rpm. mono. 10 in.   With: Hager, F.W. Swanee smiles.   Husk O'Hare's Super Orchestra of Chicago.   Recorded in New
York Oct. 19, 1922.--cf. B. Rust, Jazz records, 1978. 19221019 3804. N4.   Acoustic recording.   Gennett 4983 ([Side] B:
(4983-B) ; Mx. 8075--B (62 mm.) : label (blue, gold print), shellac (black). IJS).   Jazz ensembles.   Dance-orchestra
music.   O'Hare, Husk, 1890-1970, director.   Husk O'Hare's Super Orchestra of Chicago.
oclc4384227

IJS D000026.01
Lady of the evening; fox trot. [Sound recording]   Berlin, Irving, 1888-   Gennett 5002. [1922?] 8106-B.   on side 1 of
1 disc. 78 rpm. mono. 10 in.   With: Davis, B. Carolina home.   Glantz's Metropolitan Players.   Recorded in New York
ca. Nov. 15, 1922.--cf. B. Rust, American dance band discography. 19221115 3804. N4.   Acoustic recording.   Gennett 5002
([Side] A: (5002-A) ; Mx. 8106--B (66 mm.) : label (blue, gold print), shellac (black). IJS).   Jazz ensembles.
Dance-orchestra music.   Glantz, Nathan, director.   Nathan Glantz and his orchestra.
oclc4384231

IJS D000026.02
Carolina home; fox trot [by] Davis [and] Silver. [Sound recording]   Davis, Benny, 1895-   Gennett 5002. [1922?] 8099[-A]
    on side 2 of 1 disc. 78 rpm. mono. 10 in.   With: Berlin, I. Lady of the evening.   Bailey's Lucky Seven. [Includes
Phil Napoleon, trumpet; possibly Charlie Panelli, trombone; Jimmy Lytell, clarinet or alto sax; Benny Krueger, alto sax;
possibly Nick Lucas, banjo; Jack Roth, drums.]--cf. B. Rust, Jazz records, 1978.   Recorded in New York ca. Nov. 10,
1922.--cf. B. Rust, Jazz records, 1978. 19221110 3804. N4.   Acoustic recording.   Gennett 5002 ([Side] B: (5002-B) ; Mx.
8099--[A] (61 mm.) : label (blue, gold print), shellac (black). IJS).   Jazz septets.   Silver, Abner, 1899-   Napoleon,
Phil, 1901- trumpet.   Panelli, Charlie, trombone.   Lytell, Jimmy, clarinet or alto sax.   Krueger, Benny, ca.
1899-1967, alto sax.   Lucas, Nick, banjo.   Roth, Jack, drums.   Bailey's Lucky Seven.
oclc4384238

IJS D000027.01
Lost, a wonderful girl; fox trot [by] Davis [and] Hanley. [Sound recording]   Davis, Benny, 1895-   Gennett 5005. [1923?]
8110--B.   on side 1 of 1 disc. 78 rpm. mono. 10 in.   With: Kalmar, B. I gave you up just before you threw me down.
Bailey's Lucky Seven. [Includes Phil Napoleon and Jules Levy, Jr., trumpet; possibly Charlie Panelli, trombone; Jimmy Lytell,
clarinet or alto sax; Loring McMurray, alto sax; possibly Nick Lucas, banjo; Jack Roth, drums.]--cf. B. Rust, Jazz records,
1978.   Recorded in New York ca. Nov. 17, 1922.--cf. E. Rust, Jazz records, 1978. 19221117 3804. N4.   Acoustic recording.
    Gennett 5005 ([Side] A: (5005-A) ; Mx. 8110--B (60 mm.) : label (blue, gold print), shellac (black). IJS).   Jazz
septets.   Hanley, James Frederick, 1892-1942.   Napoleon, Phil, 1901- trumpet.   Levy, Jules, trumpet.   Panelli,
Charlie, trombone.   Lytell, Jimmy, clarinet or alto sax.   McMurray, Loring, alto sax.   Lucas, Nick, banjo.   Roth,
Jack, drums.   Bailey's Lucky Seven.
oclc4384247

FIGURE 3. Performer/Title Entries on One Frame of the Performer/Title Index

Performer	Title	Date	Label Name	Issue #	IJS #
ARDEN, VICTOR, 1903-	OLD MAN JAZZ	19200514	Victor	18699.	D000559.02
ARDEN, VICTOR, 1903-	ROSE OF THE ORIENT	19200299	Brunswick	2037.	D000408.02
ARDEN, VICTOR, 1903-	ROSE OF WASHINGTON SQUARE	19200224	Victor	18659.	D000550.01
ARDEN, VICTOR, 1903-	ROSY CHEEKS	19210831	Victor	18801.	D000599.02
ARDEN, VICTOR, 1903-	SWANEE	19200126	Victor	18651.	D000548.02
ARDEN, VICTOR, 1903-	SWEET N PRETTY	19181203	Victor	18520.	D000536.02
ARDEN, VICTOR, 1903-	VAMPING ROSE	19210609	Victor	18787.	D000575.02
ARDEN, VICTOR, 1903-	VENETIAN MOON	19200114	Victor	18651.	D000548.01
ARDEN, VICTOR, 1903-	WHO WANTS A BABY	19200299	Brunswick	2037.	D000408.01
ARDEN, VICTOR, 1903-	WILDFLOWER	19230322	Brunswick	2422.	D000042.02
ARDEN, VICTOR, 1903-	YOU AIN'T HEARD NOTHING YET	19200224	Victor	18659.	D000550.02
ARDEN, VICTOR, 1903-	YOU'RE SOME PRETTY DOLL	19190104	Victor	18527.	D000537.02
ARDEN, VICTOR, 1903-	JERRY	19190902	Victor	18617.	D000541.02
ARDEN, VICTOR, 1903-	OLD MAN JAZZ	19200514	Victor	18699.	D000599.02
ARENBURG, BILL,	BLUE KITTEN SELECTIONS	19220399	Brunswick	2247.	D000424.01
ARENBURG, BILL,	CRAZY BLUES	19210399	Brunswick	2077.	D000418.01
ARENBURG, BILL,	DON'T LEAVE ME MAMMY	19220399	Brunswick	2246.	D000422.02
ARENBURG, BILL,	EVERYBODY STEP	19211099	Brunswick	2151.	D000415.01
ARENBURG, BILL,	GLOW LITTLE LANTERN OF LOVE	19210923	Emerson	10452.	D000833.01
ARENBURG, BILL,	HOW MANY TIMES	19211099	Brunswick	2151.	D000415.02
ARENBURG, BILL,	I'M JUST WILD ABOUT HARRY	19220599	Brunswick	2272.	D000427.02
ARENBURG, BILL,	IT'S GETTING DARK ON OLD BROADWAY	19220099	Brunswick	2340.	D000433.C2
ARENBURG, BILL,	JIMMY I LOVE BUT YOU	19220399	Brunswick	2247.	D000424.02
ARENBURG, BILL,	POOR LITTLE ME	19220399	Brunswick	2246.	D000422.02
ARENBURG, BILL,	ROYAL GARDEN BLUES	19210399	Brunswick	2077.	D000418.02
ARENBURG, BILL,	SOME OF THESE DAYS	19220599	Brunswick	2272.	D000427.01
ARENBURG, BILL,	STUMBLING	19220599	Brunswick	2340.	D000433.01
ARENBURG, BILL,	TUCK ME TO SLEEP IN MY OLE 'TUCKY HO	19210923	Emerson	10452.	D000833.02
ARMER, AL,	TELL HER IN THE SPRINGTIME	19241218	Vocalion	14955.	D000403.02
ARMER, AL,	ADORING YOU	19240715	Victor	19429.	D000717.01
ARMER, AL,	ALABAMY BOUND	19241229	Victor	19557.	D000727.01
ARMER, AL,	BY THE WATERS OF MINNETONKA	19240611	Victor	19391.	D000713.01
ARMER, AL,	CALL OF THE SOUTH	19241229	Victor	19557.	D000727.02
ARMER, AL,	GEORGE WHITE'S SCANDALS OF 1924 SOME	19240771	Victor	19414.	D000715.01
ARMER, AL,	HOODOO MAN	19240509	Victor	19339.	D000710.02
ARMER, AL,	IT HAD TO BE YOU	19240408	Victor	19339.	D000710.01
ARMER, AL,	LADY, BE GOOD	19241218	Vocalion	14955.	D000403.01
ARMER, AL,	LONELY LITTLE MELODY	19240775	Victor	19414.	D000715.02
ARMER, AL,	MEDITATION	19240611	Victor	19391.	D000713.02
ARMER, AL,	MY ROAD	19240915	Victor	19461.	D000718.02
ARMER, AL,	OH, JOSEPH	19241216	Victor	19546.	D000726.02
ARMER, AL,	ROSE-MARIE ROSE-MARIE	19240918	Victor	19461.	D000718.01
ARMER, AL,	WHERE THE DREAMY WABASH FLOWS	19240813	Victor	19546.	D000726.01
ARMER, AL,	WHERE'S MY SWEETIE HIDING	19241219	Victor	19428.	D000726.01
ARMSTRONG, LIL HARDIN, 190	ALLIGATOR HOP	19230406	Gennett	5274.	D000036.02
ARMSTRONG, LIL HARDIN, 190	CANAL STREET BLUES	19231015	Gennett	5133.	D000090.01
ARMSTRONG, LIL HARDIN, 190	CHATTANOOGA STOMP	19241222	Columbia	13003D.	D000001.02
ARMSTRONG, LIL HARDIN, 190	EARLY EVERY MORN	19241222	Gennett	3044.	D000090.01
ARMSTRONG, LIL HARDIN, 190	HIGH SOCIETY RAG	19230622	Okeh	4933.	D000351.01
ARMSTRONG, LIL HARDIN, 190	JAZZIN' BABIES' BLUES	19230623	Okeh	4975.	D000353.02
ARMSTRONG, LIL HARDIN, 190	JUST GONE	19230406	Gennett	5133.	D000036.01
ARMSTRONG, LIL HARDIN, 190	KNOCKED BLUES	19231005	Gennett	5274.	D000040.01
ARMSTRONG, LIL HARDIN, 190	NEW ORLEANS STOMP	19231016	Columbia	13003D.	D000090.02
ARMSTRONG, LIL HARDIN, 190	NOBODY KNOWS THE WAY I FEEL DIS MORN	19241222	Gennett	3044.	D000001.01
ARMSTRONG, LIL HARDIN, 190	SNAKE RAG	19230622	Okeh	4933.	D000351.02

FIGURE 4. Performer/Performing Group Entries on One Frame of the Performer/Performing Group Index

Performer	Date	Performing Group or First-Named Performer	Title	IJS #
ARMSTRONG, LOUIS, 1900-197	19381010	WALLER, FATS, 1904-1964	TIGER RAG	D001112.01
ARMSTRONG, LOUIS, 1900-197	19441207	V-DISC ALL STARS	MIDNIGHT AT V-DISC	D000936.00
ARMSTRONG, LOUIS, 1900-197	19441207	V-DISC ALL STARS	PLAY ME THE BLUES	D000936.01
ARMSTRONG, LOUIS, 1900-197	19441207	V-DISC ALL STARS	PLAY ME THE BLUES	D000936.02
ARMSTRONG, LOUIS, 1900-197	19441207	V-DISC ALL STARS	PLAY ME THE BLUES	D0000936.0
ARMSTRONG, LOUIS, 1900-197	19480602	LOUIS ARMSTRONG AND THE ALL STARS	I CRIED FOR YOU	D001087.02
ARMSTRONG, LOUIS, 1900-197	19480602	LOUIS ARMSTRONG AND THE ALL STARS	LOUIS ARMSTRONG'S ALL STARS, VOL II	D001087.00
ARMSTRONG, LOUIS, 1900-197	19480604	LOUIS ARMSTRONG AND THE ALL STARS	ME AND BROTHER BILL	D001087.04
ARMSTRONG, LOUIS, 1900-197	19480604	LOUIS ARMSTRONG AND THE ALL STARS	WHISPERING	D001087.03
ARMSTRONG, LOUIS, 1900-197	19480605	LOUIS ARMSTRONG AND THE ALL STARS	BASIN STREET BLUES	D001087.09
ARMSTRONG, LOUIS, 1900-197	19480605	LOUIS ARMSTRONG AND THE ALL STARS	DON'T FENCE ME IN	D001087.07
ARMSTRONG, LOUIS, 1900-197	19480605	LOUIS ARMSTRONG AND THE ALL STARS	HIGH SOCIETY	D001087.01
ARMSTRONG, LOUIS, 1900-197	19480605	LOUIS ARMSTRONG AND THE ALL STARS	I GOTTA RIGHT TO SING THE BLUES	D001087.06
ARMSTRONG, LOUIS, 1900-197	19480605	LOUIS ARMSTRONG AND THE ALL STARS	I GOTTA RIGHT TO SING THE BLUES	D001087.08
ARMSTRONG, LOUIS, 1900-197	19480605	LOUIS ARMSTRONG AND THE ALL STARS	JACK-ARMSTRONG BLUES	D001087.10
ARMSTRONG, LOUIS, 1900-197	19480605	LOUIS ARMSTRONG AND THE ALL STARS	LOVE ME TONIGHT LOVER	D001087.05
ARMSTRONG, LOUIS, 1900-197	19480605	LOUIS ARMSTRONG AND THE ALL STARS	MOP MOP	D001087.11
ARMSTRONG, LOUIS, 1900-197	19490800	LOUIS ARMSTRONG AND THE ALL STARS	BUGLE CALL RAG	D000986.09
ARMSTRONG, LOUIS, 1900-197	19490807	LOUIS ARMSTRONG AND THE ALL STARS	HONEYSUCKLE ROSE	D000986.03
ARMSTRONG, LOUIS, 1900-197	19490807	LOUIS ARMSTRONG AND THE ALL STARS	LITTLE BIRD TOLD ME	D000986.04
ARMSTRONG, LOUIS, 1900-197	19490807	LOUIS ARMSTRONG AND THE ALL STARS	LOUIS ARMSTRONG ALL STARS, PHILADELP	D000986.01
ARMSTRONG, LOUIS, 1900-197	19490807	LOUIS ARMSTRONG AND THE ALL STARS	ONE O'CLOCK JUMP	D000986.02
ARMSTRONG, LOUIS, 1900-197	19490807	LOUIS ARMSTRONG AND THE ALL STARS	STATE FAIR THAT'S FOR ME	D000986.07
ARMSTRONG, LOUIS, 1900-197	19490809	LOUIS ARMSTRONG AND THE ALL STARS	GOING PLACES JEEPERS CREEPERS	D000986.11
ARMSTRONG, LOUIS, 1900-197	19490809	LOUIS ARMSTRONG AND THE ALL STARS	NO, NO, NANETTE TEA FOR TWO	D000986.09
ARMSTRONG, LOUIS, 1900-197	19590999	ARMSTRONG, LOUIS, 1900-1971	CHIMES BLUES	D000986.12
ARMSTRONG, LOUIS, 1900-197	19590999	ARMSTRONG, LOUIS, 1900-1971	DR JAZZ	D000916.06
ARMSTRONG, LOUIS, 1900-197	19550999	ARMSTRONG, LOUIS, 1900-1971	DROP THAT SACK	D000916.05
ARMSTRONG, LOUIS, 1900-197	19590999	ARMSTRONG, LOUIS, 1900-1971	I AIN'T GOT NOBODY	D000916.02
ARMSTRONG, LOUIS, 1900-197	19590999	ARMSTRONG, LOUIS, 1900-1971	I WANT A BIG BUTTER AND EGG MAN	D000916.03
ARMSTRONG, LOUIS, 1900-197	19590999	ARMSTRONG, LOUIS, 1900-1971	JELLY ROLL BLUES	D000916.07
ARMSTRONG, LOUIS, 1900-197	19590999	ARMSTRONG, LOUIS, 1900-1971	NEW ORLEANS STOMP	D000916.0
ARMSTRONG, LOUIS, 1900-197	19590999	ARMSTRONG, LOUIS, 1900-1971	NEW ORLEANS STOMP	D000916.04
ARMSTRONG, LOUIS, 1900-197	19590999	ARMSTRONG, LOUIS, 1900-1971	OLD KENTUCKY HOME	D000916.08
ARMSTRONG, LOUIS, 1900-197	19590999	ARMSTRONG, LOUIS, 1900-1971	PANAMA	D000916.00
ARMSTRONG, LOUIS, 1900-197	19550999	ARMSTRONG, LOUIS, 1900-1971	SNAKE RAG	D000916.01
ARMSTRONG, LOUIS, 1900-197	19590999	ARMSTRONG, LOUIS, 1900-1971	SNAKE RAG	D000916.10
ARMSTRONG, LOUIS, 1900-197	19590999	ARMSTRONG, LOUIS, 1900-1971	ST JAMES INFIRMARY	D000916.11
ARMSTRONG, LOUIS, 1900-197	19590999	ARMSTRONG, LOUIS, 1900-1971	THER'LL BE A HOT TIME IN THE OLD TO	D000916.11
ARNDT, FELIX, 1889-1918,	19110131	VAN EPS, FRED, BANJO	RAG PICKINGS	D000517.02
ARNDT, FELIX, 1889-1918,	19140925	VAN EPS TRIO	NOTORIETY RAG	D000521.02
ARNDT, FELIX, 1889-1918,	19140925	VAN EPS BANJO ORCHESTRA	SOUP TO NUTS	D000133.01
ARNDT, FELIX, 1889-1918,	19140925	VAN EPS BANJO ORCHESTRA	I WANT TO GO BACK TO MICHIGAN	D000133.02
ARNDT, FELIX, 1889-1918,	19150127	VAN EPS TRIO	ORIGINAL FOX TROT	D000523.01
ARNHEIM, GUS, 1897-1955,	19240309	LYMAN'S CALIFORNIA AMBASSADOR ORCHESTR	CUT YOURSELF A PIECE OF CAKE	D000448.02
ASH, PAUL, 1891-1958,	19240509	PAUL ASH AND HIS GRANADA ORCHESTRA	MY BEAUTIFUL MEXICAN ROSE	D000473.01
ASH, PAUL, 1891-1958,	19240509	PAUL ASH AND HIS GRANADA ORCHESTRA	ORIENTAL LOVE DREAMS	D000473.02
ASHBY, HAROLD	19690509	ELLINGTON, DUKE, 1899-1974	BLACK BUTTERFLY	D000904.04
ASHBY, HAROLD	19700615	DUKE ELLINGTON AND HIS ORCHESTRA	LOVE IS JUST AROUND THE CORNER	D000904.08
ASHBY, HAROLD	19700615	DUKE ELLINGTON AND HIS ORCHESTRA	MENDOZA	D000904.09
ASHBY, HAROLD	19701209	DUKE ELLINGTON AND HIS ORCHESTRA	BATEAU	D000904.05

FIGURE 5. Performing Group Entries on One Frame of the Performing Group Index

Performing Group	Date	Title	Label Name	Issue #	IJS #
BEN SELVIN AND HIS ORCHESTRA.	19230599	YES, WE HAVE NO BANANAS	Vocalion	14590.	D000367.01
BEN SELVIN AND HIS ORCHESTRA.	19230999	MAMMA'S GONNA SLOW YOU DOWN	Vocalion	14669.	D000386.01
BEN SELVIN AND HIS ORCHESTRA.	19230999	WALK, JENNY, WALK	Vocalion	14669.	D000386.02
BEN SELVIN AND HIS ORCHESTRA.	19239999	BARNEY GOOGLE	Vocalion	14556.	D000376.01
BEN SELVIN AND HIS ORCHESTRA.	19239999	BARNEY GOOGLE	Vocalion	14556.	D000377.01
BEN SELVIN AND HIS ORCHESTRA.	19239999	BESIDE A BABBLING BROOK	Vocalion	14558.	D000378.01
BEN SELVIN AND HIS ORCHESTRA.	19239999	I LOVE ME	Vocalion	14556.	D000376.02
BEN SELVIN AND HIS ORCHESTRA.	19239999	I LOVE ME	Vocalion	14556.	D000377.02
BEN SELVIN AND HIS ORCHESTRA.	19239999	IF I KNEW YOU THEN AS I KNOW YOU NOW	Vocalion	14630.	D000381.01
BEN SELVIN AND HIS ORCHESTRA.	19239999	JUST A GIRL THAT MEN FORGET	Vocalion	14630.	D000381.02
BEN SELVIN AND HIS ORCHESTRA.	19239999	WHO'S SORRY NOW	Vocalion	14558.	D000378.02
BEN SELVIN AND HIS ORCHESTRA.	19249999	WHAT'S TODAY GOT TO DO WITH TOMORROW	Vocalion	14797.	D000394.02
BEN SELVIN AND HIS ORCHESTRA.	19250410	ALL ABOARD FOR HEAVEN	Columbia	355-D.	D000086.01
BEN SELVIN AND HIS ORCHESTRA.	19250410	ORIGINAL CHARLESTON	Columbia	355-D.	D000086.02
BEN SELVIN AND HIS ORCHESTRA.	19251214	NOBODY'S BUSINESS	Domino	3629	D001044.02
BEN SELVIN AND HIS ORCHESTRA.	19251214	SUNNY WHO	Domino	3629	D001044.01
BEN SELVIN AND HIS ORCHESTRA.	19200999	JANE	Velvet Tone	1770-V.	D000982.01
BENNY CARTER AND HIS ORCHESTRA.	19370817	SKIP IT	Vocalion	S.126.	D000678.01
BENNY CARTER AND HIS ORCHESTRA.	19370818	PARDON ME, PRETTY BABY	New World Records	NW 274.	D000315.05
BENNY CARTER AND HIS ORCHESTRA.	19370818	PARDON ME, PRETTY BABY	New World Records	NW 274.	D000315.05
BENNY CARTER AND HIS ORCHESTRA.	19370818	PARDON ME, PRETTY BABY	Vocalion	S.126.	D000678.02
BENNY GOODMAN AND HIS ORCHESTRA.	19340911	SOLITUDE	Banner	33192.	D000942.02
BENNY GOODMAN AND HIS ORCHESTRA.	19410303	SOLO FLIGHT	Beppo	14800.	D001002.02
BENNY GOODMAN AND HIS ORCHESTRA.	19410699	SOLO FLIGHT	Beppo	14800.	D001002.01
BENNY GOODMAN SEXTET.	19391002	FLYING HOME	Columbia	36721.	D000706.01
BENNY GOODMAN SEXTET.	19400115	I FOUND A NEW BABY	Columbia	36039.	D000707.01
BENNY GOODMAN SEXTET.	19401219	BREAKFAST FEUD	Columbia	36039.	D000707.02
BENNY GOODMAN SEXTET.	19410115	I FOUND A NEW BABY	Columbia	36721.	D000706.02
BENNY GOODMAN SEXTET.	19410115	I'VE FOUND A NEW BABY	New World Records	NW 274.	D000315.07
BENNY KRUEGER AND HIS ORCHESTRA.	19200199	SINGIN' THE BLUES	Brunswick	2066.	D000412.02
BENNY KRUEGER AND HIS ORCHESTRA.	19210399	CRAZY BLUES	Brunswick	2077.	D000418.01
BENNY KRUEGER AND HIS ORCHESTRA.	19210399	ROYAL GARDEN BLUES	Brunswick	2077.	D000418.02
BENNY KRUEGER AND HIS ORCHESTRA.	19210923	GLOW LITTLE LANTERN OF LOVE	Emerson	10452.	D000833.02
BENNY KRUEGER AND HIS ORCHESTRA.	19210923	TUCK ME TO SLEEP IN MY OLD 'TUCKY HO	Emerson	10452.	D000833.01
BENNY KRUEGER AND HIS ORCHESTRA.	19211099	EVERYBODY STEP	Brunswick	2151.	D000415.01
BENNY KRUEGER AND HIS ORCHESTRA.	19211099	HOW MANY TIMES	Brunswick	2151.	D000415.02
BENNY KRUEGER AND HIS ORCHESTRA.	19220399	BLUE KITTEN SELECTIONS	Brunswick	2247.	D000424.01
BENNY KRUEGER AND HIS ORCHESTRA.	19220399	DON'T LEAVE ME MAMMY	Brunswick	2246.	D000422.02
BENNY KRUEGER AND HIS ORCHESTRA.	19220399	JIMMY I LOVE BUT YOU	Brunswick	2247.	D000424.02
BENNY KRUEGER AND HIS ORCHESTRA.	19220399	POOR LITTLE ME	Brunswick	2246.	D000422.01
BENNY KRUEGER AND HIS ORCHESTRA.	19220599	I'M JUST WILD ABOUT HARRY	Brunswick	2272.	D000427.02
BENNY KRUEGER AND HIS ORCHESTRA.	19220599	SOME OF THESE DAYS	Brunswick	2340.	D000433.01
BENNY KRUEGER AND HIS ORCHESTRA.	19220599	STUMBLING	Brunswick	2272.	D000427.01
BENNY KRUEGER AND HIS ORCHESTRA.	19231220	IT'S GETTING DARK ON OLD BROADWAY	Brunswick	2340.	D000433.02
BENNY KRUEGER AND HIS ORCHESTRA.	19240227	LINGER AWHILE	Brunswick	2526.	D000456.01
BENNY KRUEGER AND HIS ORCHESTRA.	19240227	WHY DID I KISS THAT GIRL	Brunswick	2576.	D000459.01
BENNY KRUEGER AND HIS ORCHESTRA.	19240303	I WONDER WHO'S DANCING WITH YOU TONI	Brunswick	2576.	D000459.02
BENNY KRUEGER AND HIS ORCHESTRA.	19240724	CHARLEY, MY BOY	Brunswick	2667.	D000472.01
BENNY KRUEGER AND HIS ORCHESTRA.	19240724	PLEASURE MAD	Brunswick	2667.	D000472.02
BENNY KRUEGER AND HIS ORCHESTRA.	19240801	I WONDER WHAT'S BECOME OF SALLY	Brunswick	2682.	D000478.01
BENNY KRUEGER AND HIS ORCHESTRA.	19240806	SUSQUEHANNA HOME	Brunswick	2682.	D000478.02
BENNY KRUEGER AND HIS ORCHESTRA.	19250428	TELL ME MORE SELECTIONS	Brunswick	2910.	D000497.02
BENNY KRUEGER AND HIS ORCHESTRA.	19250428	TELL ME MORE WHY DO I LOVE YOU	Brunswick	2910.	D000497.01
BENSON ORCHESTRA OF CHICAGO.	19200920	PAIR ONE	Victor	18697.	D000557.01
BENSON ORCHESTRA OF CHICAGO.	19200921	CHILI BEAN	Victor	18698.	D000558.01

FIGURE 6. Title Entries on One Frame of Title Index

Title	Date	Performing Group or Featured Performer	Label Name	Issue #	IJS #
APPLE SAUCE;	19230226	VIRGININANS (MUSICAL GROUP)	Victor	19032.	D000647.02
APRIL	19580809	TRISTANO, LENNIE	Bombasi	11:235	D001082.08
APRIL BLOSSOMS.	19230322	CARL FENTON AND HIS ORCHESTRA	Brunswick	2422.	D000442.02
APRIL BLOSSOMS.	19230426	GREAT WHITE WAY ORCHESTRA	Victor	19077.	D000658.01
APRIL IN PARIS	19450907	GARNER, ERROLL, 1923- PRF	Jazz Connoisseur	JC 002	D000970.06
APRIL IN PARIS	195006--	CHARLIE PARKER QUINTET PRF	Crazed Olaf	CPACS 195	D001094.02
APRIL IN PARIS	195006--	CHARLIE PARKER QUINTET PRF	Crazed Olaf	CPACS 195	D01094.02
APRIL SHOWERS;	19211027	PAUL WHITEMAN ORCHESTRA	Victor	18825.	D000588.02
APRIL SHOWERS;	19211199	GENE RODEMICH AND HIS ORCHESTRA	Brunswick	2169.	D000417.02
ARABIA;	19210299	GBEN BROTHERS NOVELTY BAND	Brunswick	2086.	D000413.02
ARE YOU PLAYING FAIR;	19220629	ZEZ CONFREY AND HIS ORCHESTRA	Victor	18921.	D000614.02
ARKANSAS BLUES	19210928	MARY STAFFORD AND HER JAZZ BAND	Columbia	A3493.	D000207.01
ARKANSAS BLUES.	19210299	LUCILLE HEGAMIN AND HER BLUE FLAME SYN	Black Swan	2032	D000738.01
ARKANSAS BLUES;	19240703	LITTLE RAMBLERS	Columbia	175-D.	D000073.02
ARKANSAW MULE;	19240999	CHARLEY STRAIGHT AND HIS ORCHESTRA	Claxtonola	40264.	D000920.01
ARKANSAW [SIC] BLUES;	19240223	MOUND CITY BLUE BLOWERS	Brunswick	2581	D000461.01
ASSUNTA;	19621227	HUBBARD, FREDDIE, TRUMPET	Blue Note.	BN-LA96-H2.	D000279.06
AT THE FUNNY PAGE BALL.	19180007	WILBUR SWEATMAN'S ORIGINAL JAZZ BAND	Columbia	A2663.	D000149.02
AT THE HIGH BROWN BABIES' BALL.	19190902	ALL STAR TRIO	Victor	18617.	D000541.02
AT THE JAZZ BAND BALL;	19180318	ORIGINAL DIXIELAND JAZZ BAND	Victor	18457.	D000533.01
AFW USA.	19640428	CHARLES MINGUS JAZZ WORKSHOP PRF	Unique Jazz	UJ 009	D001096.01
AFW YOU USA.	19640428	CHARLES MINGUS JAZZ WORKSHOP PRF	Unique Jazz	UJ 009	D001096.01
AUNT HAGAR'S BLUES.	19210899	LADD'S BLACK ACES	Gennett	9150.	D000055.01
AUNT HAGAR'S BLUES.	19221199	ISHAM JONES AND HIS ORCHESTRA	Brunswick	2358.	D000436.02
AUNT HAGAR'S BLUES;	19230201	VIRGININANS (MUSICAL GROUP)	Victor	19021.	D000644.02
AUNT HAGAR'S BLUES;	19230416	TED LEWIS AND HIS BAND	Columbia	A3879.	D000241.02
AUNT HAGAR'S CHILDREN BLUES	19210801	LANIN'S SOUTHERN SERENADERS	Emerson	10439.	D000832.02
AUNT HAGAR'S CHILDREN BLUES.	19300830	LANIN'S SOUTHERN SERENADERS	Black Swan	2034.	D000739.01
AUNT HAGAR'S CHILDRENS BLUES;	19210899	LADD'S BLACK ACES	Gennett	9150.	D000055.01
AUNT HAGERS BLUES.	19300830	LANIN'S SOUTHERN SERENADERS	Black Swan	2034.	D000739.01
AUNT HAGERS' CHILDREN BLUES;	19221199	ISHAM JONES AND HIS ORCHESTRA	Brunswick	2358.	D000436.02
AUTOLIEBCHEN;	19139999	CONWAY'S BAND	Victor	17392.	D000520.01
AVALON:	19200001	ART HICKMAN AND HIS ORCHESTRA	Columbia	A3322.	D000190.01
AVALON;	19201001	ART HICKMAN AND HIS ORCHESTRA	Columbia	A3322.	D000190.02
AVALON;	19209999	ISHAM JONES AND HIS RAINBO ORCHESTRA	Brunswick	5027.	D000501.01
AWAY DOWN EAST IN MAINE;	19221128	JOSEPH SAMUELS AND HIS ORCHESTRA	Perfect	14082	D001061.01
AWAY DOWN SOUTH;	19230999	ISHAM JONES AND HIS ORCHESTRA	Brunswick	2302.	D000429.01
AWFUL MOANIN' BLUES.	19230913	SMITH, CLARA, SINGER	Columbia	A4000.	D000271.02
BABY BLUE EYES;	19230214	GREAT WHITE WAY ORCHESTRA	Victor	19009.	D000642.02
BABY WON'T YOU PLEASE COME HOME BLUE	19230411	SMITH, BESSIE, 1898-1937, SINGER	Columbia	A3888.	D000242.01
BABY WON'T YOU PLEASE COME HOME BLUE	19230411	SMITH, BESSIE, 1898-1937, SINGER	Columbia	A3888.	D000243.01
BABY;	19281127	JIMMY MCHUGH'S BCSTONIANS	Harmony	795-H.	D000813.02
BABY;	19441202	TEAGARDEN, JACK, 1905-1964	Pumpkin	106.	D000972.04
BABY, WON'T YOU PLEASE COME HOME	19450830	GARNER, ERROLL, 1923- PRF	Jazz Connoisseur	JC 001	D000969.15
BABY, WON'T YOU PLEASE COME HOME	19500406	SIDNEY BECHET AND HIS ALL STARS PRF	Transakt	1000	D001105.14
BABY, WON'T YOU PLEASE COME HOME.	19230411	SMITH, BESSIE, 1898-1937, SINGER	Columbia	A3888.	D000242.01
BABY, WON'T YOU PLEASE COME HOME.	19230411	SMITH, BESSIE, 1898-1937, SINGER	Columbia	A3888.	D000243.01
BABY, WON'T YOU PLEASE COME HCME.	19221125	TAYLOR, EVA, 1896-1977, SINGER	Okeh	4740.	D000342.02
BABY'S GOT THE BLUES	19230915	MILES, JOSI, SINGER	Gennett	5261.	D000038.01
BACK O' TOWN BLUES;	19230999	COTTON PICKERS (MUSICAL GROUP)	Brunswick	2486.	D000449.02
BACK WHERE THE DAFFODILS GROW;	19241030	STATLER HOTEL DANCE ORCHESTRA	Cameo	621.	D000893.02
BACK WHERE THE DAFFODILS GROW;	19241107	VAGABONDS (MUSICAL GROUP)	Claxtonola	40397.	D000930.01
BAGDAD;	19240805	RAY MILLER AND HIS ORCHESTRA	Brunswick	2681.	D000477.01
BALLIN' THE JACK	19441216	TEAGARDEN, JACK, 1905-1964	Pumpkin	106.	D000972.07
BALTIMORE BUZZ;	19210503	SISSLE'S SIZZLING SYNCOPATORS	Emerson	10385.	D000830.01

FIGURE 7. Composer, Director, Arranger Entries on One Frame of the Composer Index

Composer	Title	Date	Label Name	Issue #	IJS #
BAKER, PHIL, 1896-1963	BLACK SHEEP BLUES	19231019	Claxtonola	40272.	D000921.01
BAKER, PHIL, 1896-1963	LOOK AT THOSE EYES	19250404	Victor	19648	D000731.02
BARBOUR, J BERNI	MY MAN ROCKS ME WITH A STEADY ROLL	19220999	Paramount	12164.	D000293.02
BARD, LARRY	FROM ONE 'TILL TWO, I ALWAYS DREAM O	19240321	Victor	19304.	D000708.01
BARD, LARRY	FROM ONE 'TILL TWO, I ALWAYS DREAM O	19240423	Brunswick	2613.	D000470.02
BARGY, ROY, D 1974	LOTS O' MAMA	19240423	Brunswick	2613.	D000470.01
BARGY, ROY, D 1974	FOOLISH CHILD	19230827	Victor	19136.	D000672.01
BARGY, ROY, D 1974	FOOLISH CHILD	19230831	Perfect	10 in.	D001066.02
BARGY, ROY, D 1974	FOOLISH CHILD	19230899	Cameo	446.	D000861.01
BARGY, ROY, D 1974	PIANOFLAGE	19220999	Brunswick	2344.	D000434.01
BARGY, ROY, D 1974,	RUFENEDDY	19220999	Brunswick	2344.	D000434.02
BARON, MAURICE, 1889-1964, director.	THAT OLD GANG OF MINE	19230827	Brunswick	19136.	D000672.02
BARRETT, EMMA, arranger.	RAILRCAL BLUES	19219999	Victor	18850.	D000591.02
BARRETT, EMMA, arranger.	KISS A MISS	19201199	Brunswick	2066.	D000412.01
BARRETT, EMMA, arranger.	CHIME BLUES	19641018	Preservation Hall	VPS-2.	D000275.03
BARRIS, HARRY, 1905-1962	JUST A CLOSER WALK WITH THEE	19641018	Preservation Hall	VPS-2.	D000275.04
BARRIS, HARRY, 1905-1962	SAINTS	19641018	Preservation Hall	VPS-2.	D000275.08
BARRIS, HARRY, 1905-1962	I SURRENDER DEAR	19470126	Big Chief Jerollom	SBBH 1947.	D001081.07
BASIE, COUNT, 1904-	I SURRENDER DEAR	19470913	Bombasi	11;235.	D001082.02
BASIE, COUNT, 1904-	PLAY IT RED	19270526	Harmony	432-H.	D000794.01
BASIE, COUNT, 1904-	BASES LOADED	19530106	Unique Jazz	UJ 005	D001091.06
BASIE, COUNT, 1904-	BASIE ELUES	19530107	Unique Jazz	UJ 005	D001091.09
BASIE, COUNT, 1904-	BASIE ENGLISH	19530106	Unique Jazz	UJ 005	D001091.01
BASIE, COUNT, 1904-	BASIE ENGLISH	19530113	Unique Jazz	UJ 004.	D001089.07
BASIE, COUNT, 1904-	BASIE JONES	19530107	Unique Jazz	UJ 005	D001091.07
BASIE, COUNT, 1904-	BREAC	19530108	Unique Jazz	UJ 004.	D001089.11
BASIE, COUNT, 1904-	EVERY TUB	19380216	Decca	1728	D000316.11
BASIE, COUNT, 1904-	EVERY TUB	19380216	New World Records	NW 274.	D000315.01
BASIE, COUNT, 1904-	EVERY TUB	19530107	Unique Jazz	UJ 005	D001091.11
BASIE, COUNT, 1904-	EVERY TUB	19530114	Unique Jazz	UJ 005	D001091.12
BASIE, COUNT, 1904-	GOOD BAIT	19510113	Oberon	5100.	D001086.05
BASIE, COUNT, 1904-	HOBNAIL FOOGIE	19510113	Unique Jazz	UJ 004.	D001089.04
BASIE, COUNT, 1904-	I LEFT MY BABY	19391106	New World Records	NW 295.	D000808.02
BASIE, COUNT, 1904-	JUMPIN' AT THE WOODSIDE	19530101	Unique Jazz	UJ 004.	D001089.08
BASIE, COUNT, 1904-	JUMPIN' AT THE WOODSIDE	19770629	Atlantic	SD 8800.	D000278.06
BASIE, COUNT, 1904-	KING	19651126	Pumpkin	108.	D000998.03
BASIE, COUNT, 1904-	CNE O'CLOCK JUMP	19450708	Unique Jazz	UJ 006.	D000997.31
BASIE, COUNT, 1904-	CNE O'CLOCK JUMP	19490807	Jazz Connoisseur	JC 005.	D000986.01
BASIE, COUNT, 1904-	CNE O'CLOCK JUMP	19530101	Unique Jazz	UJ 004.	D001089.01
BASIE, COUNT, 1904-	CNE O'CLOCK JUMP	19530106	Unique Jazz	UJ 005	D001091.06
BASIE, COUNT, 1904-	PARADISE SCUAT	19530107	Unique Jazz	UJ 005	D001091.10
BASIE, COUNT, 1904-	FREVIEW	19530101	Unique Jazz	UJ 004.	D001089.01
BASIE, COUNT, 1904-	SHOE-SHINE SWING	19370208	Jazz Archives	JA-16.	D000288.01
BASIE, COUNT, 1904-	SWINGING AT THE DAISY CHAIN	19370110	Jazz Archives	JA-16.	D000288.10
BASKETTE, BILLY, 1884-1949	EVERYBODY WANTS A KEY TO MY CELLAR	19190404	Columbia	A2750.	D000156.01
BASKETTE, BILLY, 1884-1949	JERRY	19190902	Victor	18617.	D000541.02
BASKETTE, BILLY, 1884-1949	WAITIN' FOR THE EVENIN' MAIL	19230525	Victor	19086.	D000660.02
BASKETTE, BILLY, 1884-1949	WAITIN' FOR THE EVENIN' MAIL	19230626	Victor	19909.	D000664.01
BASKETTE, BILLY, 1884-1949	WAITIN' FOR THE EVENIN' MAIL	19231001	Columbia	13002D.	D000089.02
BATES, CHARLES	HARD HEARTED HANNAH	19240724	Columbia	14311.	D001076.02
BATES, CHARLES	HARD HEARTED HANNAH	19240106	Perfect	624.	D000897.01
BAUER, ABEL, 1893-	LET ME LINGER LONGER IN YOUR ARMS	19250602	Cameo	19692.	D000736.01
BAYES, NORA, 1880-1928	FROHIBITION BLUES	19190718	Victor	A2823.	D000174.01
BAYHA, CHARLES A, 1891-195	NCT SO LONG AGO	19210225	Columbia	A3429.	D000200.01
BECHET, SIDNEY	LC THAT THING	19240528	Vocalion	14838.	D000398.01

FIGURE 8. Brunswick Issue Numbers Listed on One Frame of the Label Name and Issue Number Index

Label Name	Issue #	Title	Performing Group	OCLC #	IJS #
Brunswick	2733.	TELL ME WHAT TO DO	Vic Meyers and his orchestra.	5117993	D000482.01
Brunswick	2752.	COPENHAGEN	Oriole Terrace Orchestra.	5072260	D000483.02
Brunswick	2752.	MY ROSE MARIE	Oriole Terrace Orchestra.	5072145	D000483.01
Brunswick	2753.	I DIDN'T CARE TILL I LOST YOU	Ray Miller and his orchestra.	5112660	D000484.01
Brunswick	2753.	ME AND THE BOY FRIEND	Ray Miller and his orchestra.	5112845	D000484.02
Brunswick	2766.	JIMTOWN BLUES	Cotton Pickers (Musical group)	5072035	D000480.02
Brunswick	2767.	PRINCE OF WAILS	Cotton Pickers (Musical group)	5076697	D000480.01
Brunswick	2767.	DOO WACKA DOO	Isham Jones and his orchestra.	5150627	D000485.02
Brunswick	2778.	HONEST AND TRULY	Isham Jones and his orchestra.	5150510	D000485.01
Brunswick	2778.	BY THE LAKE	Ray Miller and his orchestra.	5140683	D000486.01
Brunswick	2788.	NOBODY KNOWS WHAT A RED HEAD MAMA CA	Ray Miller and his orchestra.	5140841	D000486.02
Brunswick	2788.	I'LL SEE YOU IN MY DREAMS	Ray Miller and his orchestra.	5145778	D000487.01
Brunswick	2804.	WHY COULDN'T IT BE POOR LITTLE ME	Ray Miller and his orchestra.	5145638	D000487.02
Brunswick	2804.	DEEP SECOND STREET BLUES	Mound City Blue Blowers.	5140999	D000488.02
Brunswick	2818.	TIGER RAG	Mound City Blue Blowers.	5140949	D000488.01
Brunswick	2818.	JACKSONVILLE GAL	Cotton Pickers (Musical group)	5141049	D000489.01
Brunswick	2847.	MISHAWAKA BLUES	Cotton Pickers (Musical group)	5141126	D000489.02
Brunswick	2847.	I'LL TAKE HER BACK IF SHE WANTS TO C	Ray Miller and his orchestra.	5155313	D000490.02
Brunswick	2849.	WE'RE BACK TOGETHER AGAIN	Ray Miller and his orchestra.	5141233	D000490.01
Brunswick	2849.	GETTIN' TOLD	Mound City Blue Blowers.	5151115	D000491.01
Brunswick	2854.	PLAY ME SLOW	Mound City Blue Blowers.	5151058	D000491.02
Brunswick	2854.	RIVERBOAT SHUFFLE SOUND RECORDING	Isham Jones and his orchestra.	5150845	D000492.02
Brunswick	2855.	SWANEE BUTTERFLY	Isham Jones and his orchestra.	5150950	D000492.01
Brunswick	2855.	LET IT RAIN, LET IT POUR	Ray Miller and his orchestra.	5145499	D000493.01
Brunswick	2866.	RED HOT HENRY BROWN	Ray Miller and his orchestra.	5145566	D000493.02
Brunswick	2866.	JUST A LITTLE DRINK	Ray Miller and his orchestra.	5145281	D000494.02
Brunswick	2879.	MOONLIGHT AND ROSES	Ray Miller and his orchestra.	5145159	D000494.01
Brunswick	2879.	DOWN AND OUT BLUES	Cotton Pickers (Musical group)	5156583	D000495.01
Brunswick	2898.	THOSE PANAMA MAMAS	Cotton Pickers (Musical group)	5156651	D000495.02
Brunswick	2898.	HOLD ME IN YOUR ARMS	Ray Miller and his orchestra.	5158907	D000496.01
Brunswick	2910.	PHOEBE SNOW	Ray Miller and his orchestra.	5159101	D000496.02
Brunswick	2910.	TELL ME MORE SELECTIONS	Benny Krueger and his orchestra.	5159194	D000497.02
Brunswick	2913.	TELL ME MORE WHY DO I LOVE YOU	Benny Krueger and his orchestra.	5159309	D000497.01
Brunswick	3567.	COLLEGIATE	Carl Fenton and his orchestra.	5155591	D000498.01
Brunswick	3567.	SWEET GEORGIA BROWN	Isham Jones and his orchestra.	5155683	D000498.02
Brunswick	3567.	MELANCHOLY	Johnny Dodds' Black Bottom Stompers.	5512932	D000675.02
Brunswick	3567.	MELANCHOLY	Johnny Dodds' Black Bottom Stompers.	5512989	D000676.02
Brunswick	5012.	WILD MAN BLUES	Johnny Dodds' Black Bottom Stompers.	5619873	D000675.01
Brunswick	5026.	WILD MAN BLUES	Johnny Dodds' Black Bottom Stompers.	5657150	D000676.01
Brunswick	5026.	JEAN	Isham Jones and his Rainbo Orchestra.	5174898	D000499.02
Brunswick	5027.	SAHARA ROSE	Isham Jones and his Rainbo Orchestra.	5174817	D000499.01
Brunswick	5027.	JAPANESE SANDMAN	Isham Jones and his Rainbo Orchestra.	5175509	D000500.01
Brunswick	5045.	KOCLEMOFF	Isham Jones and his Rainbo Orchestra.	5175651	D000500.02
Brunswick	5045.	AVALON	Isham Jones and his Rainbo Orchestra.	5175919	D000501.01
Brunswick	5049.	WISHING	Isham Jones and his orchestra.	5176012	D000501.02
Brunswick	5049.	LOOK FOR THE SILVER LINING	Isham Jones and his orchestra.	5176218	D000502.01
Brunswick	5052.	WHIP-POOR-WILL	Isham Jones and his orchestra.	5176123	D000502.02
Brunswick	5052.	DO YOU EVER THINK OF ME	Isham Jones and his orchestra.	5176424	D000503.01
Brunswick	5065.	MAKE BELIEVE	Isham Jones and his orchestra.	5763334	D000503.01
Brunswick	5065.	ALL SHE'D SAY WAS UMH HUM	Isham Jones and his orchestra.	5176595	D000504.02
Brunswick	5065.	UNDERNEATH HAWAIIAN SKIES	Isham Jones and his orchestra.	5176535	D000504.01
Brunswick	5065.	MA	Isham Jones and his orchestra.	5178366	D000505.01
Brunswick	5065.	MA	Isham Jones and his orchestra.	5179065	D000505.02
Brunswick	5065.	WABASH BLUES	Isham Jones and his orchestra.	5178448	D000506.02
Brunswick	5065.	WABASH BLUES	Isham Jones and his orchestra.	5179220	D000506.02

NOTES

1. This project was initiated in May 1978 under Grant RC-30601-78-597, Research Collections Program, National Endowment for the Humanities.

2. This project was continued in August 1979 under Grant RC-00105-79-1403, Research Collections Program, National Endowment for the Humanities.

3. *Anglo-American Cataloging Rules,* North American text (Chicago: American Library Association, 1967) and, since 1 January 1981, *Anglo-American Cataloguing Rules,* 2nd ed. (Chicago: American Library Association, 1978).

4. Associated Audio Archives (ARSC), *Rules for Archival Cataloging of Sound* Recordings (Manassas, Va.: Association for Recorded Sound Collections, 1978).

5. OCLC Online Computer Library Center, Inc., January 1981-. Established in 1967 as the Ohio College Library Center, the bibliographic network is commonly identified as OCLC since its incorporation as OCLC, Inc., in 1977.

6. Library of Congress, MARC Development Office, *Music: a MARC Format* (Washington, D.C.: for sale by the Superintendent of Documents, U. S. Government Printing Office, 1976) and Addenda 1-3 (Washington, D.C.: Library of Congress, 1976-1980). The acronym MARC translates to "machine-readable-cataloging."

7. *Anglo-American Cataloguing Rules,* 2nd ed. (Chicago: American Library Association, 1978).

8. Representation in Machine-Readable Form of Bibliographic Information Committee, an interdivisional committee of the American Library Association. The author is the Music Library Association representative to the MARBI Committee.

9. *Anglo-American Cataloging Rules,* 1967, have been replaced as the national standard, effective 1 January 1981, by *Anglo-American Cataloguing Rules,* 2nd ed. Also, effective 1 January 1981, *Music: A MARC Format* has been incorporated into the composite MARC document *MARC Formats for Bibliographic Data* (Washington, D.C.: Library of Congress, 1980).

10. Authority control is the library term for the method used to ensure consistency of entries, also called headings, for personal names, corporate names, uniform titles, and uniform titles associated with names. In computer terminology entries are called access points.

11. *Anglo-American Cataloguing Rules,* 2nd ed., was published in 1978 and originally scheduled for implementation on 1 January 1980. However, in response to requests from the Association of Research Libraries and the bibliographic utilities, implementation was postponed until 1 January 1981.

12. Library of Congress, MARC Development Office, *Authorities: A MARC Format* (Washington, D.C.: for sale by the Superintendent of Documents, U. S. Government Printing Office, 1976) and Addenda 1-3 (Washington, D.C.: Library of Congress, 1976-1980) provide documentation for the MARC authority file, which is distributed on magnetic tape by the Library of Congress. This preliminary edition has been revised for reissue in 1981.

13. Coded data, which is included in the catalogue-record to facilitate machine-retrieval, does not normally appear in the *IJS Jazz Register.* Certain coded data, such as the data of performance coded YYYYMMDD (for example, May 17, 1923 = 19230517), which is used in the indexes, does appear in pre-1981 entries because the coded field had not yet been defined for the MARC music format.

14. Judith G. Schmidt, "Library of Congress Plans for the National Union Catalog," *LC Information Bulle-*

tin, vol. 40, no. 3 (January 16, 1981): pp. 35-36; J. McRee Elrod, "Universal Availability of Bibliographic Records," *IFLA Journal,* no. 4 (1978): pp. 347-350.

15. "Library Service Enters Home via Interactive, Cable Television Program in Columbus," *OCLC Newsletter,* no. 124 (1979 August 13): pp. 1-2.

16. William Saffady, *Computer-Output Microfilm: Its Library Applications* (Chicago: American Library Association, 1978): p. 103.

17. Samples may be requested by writing: Marie P. Griffin, Librarian, Institute of Jazz Studies, Rutgers University, 135 Bradley Hall, Newark, N.J. 07102.

18. Marie Griffin, "Proposal for a Union Catalog of Jazz Sound Recordings," (13 pp. including sample worksheets) sent to cooperating archives 1 August 1980 in partial fulfillment of the provisions of Grant RC-00105-79-1404, National Endowment for the Humanities.

19. Cathleen C. Flanagan, "The Use of Commercial Sound Recordings in Scholarly Research," *Association for Recorded Sound Collections - Journal,* vol. 11, no. 1 (1979): pp. 4-11.

20. Rudi Blesh, "The Birth of Discography," *Studies in Jazz Discography I* (New Brunswick, N.J.: Rutgers University, 1971): pp. 34-35.

21. Charles Delaunay, *Hot Discography,* edited by Hot Jazz (Paris: 1936).

22. William M. Weinberg, "Introduction," *Studies in Jazz Discography I:* p. [iv].

NORMAN P. GENTIEU

NOTES FOR A BIO-DISCOGRAPHY
OF JOE SULLIVAN

PART II: NEW YORK AND
LOS ANGELES, 1928-1938

This is the second in a series of articles drawn from Norman P. Gentieu's book-length study of Joe Sullivan's life and recording history. "Part I: Chicago, 1906-1928" appeared in the Journal of Jazz Studies *vol. 4, no. 2 (Spring/Summer 1977), pp. 33-42.*
—*The Editors*

The Twenties brought unprecedented prosperity to this country, and Herbert Hoover, in a 1928 campaign speech, lauded "the American system of rugged individualism." But economic forces were at work that would create increasing hardships for jazz musicians. The radio, for example, had put the piano and the phonograph in almost total shadow.

> In 1919, consumers spent $204 million for pianos. By 1929, when radio sales were at their pre-World War II peak, piano sales had dropped to $87 million, and in 1933 to $17 million. Sales of phonographs and records declined from $339 million in 1919 to $153 million in 1929 and by 1933 sank to $6 million.[1]

Joe Sullivan moved to New York City in 1928, one year before the Great Depression, and played with groups some of which would have ill-fitted the category of jazz. One of his early jobs in Manhattan, however, must have been to his liking. In July 1928, McKenzie and Condon's Chicagoans played a two-week engagement at the Palace Theatre, backing the dance team of Charles Sabin and Barbara Bennett and offering instrumental selections as a respite for the dancers. On July 21, *Billboard* referred to the "commendable seven-man musical unit," and was even more enthusiastic a week later:

> Sandwiching the team's bits are numbers by the seven-piece band. Why these multi-clothed boys are billed as a Pancho Orchestra is one of the week's puzzles. They are a corking unit, playing the slow and syncopated arrangements with excellent results. In fact, their accompaniment for Sabin's brief solo is more stimulating than the efforts of the stepper. The act was loudly applauded here, but it is doubtful whether the success will be duplicated in houses catering to family audiences. . . .

Although a planned engagement at the Chateau Madrid failed to materialize, there were

---

Norman P. Gentieu has written extensively on jazz since the 1930s, when his first articles appeared in *Metronome*. He has blended his musical interests with a career in science writing about topics in chemistry and metallurgy. His extensive studies on Joe Sullivan were commissioned by the Hot Platter Club of Central Jersey as a memorial to William G. Cleland, a dedicated Sullivan collector.

compensations for Sullivan, including opportunity to continue his informal education with the masters of stride piano in Harlem, particularly Thomas "Fats" Waller.

> . . . the gin mills in Harlem. . . . That's where I learned so much from the very fine Negro pianists Art Tatum and Willie 'The Lion' Smith. . . .[2]

> . . . New York when Harlem was so wonderful. Connie's Inn and the little club down stairs just a short walk from Sugar Hill [Pod's and Jerry's] where The Lion was playing and Fats and I'd drop in and Fats and Lion would have a cuttin' contest. Man! what piano playing they indulged in![3]

> . . . occasionally they'd let me sit in and afterwards, oh, five or six o'clock in the morning we'd usually go and get chili ribs or something like that and then Fats would take me up to this wonderful theatre where they had this big beautiful organ. . . .[4]

> Fats and I'd drop in at the old Lafayette theatre . . . and he'd play the organ and the women cleaning up in the balcony would stop and call out "Oh play it Mr. Fats, play it some more!"[5]

> Fats would play the most marvelous music and I was sitting right back of him and of course we had our jug over on the side you know. I never heard anybody play organ like he did. I believe he played it almost equally as well as he did piano because I think he could get a little more oomph in it. . . . I don't think the records did him justice at all. I don't think he had the feeling. He was more relaxed, I know, at six or seven o'clock in the morning. Naturally, you know, everybody is if you've made a night of it. But when you go in cold into a studio and sit down and try to play, it's like the Jitterbug Waltz. And then he kidded around so much I don't think anyone took him seriously. They should have heard him when he was really playing. Magnificent, he really was.[6]

FIRST NEW YORK RECORDINGS

Sullivan's engagements in Manhattan proved to be diverse, if not always a jazzman's Utopia. He continued to visit the recording studios with such jazz musicians as Red Nichols, Benny Goodman, and Jack Teagarden. He played with Red Nichols's band at the Hollywood Restaurant and toured New England with Nichols in 1929. He recorded with Louis Armstrong the same year. Sometime in 1930, he played in a band at Jimmy Plunkett's speakeasy, listed in the telephone directory as "The Trombone Club" in honor of Tommy Dorsey, at 205½ West 53rd Street, where Bix Beiderbecke was a frequent customer. Joe played in Roger Wolfe Kahn's Orchestra, then joined Red McKenzie's Mound City Blue Blowers for a steady job at Sherman Billingsley's Stork Club until the forces of law and order closed that spa early in 1932. Other groups, some rather improbable, that Joe played with included Ozzie Nelson, Russ Columbo, the Dorsey Brothers, and Joe Sanders.

By early July 1928, only ten weeks after his last Chicago recording date, Sullivan made his first New York record, with some of the same performers—Gene Krupa, Eddie Condon, and Frank Teschemacher. Other opportunities followed quickly.

Kaiser Marshall has described the circumstances surrounding the Armstrong session of March 5, 1929:

> We had been working the night before and the record date was for eight in the morning, so we didn't bother about going to bed. I rode the boys around in my car . . . and we had breakfast about six so we could get to the studio at eight. We took a gallon jug of whiskey with us.[7]

LOST TRANSCRIPTIONS

After the blues had been committed to wax, Armstrong was asked for its title. Momentarily stumped, he found the answer in the depleted whisky container: "We sure knocked that jug—you can call it "Knockin' A Jug."

Sullivan's 1930 recordings with Red Nichols included numerous transcriptions for the National Radio Advertising Company. Red Nichols made at least 54 transcriptions for N.R.A.C., but only three of these (listed in the discography which follows) are known to have been retrieved from oblivion, a somber fact that should cause Sullivan (and Red Nichols) collectors hope and frustration in about equal proportions. For further information on this subject, readers are referred to the well-researched liner notes on Broadway BR-101.[8]

There is a possibility that Joe Sullivan played piano for a Gershwin musical comedy. On October 14, 1930, *Girl Crazy* opened at the Alvin Theatre. The cast included Ethel Merman, Ginger Rogers, Allen Kearns, and Willie Howard. But equivalent stars were in the pit orchestra—Benny Goodman, Glenn Miller, Red Nichols, Gene Krupa, Jack Teagarden, and Jimmy Dorsey. Nichols recorded two of the show's twelve musical numbers ("Embraceable You" and "I Got Rhythm") with most of this group and Jack Russin on piano, on October 23, 1930. Is it not reasonable to suppose that Nichols, familiar with Sullivan's professionalism on recent recordings, would have availed himself of this proved musician for at least part of an engagement of a show that ran for 272 performances?

A BIXIAN LEGEND

Two episodes in 1931 involved Beiderbecke. One was a record date, which has been described by Condon.[9] At first glance, the story appears to be another exhibit in the lax museum of Bixian apocrypha, to be taken with a measure of skepticism for Condon's hyperbole.

> [Bix] couldn't go back to Whiteman; he didn't have the stamina for the job, or the ability to concentrate. He played college dates and made a few records: one day he ruined twenty-eight masters trying to get a solo right. Joe Sullivan was in the band; he almost cried when he told me about it.

Fact or fantasy? The incident acquires a certain verisimilitude in this commentary by Sullivan himself:

I recorded with Bix in the late 20s. The two dates were never released, too much drinking. One early Saturday A.M. 19 or 20 takes were thrown out. The other trumpet player can't think of his name spoiled as many as Bix did.[10]

This episode eventually became transmogrified into the fatal but mythical August 1931 date. The truth is that on May 1, 1931, Bix led a group fronted by Benny Goodman at a house party at Princeton University's Cottage Club. The group also included Charlie Teagarden, Will Bradley, Bud Freeman, John Geller, Joe Sullivan, Bill Challoner (guitar) and Johnny Powell (drums). The next night the same band, with Jimmy Dorsey replacing Goodman, played at the Charter Club. After finishing this gig, the musicians were easily persuaded to move to Byrnes McDonald's home where they continued the session.[11]

Two events of 1932 are noteworthy. Sullivan opened at Joe Helbock's Onyx Club, a walk-up-one-flight speakeasy on the north side of 52nd Street. Helbock's motive was refreshingly ulterior—he hired Sullivan because he liked good jazz. And Eddie Condon has described the epic celebration of Joe Sullivan's 26th birthday at the apartment the two Chicagoans shared at the rear of a building on 54th Street.[12] The chapter entitled ''A Birthday for Joe'' is recommended reading for those nostalgia buffs who yearn for the good old days of Prohibition and the carefree carousings it engendered.

Quandaries confront discographers—for example, the identity of the pianist for Billy Banks on April 13, 1932. Five days later, Joe Sullivan appeared with Billy Banks and a pickup group for the first of two recording sessions. On such flimsy evidence, one can only offer the possibility that Joe might have accompanied the aspiring Banks earlier.

COLUMBO DAYS

Sullivan performed with Russ Columbo's orchestra for much of 1932, but the personnel of the recording dates which produced eleven sides in June, August, and November is uncertain, although the discography suggests a possible lineup.[13] Sullivan fans hopeful of hearing his jazz piano on records made by the ''crooner of sentimental songs,'' however, are advised by Brian Rust to forget it: ''Although Russ Columbo's Orchestra in the Park Central Hotel in New York (1932-1933) included Benny Goodman-cl, Joe Sullivan-p, and Gene Krupa-d, there is no evidence of their presence on any of his records.''[14] Given Columbo's romantic vocalizing, the nervous conservatism of Victor recording directors, and the desperate economic condition at that time, opportunities for Sullivan to surface for a jazz solo were skimpy. Since the band, assembled by Goodman at Columbo's request, was remarkable, Victor's failure to give the group its head, or at least to permit one instrumental session, is a cause for regret.

The Columbo band, with personnel somewhat different from the recording group, played at the Waldorf-Astoria in early 1932. Then, after some vaudeville dates, it opened in mid-May at the Woodmansten Inn in the Bronx, N.Y. Benny left before the month was out, but he remembers the date well:

Joe Sullivan was on piano and they wanted two pianists. I said how the hell are you gonna have two pianos with Joe Sullivan?

I had a friend, a real nice guy named Roland Wilson. (We called him "Whiskey" Wilson. His family had owned the whiskey called "Wilson's, That's All!" but lost most of their money in the market crash.) I said: "Roland, you got a job, only on one condition." He said: "What's that?" I said: "If I ever hear you, you're fired!"

We used to rock the Woodmansten Inn. . . .[15]

Joe rejoined Roger Wolfe Kahn in the spring of 1933 and recounts:

I was down in New Orleans with Roger Wolfe Kahn's band, and Artie Shaw, by the way, was in that band. Oh, that was wonderful. We used to look over there. He was the highest paid musician in the band, and Charlie Teagarden and I, we were almost like little old sidemen . . . so here would be Artie Shaw—the music stand is here and he's having all these books, you know, which were too deep for me even to understand. And someone would have to punch him. We had all those big arrangements [that] cost Roger Wolfe Kahn thousands of dollars and Artie'd pick up the clarinet; he'd go through the things and put it down and start reading again.[16]

LOS ANGELES AND HOLLYWOOD

Joe Sullivan's first visit east ended after about five years of uncommonly varied experience and several outstanding recordings. According to Connor and Hicks,[17] he left New York City for California in October 1933. But there must have been previous journeys west, and subsequent returns to the East Coast. The 1933 recording dates with Bing Crosby and others show this to be so. And Oro "Tut" Soper remembers that Joe played for lunch and dinner at the Werner-Kelton Hotel in Hollywood in late 1930-1931 when Soper stayed there.[18]

Joe arrived in Los Angeles in the fall of 1933 and, after auditioning, joined Bing Crosby's first studio orchestra. He worked regularly as Bing's accompanist, appearing in his films, and also played in Georgie Stoll's studio and recording orchestra. Among the Bing Crosby movies that Joe played for were: *Anything Goes* (Cole Porter composed the score for this film, but Hoagy Carmichael wrote the special number that will long be associated with Joe, "Moonburn") and *Pennies from Heaven* (Louis Armstrong and Lionel Hampton also appeared in this one). Joe may also have played on the soundtrack of the Harry Richman film, *The Music Goes 'Round,* which also starred the Onyx Club band of Eddie Farley and Mike Riley. All three films were released in 1936. On the February 5, 1936, Kraft Music Hall radio program, Joe and Bing again did "Moonburn." An air check of this program exists.

The first Los Angeles listing in the discography which follows—"I Guess It Had To Be That Way" on August 27, 1933—appears in Rust. The following listings for the same date reflect more recent research, which indicates that Sullivan played on this side and three others as the pianist with Jimmy Grier and his Orchestra, the group accompanying Bing.[19]

FIRST SOLO RECORDINGS

The September 26, 1933, session produced Sullivan's first appearance on records as a solo pianist, without benefit of a rhythm section. Three of the tunes are Joe's; the other is Fats Waller's evergreen classic, "Honeysuckle Rose." All in all, the four sides present a thoroughly creditable performance, in spite of Donald Biggar's criticism that "they are somewhat too studied to pass as genuine tavern piano."[20] They are "studied" only if the term is meant clear articulation of the notes. Biggar fails to define "genuine tavern piano." At any rate, Sullivan should have been proud of this debut. His fire, feeling, and imagination are all on display, and implicit here is a promise of future triumphs.

By the time he recorded his second quartet of solos in August 1935, Joe Sullivan had matured into a pianist of superlative artistry. "Minor Mood", for example, with its jazz interpretation of Rachmaninoff's Prelude in C-sharp minor, in which even Chopin is quoted with a genuine jazz accent, has moved far beyond the comparatively routine and primitive syncopation of George L. Cobb's "Russian Rag."

A surprise lurks in this group of pieces. The 1933 version of "Little Rock Getaway" has been trimmed down to its skeleton and practically re-written—transformed into a composition of far greater interest harmonically than its predecessor. Sometime between 1933 and 1935, Sullivan must have listened to, absorbed, and transmuted two classics of piano jazz: "Buddy's Habits" by Arnett Nelson and "Carolina Shout" by James P. Johnson. This example of musical evolution and synthesis has been well demonstrated by Don Ewell on "A Jazz Portrait of the Artist" (Chiaroscuro CR 106), an LP that had its origin in a suggestion by the late Sherman Fairchild in August 1970 that some tunes associated with Joe Sullivan be recorded. These sides were remarkable achievements in 1935; now, over forty years later, they have lost none of their excitement or essential jazz quality, which is to say, their timelessness.

FROM BING TO BOB

Joe Sullivan returned to New York City in the summer of 1936 and joined Bob Crosby and his Orchestra for an engagement at the Hotel Lexington. In mid-September, they appeared at the Earle Theatre in Philadelphia. The author remembers hearing this excellent band at the Earle. Joe was featured on "Pagan Love Song" and played a dozen or so choruses on that saccharine and unpaganlike theme, producing some of the gutsiest jazz ever heard.

Did this music turn the local music appreciators on? Hardly. The critic from the *Evening Bulletin* wrote a review notable not only for its lukewarm enthusiasm but also for the unintentional disclosure of its writer's fusty taste:

> The main attraction billed for the stage is Bob Crosby, brother of Crooner Bing, who leads his own band through the latest swing music. The selections presented, however, lack in originality of treatment and, in almost all instances, are irritating to the ear. The Crosby "swing music" is indeed jazz at about its lowest level with none of the later Paul Whiteman

refinements. Although the music is weak and trying on the nerves, a first-class dancing team, Ray and Grace MacDonald, inject life to the boards. Kay Weber is the vocalist.[21]

As a tiger among the Bob Crosby Bobcats, Sullivan appeared to be finally on his way to fame if not fortune in the fall of 1936. Unfortunately, a near-fatal illness brought his career to a shuddering halt. While the band was playing an engagement at the Adolphus Hotel in Dallas in December 1936, the pianist collapsed. Sullivan had fallen prey to tuberculosis. Instead of riding the crest of the Crosby band's popularity, he spent most of 1937 in the Dore Sanitarium at Monrovia, California (near Los Angeles).

Very little information on his stay at Dore Sanitarium has come to light. In his introduction to the Joe Sullivan piano folio, D.D. (presumably Dave Dexter) stated that "though very ill with tuberculosis, which almost proved fatal, while featured with Bob Crosby, he practiced diligently in the sanitorium on a dummy keyboard Benny Goodman sent him."[22] An inquiry to D. Russell Connor, an expert on Goodman, elicited this reply: "I'm sorry, I cannot confirm the story that Benny Goodman had a dummy keyboard sent to Joe Sullivan when Joe was hospitalized. I mentioned it to Benny but just drew a blank. This is not to say it did not happen, but . . ."[23]

Given Joe Sullivan's temperament, the silent keyboard would have been a godsend and quite possibly an essential ingredient in his recovery. For this was the second traumatic experience in his life. (The first had been an injury in the early 1920s that left his eyes crossed. Sullivan himself described this ordeal: "I was so self-conscious that I was afraid to look at anybody head on. I always talked to people sideways. But most of this shy feeling went away after I got to New York a couple of years later and had my eyes straightened by surgery."[24])

The March 1937 issue of *Tempo* reported that Joe Sullivan was on the road to recovery and expected "to be back in good shape soon." This news item included a message from Joe:

> He extends his thanks to the many who wrote to him at suggestion of TEMPO. Joe says he has had a "flood of letters," too many to answer personally, but that every one is appreciated.

A FIVE-HOUR BENEFIT CONCERT

On Sunday, May 23, 1937, a "swing concert" organized by Bing Crosby was given to help pay Joe's expenses at Dore Sanitarium[25]—a fine altruistic gesture in view of the pianist's economic adversity and the high cost of his prolonged confinement and medical treatment. Some 4,000 people bought tickets for the concert at Pan-Pacific Auditorium in Los Angeles at prices of 50 cents, $1.00 and $1.50; another 4,000 or so were turned away. The show grossed over $4,000, with a net of $3,086 in pre-World War II dollars left for Joe. Crosby, who appeared and sang several songs, read a wire of appreciation from Sullivan, who was listening, and introduced Mrs. Sullivan, who was in the audience.

It was the biggest, the longest, and the most successful musical benefit ever staged up to that time. And, as even a cursory glance at the program shows, it was brimming with what a future generation would call superstars, among them: Seger Ellis and his saxless band; Louis Prima and band; Phil Harris; Jimmy Grier and orchestra; Jimmy Dorsey and orchestra, then playing nightly at the Pan-Pacific. Johnny Mercer did a special tune with Dorsey called "Boogie Woogie," based on "Pinetop's Boogie Woogie," for which he had written words "all about Pinetop and Joe." Unfortunately, a large part of this song was cut out during the broadcast to make way for station announcements.

Also on hand were Art Tatum; Ben Pollack with a band specially organized for the occasion, with eight brass and eight saxes and featuring Muggsy Spanier on cornet and Archie Rosate on clarinet; Ray Noble and orchestra, with Ella Logan as vocalist; Victor Young and his orchestra of around 50 pieces, with Dorothy Lamour as vocalist and a trumpet man who played the Bix chorus on "Sweet Sue." Earl Hines, with vocals by Ida Mae James, closed the show. This list is incomplete—many other musicians also appeared during a tribute that lasted more than five hours.

There was one item in the *Tempo* write-up that must have appealed to Sullivan's sense of humor: "Men's rest room was unusually crowded with musicians during offering of one ultra-commercial band."

Sullivan was discharged as cured late in December 1937, just about a year after he was first stricken in Dallas. The January 1938 *Tempo* reported that Sullivan had "left the sanitarium during the latter part of December and was at his new home in North Hollywood for Christmas. Though not entirely recovered, Sullivan is convalescing rapidly and may be able to return to musical activity in a few months."

Happily, this tentative prediction was fulfilled; Joe did resume playing in 1938. Almost 25 years of creative activity, during which many of the great jazz pianist's finest improvisations were to be recorded, lay ahead.

EXPLICATION OF RECORD LISTINGS (July 6, 1928—March 31, 1936)

Name of recording group/place/date

Personnel (The conventional sequence of naming players—brass, reeds, rhythm—has been abandoned to list Sullivan and his rhythm section first, a logical modification in view of the primary emphasis of this article.)

Matrix and take	*Title*	*Original label and number*	*LP (if known)*

(Original label and number is generally limited to the record which was first issued commercially, although a few exceptions have been made. With this information, readers will be able to use Rust, Jepsen, and other discographies to investigate record issues in depth.)

MIFF MOLE'S LITTLE MOLERS   NEW YORK, JULY 6, 1928

p-Joe Sullivan, d-Gene Krupa, bj-Eddie Condon, c-Red Nichols, tb-Miff Mole, cl-Frank
Teschemacher.

| 400849-C | Windy City Stomp (also, *One Step to Heaven) | HRS 15, *Columbia 35953 | LP: Columbia CL 632 |
| 400850-A | Shim-me-sha-wabble | Okeh 41445, *Columbia 35953 | LP: Columbia CL 632 |

EDDIE CONDON QUARTET   NEW YORK, JULY 28, 1928

p-Joe Sullivan, d-Gene Krupa, bj-Eddie Condon, cl & as-Frank Teschemacher.

| 400899-A | Oh! Baby | Parlophone R-2932 | LP: Columbia CL 632, C3L 32 |
| 401035-A | Indiana (voc-Eddie Condon) | Parlophone R-2932 | LP: Columbia CL 632, C3L 32, KG 31564 |

EDDIE CONDON AND HIS FOOTWARMERS   NEW YORK, OCTOBER 30, 1928

p-Joe Sullivan, D-Johnny Powell, b-Art Miller, bj-Eddie Condon, c-Jimmy McPartland,
tb-Jack Teagarden, cl-Mezz Mezzrow.

| 401277-A | I'm Sorry I Made You Cry (voc-Eddie Condon) | Okeh 41142 | |
| 401278-A | Makin' Friends (voc-Jack Teagarden) | Okeh 41142 | LP: Columbia CL 632 |

EDDIE'S HOT SHOTS   NEW YORK, FEBRUARY 8, 1929

p-Joe Sullivan, d-George Stafford, bj-Eddie Condon, t-Leonard Davis, tb-Jack
Teagarden, cs-Mezz Mezzrow, ts-Happy Caldwell.

48345-1	I'm Gonna Stomp, Mr. Henry	Victor V-38046	
48345-2	Lee (voc-Jack Teagarden)	Bluebird B-10168	LP: RCA LX-3005, LPV 528
48346-1	That's a Serious Thing (voc-Jack Teagarden)	Bluebird B-10168	LP: REA LX-3005, LPV 528
48346-2		Victor V-38046	

LOUIS ARMSTRONG AND HIS ORCHESTRA   NEW YORK, MARCH 5, 1929

p-Joe Sullivan, d-Kaiser Marshall, g-Eddie Lang, t-Louis Armstrong, tb-Jack
Teagarden, ts-Happy Caldwell.

| 401688-B | I'm Gonna Stomp, Mr. Henry Lee | Unissued | |
| 401689-B | Knockin' a Jug | Okeh 8703 | LP: Columbia CL 854, Folkways 2807 |

(A copy of a test pressing, possibly of Take A, exists.)

LOUISIANA RHYTHM KINGS **NEW YORK, JUNE 11, 1929**

p-Joe Sullivan, d-Dave Tough, c-Red Nichols, tb-Jack Teagarden, cl-Pee Wee
Russell, ts-Bud Freeman.

E-30029-?	That Da Da Strain	Vocalion 15828	
E-30030-?	Basin Street Blues (voc-Jack Teagarden)	Vocalion 15815	LP: Ace of Hearts AH-168, Decca DL 4540
E-30031-?	Last Cent	Vocalion 15815	

RED NICHOLS AND HIS FIVE PENNIES **NEW YORK, JUNE 12, 1929**

p-Joe Sullivan, d-Dave Tough, b-Art Miller, bj-Tommy Felline, t-Red Nichols,
Manny Klein, Tommy Thunen; tb-Jack Teagarden, Glenn Miller, Herb Taylor; cl-Pee
Wee Russell, ts-Bud Freeman.

E-30056-A	Who Cares? (voc-Red McKenzie)	Brunswick 4778

(unnumbered non-vocal master made, but never issued)

E-30057-A	Rose of Washington Square	Brunswick 4778

BENNIE GOODMAN'S BOYS **CHICAGO, AUGUST 13, 1929**

p-Joe Sullivan, d-Bob Conselman, b-Harry Goodman, bj-Herman Foster, t-Wingy Manone,
cl-Benny Goodman, ts-Bud Freeman.

C-4035-A	After a While (voc-Wingy Manone)	Brunswick 4968	LP: Brunswick BL 54010, BL 58015
C-4036-A	Muskrat Scramble	Brunswick 4968	LP: Brunswick BL 54010, BL 58015, Decca DL 8398

RED NICHOLS AND HIS FIVE PENNIES **NEW YORK, JULY 2, 1930**

p-Joe Sullivan, d-Gene Krupa, b-Art Miller, bj-Teg Brown, t-Red Nichols, Ruby
Weinstein, Charlie Teagarden; tb-Jack Teagarden, Glenn Miller; cl-Benny Goodman,
as-Sid Stoneburn, ts-Babe Russin.

E-33304-A	Peg O' My Heart	Brunswick 4877	
E-33304-B		Brunswick 80004	LP: Brunswick BL 58008
E-33305-A	Sweet Georgia Brown	Brunswick 4944	
E-33306-A	China Boy	Brunswick 4877	LP: Brunswick BL 54008, BL58008
E-33307-A,B	Chong (He Came From Hong Kong)	Unissued	

RED NICHOLS AND HIS FIVE PENNIES   NEW YORK, JULY 3, 1930

p-Joe Sullivan, d-Gene Krupa, b-Art Miller, bj-Teg Brown, t-Red Nichols, Ruby
Weinstein, Charlie Teagarden; tb-Jack Teagarden, Glenn Miller; cl-Benny Goodman,
as-Sid Stoneburn, ts-Babe Russin.

E-33333-A	The Sheik of Araby (voc-Jack Teagarden, Teg Brown)	Brunswick 4885	LP: Brunswick BL54010, BL58008
E-33334-A	Shim-Me-Sha-Wabble	Brunswick 4885	
E-33334-B		Brunswick 80005	LP: Brunswick BL54047, BL58008

RED NICHOLS AND HIS ORCHESTRA   NEW YORK, c. AUGUST 1, 1930

p-Joe Sullivan, d-Gene Krupa, g-Teg Brown, c-Red Nichols, unknown; tb-Glenn Miller,
as & cl-Benny Goodman, ts-Bud Freeman, bs-Adrian Rollini, v-two unknown.

XE-33548   St. Louis Blues

(Part 2 of Program E, National Radio Advertising Co.)

XE-33549   Call of the Freaks   LP: Broadway BR-101

(Part 3 of Program E, National Radio Advertising Co.)

RED NICHOLS AND HIS ORCHESTRA   NEW YORK, c. AUGUST 25, 1930

p-Joe Sullivan, d-Gene Krupa, g-Teg Brown, c-Red Nichols, unknown; tb-Glenn Miller,
as & cl-Benny Goodman, ts-Bud Freeman, bs-Adrian Rollini, v-two unknown.

XE-34058   Ballin' the Jack/ Walking   LP: Broadway BR-101
             the Dog/Ballin' the Jack

(Part 3 of Program I, National Radio Advertising Co.)

RED NICHOLS AND HIS FIVE PENNIES   NEW YORK, AUGUST 27, 1930

p-Joe Sullivan, d-Gene Krupa, t-Red Nichols, Charlie Teagarden; tb-Jack Teagarden,
Glenn Miller; cl-Benny Goodman, ts-Bud Freeman, bs-xyl-Adrian Rollini.

E-34109-A	Carolina in the Morning	Brunswick 4925
E-34110-?	How Come You Do Me Like You Do?	Unissued
E-34111-A	Who?	Brunswick 4925
E-34112-?	By the Shalimar	Brunswick 4944

(Note: According to Connor and Hicks, Charlie Butterfield rather than Jack
 Teagarden may have been Glenn Miller's section mate.)

RED NICHOLS AND HIS FIVE PENNIES **NEW YORK, DECEMBER 1, 1930**

p-Joe Sullivan, d-Gene Krupa, b-Art Miller; t-Red Nichols, Charlie Teagarden,
Wingy Manone, tb-Glenn Miller; cl & as-Jimmy Dorsey, ts-Babe Russin.

| E-35618-A | My Honey's Lovin' Arms | Brunswick 6012 | LP: | Sunbeam MFC 12 |
| E-35619-A | Rockin' Chair | Brunswick 6012 | LP: | Sunbeam MFC 12 |

BILLY BANKS, VOCAL, ACC. BY: **NEW YORK, APRIL 13, 1932**

p-Joe Sullivan (?)

| 1128 | Sleepy Time Down South | Victor test |
| 1129 | Dinah/I Got Rhythm | Victor test |

BILLY BANKS AND HIS ORCHESTRA **NEW YORK, APRIL 18, 1932**

p-Joe Sullivan, d-Zutty Singleton, b-Al Morgan, g-Jack Bland, bj-Eddie Condon,
t- Henry Allen, cl & ts-Pee Wee Russell.

11716-1	Bugle Call Rag	Banner 32459 Perfect 15615 UHCA 109	LP:	IAJRC #4
11717-1	Oh! Peter (You're So Nice)(voc-Henry Allen)		LP:	OFC 9; Jazz Archives JA-1, IAJRC #4
11717-2		Columbia 35841	LP:	Jazz Archives JA-1
11718-1	Margie (voc- Billy Banks)	Banner 32462 Perfect 15620 UHCA 110	LP:	IAJRC #4
11719-2	Spider Crawl (voc-Billy Banks)	Unissued		

BILLY BANKS AND HIS ORCHESTRA **NEW YORK, MAY 23, 1932**

p-Joe Sullivan, d-Zutty Singleton, b-Al Morgan, g-Jack Bland, bj-Eddie Condon,
t-Henry Allen, cl & ts-Pee Wee Russell.

| 11717-3 | Oh! Peter (You're
So Nice) (voc-Billy
Banks) | Banner 32462
Columbia 35841
Perfect 15620
UHCA 110 | LP: | Jazz Archives
JA-1,
IAJRC #4 |
| 11717-4 | | | LP: | Jazz Archives
JA-1 |

11719-4	Spider Crawl (voc-Billy Banks)	Banner 32459 Perfect 15615 UHCA 109	LP: IAJRC #4
11881-1	Who's Sorry Now? (voc-Billy Banks)	Domino 123 Perfect 15642 UHCA 112	LP: IAJRC #4
11882-1	Take It Slow and Easy (voc-Billy Banks)	HRS 17	LP: IAJRC #4
11883-1	Bald Headed Mama (voc-Billy Banks)	Domino 123 Perfect 15642 UHCA 112	LP: IAJRC #4

RUSS COLUMBO AND HIS ORCHESTRA   NEW YORK, JUNE, AUGUST, AND NOV., 1932

p-Joe Sullivan, Marlin Skiles; d-Gene Krupa, b-Harry Goodman, g-Perry Botkin,
t-Eddie Petrowicz, Bo Ashford, Jimmy McPartland; tb-Herb Winfield and/or Artie
Foster; as-Jess Carneol, Pete Pumiglio; ts-Babe Russin; all arrangements by Marlin
Skiles.   **JUNE 16, 1932**

73017-1	Just Another Dream of You	Victor 24045	LP: RCA CPL1-1756(e)
73018-1	I Wanna Be Loved	Unissued	
73019-1	Living in Dreams	Victor 24045	LP: RCA Victor LPM-2072, LSA 3066

AUGUST 3, 1932

73148-1	My Love	Victor 24077	LP: RCA CPL1-1756(e)
73149-1	As You Desire Me	Victor 24076	
73150-1	Lonesome Me	Victor 24077	
73151-1	The Lady I Love	Victor 24076	

NOVEMBER 23, 1932

73995-1	Street of Dreams	Victor 24194	
73996-1	Make Love the Thing	Victor 24195	
73997-1	I Called to Say Goodnight	Victor 24195	
73998-1	Lost in a Crowd	Victor 24194	

BING CROSBY, ACC. BY GEORGIE STOLL AND HIS ORCHESTRA   LOS ANGELES,
AUGUST 27, 1933

p-Joe Sullivan; other players unidentified.

| LA-3-A | ~~I Guess It Had to Be~~
That Way | ~~Brunswick 6644~~ | |

BING CROSBY, ACC. BY JIMMY GRIER AND HIS ORCHESTRA   LOS ANGELES,
                                                          AUGUST 27, 1933

p-Joe Sullivan.

LA-1-A	Thanks	Brunswick 6643	LP:	Columbia Special Products P 13156 (in Set P4 13153)
LA-2-A	The Day You Came Along	Brunswick 6644	LP:	Columbia Special Products P 13156 (in Set P4 13153)
LA-3-A	I Guess It Had to Be That Way	Brunswick 6644	LP:	Columbia Special Products P 13157 (in Set P4 13153)
LA-4-A	Black Moonlight	Brunswick 6643	LP:	Columbia Special Products P 13157 (in Set P4 13153)
LA-4-B		Brunswick 6643		

JOE SULLIVAN   NEW YORK, SEPTEMBER 26, 1933

265139-2	Honeysuckle Rose	Columbia 2876-D	LP:	Epic L2N 6072, Prestige 7646/CSP P2 12854*, Columbia PG 32355
265140-2	Gin Mill Blues	Columbia 2876-D		
265141-2	Little Rock Getaway	Parlophone R-2006		
265142-2	Onyx Bringdown	Parlophone R-2006 Columbia 2925-D	LP:	Jazum 9 (erroneously titled "Onyx Breakdown")

* Part of the Columbia Special Products Album, Encores from the 30's. Volume 1, 1930-1935.

JOE VENUTI AND HIS BLUE SIX   NEW YORK, OCTOBER 2, 1933

p-Joe Sullivan, d-Neil Marshall, g-Dick McDonough, v-Joe Venuti, cl-Benny Goodman, ts-Bud Freeman, bs-Adrian Rollini.

265146-2	Sweet Lorraine	Columbia (Eng) CB-708, Decca 18167	LP:	Decca DL5383, Prestige 7644
265147-2	Doin' the Uptown Lowdown	Columbia 2834-D, Decca 18167	LP:	Decca DL5383, Prestige 7644
265148-2	The Jazz Me Blues	Columbia (Eng) CB-686, Decca 18168	LP:	Decca DL5383, Prestige 7644
265149-2	In De Ruff	Columbia (Eng) CB:686, Decca 18168	LP:	Decca DL5383, Prestige 7644

BENNY GOODMAN AND HIS ORCHESTRA   NEW YORK, OCTOBER 18, 1933

p-Joe Sullivan, d-Gene Krupa, b-Artie Bernstein, g-Dick McDonough, t-Charlie
Teagarden, Manny Klein; tb-Jack Teagarden, cl-Benny Goodman, ts-Art Karle.

265164-2	I Gotta Right to Sing the Blues (voc-Jack Teagarden)	Columbia 2835-D	LP: Jazz Panorama JP1807, Jolly Roger JR5023, Prestige 7644, Jazum 1
265165-1 265165-2	Ain'tcha Glad? (voc-Jack Teagarden)	Columbia 2835-D	LP: Jazum 1 LP: Epic LN24046 (Set SN6044), Prestige 7644, Jazum 1

EDDIE CONDON AND HIS ORCHESTRA   NEW YORK, NOVEMBER 17, 1933

p-Joe Sullivan, d-Sid Catlett, b-Artie Bernstein, bj-Eddie Condon, t-Max Kaminsky,
tb-Floyd O'Brien, cl-Pee Wee Russell, ts-Bud Freeman.

14193-C	The Eel	Brunswick 6743	LP: Epic LN24027, SN6042
14196-B	Home Cooking	Brunswick 6743	LP: Epic LN24027, SN6042

ETHEL WATERS, ACC. BY BENNY GOODMAN AND HIS ORCHESTRA   NEW YORK, NOVEMBER 27, 1933

p-Joe Sullivan, d-Gene Krupa, b-Artie Bernstein, g-Dick McDonough, t-Charlie
Teagarden, Shirley Clay; tb-Jack Teagarden, cl-Benny Goodman, ts-Art Karle.

152566-1	I Just Couldn't Take It, Baby	Columbia 2853-D	LP: Sunbeam SB 111
152566-2		Columbia 2853-D	LP: Columbia KG 31571
152567-1	A Hundred Years From Today	Columbia 2853-D	LP: Sunbeam SB 111
152567-2		Columbia 2853-D	LP: Columbia KG 31571

BENNY GOODMAN AND HIS ORCHESTRA   NEW YORK, NOVEMBER 27, 1933

p-Joe Sullivan, d-Gene Krupa, b-Artie Bernstein, g-Dick McDonough, t-Charlie
Teagarden, Shirley Clay; tb-Jack Teagarden, cl-Benny Goodman, ts-Art Karle.

152568-3	Your Mother's Son-in-Law (voc-Billie Holiday)	Columbia 2856-D	LP: Columbia C1821 CL1758(C3L-21), CSP P 12973(in Book-of-the-Month Club album 90-5652)

BENNY GOODMAN AND HIS ORCHESTRA   **NEW YORK, DECEMBER 4, 1933**

p-Joe Sullivan, d-Gene Krupa, b-Artie Bernstein, g-Dick McDonough, t-Charlie
Teagarden, Shirley Clay; tb-Jack Teagarden, cl-Benny Goodman, ts-Art Karle.

152574-1	Tappin' the Barrel (voc-Jack Teagarden)	Columbia(Eng) DB 5014	LP: Epic LN24046 (Set SN 6044)
152574-2		Columbia 2856-D	
152575-2	Riffin' the Scotch (voc-Billie Holiday)	unissued	
152576-1	Keep on Doin' What You're Doin' (voc-Jack Teagarden)	unissued	

BENNY GOODMAN AND HIS ORCHESTRA   **NEW YORK, DECEMBER 18, 1933**

p-Joe Sullivan, d-Gene Krupa, b-Artie Bernstein, g-Dick McDonough, t-Charlie
Teagarden, Shirley Clay; tb-Jack Teagarden, cl-Benny Goodman, ts-Art Karle.

152599-1	Keep on Doin' What You're Doin' (voc-Jack Teagarden)	Columbia 2867-D	LP: Columbia CL821
152650-2	Riffin' the Scotch (voc-Billie Holiday)	Columbia 2867-D	LP: Columbia CL821
152651-1	Love Me or Leave Me	Columbia 2871-D	LP: Columbia CL821
152652-2	Why Couldn't It Be Poor Little Me?	Columbia 2871-D	LP: Columbia CL821

BING CROSBY, ACC. BY GEORGE STOLL AND HIS ORCHESTRA   **LOS ANGELES, AUGUST 8, 1934**

p-Joe Sullivan, g-Bobby Sherwood; other players unidentified.

DLA-8-A	Let Me Call You Sweetheart	Decca 101
DLA-9-A	Someday Sweetheart	Decca 101

BING CROSBY, ACC. BY GEORGIE STOLL AND HIS ORCHESTRA   **LOS ANGELES, NOVEMBER 9, 1934**

p-Joe Sullivan, g-Bobby Sherwood, other players unidentified.

DLA-72-A	Love Is Just Around the Corner	Decca 310

PINKY TOMLIN, ACC. BY JOE SULLIVAN AND OTHERS   **LOS ANGELES, JANUARY 10, 1935**

p-Joe Sullivan.

LA-317-?	A Porter's Love Song (To a Chambermaid)	Brunswick 7377

PINKY TOMLIN, ACC. BY JOE SULLIVAN AND OTHERS   LOS ANGELES,
                                                            JANUARY 11, 1935

p-Joe Sullivan.

LA-318-A   "Sittin' Bull" and "Shine"   Brunswick 7378

LA-319-?   He's a Curbstone Cutie (They   Brunswick 7377
             Call Him Jelly Bean)

LA-320-A   Ragtime Cowboy Joe   Brunswick 7378

JOE SULLIVAN   LOS ANGELES, AUGUST 8, 1935

DLA-224-A   My Little Pride and Joy   Brunswick 02136

DLA-225-B   Little Rock Getaway   Decca 600   LP: Folkways 2809

DLA-226-B   Just Strolling   Decca 600

DLA-227-A   Minor Mood   Brunswick 02099

DLA-227-B   LP: Jazz Archives
                                                             JA 1

BING CROSBY, ACC. BY GEORGIE STOLL'S INSTRUMENTAL TRIO   LOS ANGELES,
                                                               NOVEMBER 13, 1935

p-Joe Sullivan, b-unknown, g-Bobby Sherwood.

DLA-262-A   Moonburn   Brunswick 02144
DLA-262-B   Decca 617

RAY MCKINLEY'S JAZZ BAND   LOS ANGELES, MARCH 31, 1936

p-Joe Sullivan, d-Ray McKinley, b-Jim Taft, t-George Thow, tb-Joe Yukl, cl-Skeets
Herfurt.

DLA-328-A   Love in the First Degree   Decca 1019

DLA-329-A   New Orleans Parade   Decca 1019

DLA-330-A   Shack in the Back   Decca 1020
DLA-330-B   Decca Y-5894

DLA-331-A   Fingerwave   Decca 1020

NOTES

1. Julius Weinberger, "Economic Aspects of Recreation," *Harvard Business Review* 15, no. 4 (Summer 1937), p. 454.

2. Joe Sullivan, "Jazz Casual" program (NET), with Ralph Gleason (1963).

3. Letter from Joe Sullivan to William Cleland, March 4, 1971.

4. "Jazz Casual" program (NET).

5. Cleland letter.

6. "Jazz Casual" program (NET).

7. Max Jones and John Chilton, *The Louis Armstrong Story, 1900-1971* (Boston: Little, Brown and Company, 1971).

8. Letter from Stanley Hester to the author, January 16, 1977.

9. Eddie Condon, *We Called It Music* (New York: Henry Holt, 1947).

10. Letter from Joe Sullivan to Jim Gordon, June 16, 1965.

11. Richard M. Sudhalter and Philip R. Evans, *Bix: Man and Legend* (New Rochelle, New York: Arlington House, 1974).

12. Condon, *We Called It Music.*

13. Letter from Frank Driggs to the author, December 6, 1976; letter from John Liquori to the author, November 28, 1976.

14. Brian Rust, ed., *Jazz Records, 1897-1942,* rev. ed. (London: Storyville Publications and Co., 1969).

15. Mort Goode, liner notes to *Russ Columbo,* RCA CPL1-1756(e) (1976).

16. "Jazz Casual" program (NET).

17. D. Russell Connor and Warren W. Hicks, *BG—On the Record* (New Rochelle, New York: Arlington House, 1969).

18. Letter from Oro M. "Tut" Soper to the author, November 21, 1976.

19. Letter from Jim Gordon to the author, November 14, 1976.

20. Donald Biggar, "Gin Mill Joe," *Piano Jazz* (1945).

21. *The Evening Bulletin* (Philadelphia, Pa.), September 12, 1936.

22. D.D. [Dave Dexter?], *Joe Sullivan Plays Boogie Woogie and the Blues* New York: Capitol Songs, Inc., 1944).

23. Letter from D. Russell Connor to the author, November 28, 1976.

24. Richard Hadlock, "The Return of Joe Sullivan," *Down Beat* (January 2, 1964), pp. 16-17.

25. "Bing's Rhythm Concert Draws Over 4000," *Tempo* (June 1937).

CHARLES NANRY

JAZZ AND MODERNISM: TWIN-BORN
CHILDREN OF THE AGE OF INVENTION

INTRODUCTION

Few art forms are as mythopoeic, indeed mythomaniacal, as jazz. The folklore of jazz and jazz musicians is filled with legends about the players of the music and the power of the music itself.[1] The marginal (or "outside looking in") status of the music and those who played it have contributed to this conception. Identified as the music of juke joints and brothels and as the music of blacks, jazz seemed a threat to the moral order in the 1920s and, under the flag of black nationalism, a threat, albeit a weaker one, to the political and social order as recently as the 1960s.[2]

Another contributory characteristic of jazz that leads to myth-making is the tension between the inner history of the music itself and the historical context in which the music was heard and played. The development of jazz has been shaped and contained by the larger world of entertainment. (Racial discrimination in recording studio hiring practices is but one example of this containment.) Externally jazz is a music shaped and molded by the mass media—in particular radio broadcasting and phonograph recording. Most Americans first hear something called jazz on a record or over the radio. While it is true what they hear is probably not "pure" jazz, it usually is a modified version of the real thing. Since the production of records and most radio broadcasting is motivated by profit, the most widely disseminated jazz is close to current pop music. This pattern of cultural diffusion is not an unusual one in mass societies; any form that seeks a wide audience must have recognizable "popular" elements in order to be accepted.[3] This process sets up a tension between critically acclaimed jazz and the most easily understood jazz.

Jazz also has an internal dynamic. Jazz musicians have to make a living in the world of popular entertainment. While they are doing that, however, they are expected to extend and re-create jazz itself. But there is risk involved in attempting to create art in a popular context: the risk of losing one's audience if the music goes beyond what the audience understands. Unlike some "classical music" audiences who understand that "their" music is difficult and demanding intellectually, many jazz listeners "dig" jazz in an atmosphere, a context, that encourages an emotional rather than an intellectual response. Drinkers, dancers, and finger-poppers reject the "student of music" label in favor of a presumption of comprehension. This sets up a tension between the act of performance and the act of creation. This tension is nowhere more evident than in jazz, because it is a music where creation (formally, musical composition) usually occurs during performance. One of the key elements of jazz—improvisation—demands that new melodic, harmonic, and rhythmic patterns emerge in the context of performance. But limits have to be imposed both by audiences and by performers. The narrow line between authenticity

Charles Nanry is a member of the sociology faculty and dean of University College on the Newark Campus of Rutgers University. He is the author of *The Jazz Text* and editor of *American Music: From Storyville to Woodstock,* as well as numerous articles on jazz.

(true jazz) and creativity (new jazz) must be perceived and manipulated by the good jazz player.[4]

Clearly, the modern academic jazzman—Larry Ridley at Rutgers, David Baker at Indiana or Richard Davis at Wisconsin—represent a "new breed" of secure professionals protected from this phenomenon. With seats on National Endowment on the Arts panels and with tenured faculty positions, a new elite, which has "paid dues" in music departments and in bureaucratized institutional settings, may move jazz closer to other art forms. Jazz players who have gained other positions of prominence in studios or in the mass media—Billy Taylor on National Public Radio comes to mind—may also escape the danger of instant oblivion in the world of popular entertainment. These players, however, have typically also "paid heavy dues" in the world of jazz itself as have their contemporaries in the other worlds of "serious" music. Their experience is quite new in jazz. The historical context in which the music has grown up presents a dramatically different picture.

The modest task I have set for myself here is to link the historical development of jazz with the transformation of America into an urban-industrial society. This is a useful exercise insofar as it points to the nature of art as the production of symbolic representations that "come off" in sociocultural contexts. Jazz provides a useful case-study of symbolic (musical) production that came into being and was forcefully shaped by the very processes that ushered in contemporary urban-industrial American society.

ART AND THE MARKET SOCIETY

C. Wright Mills described the nineteenth century as a time in which America moved from a self-balancing society to one in which all parts of society became interlocked.[5] For Mills "self-balancing" meant the conditions under which various groups, regions, and segments of society could maintain relative autonomy. The industrial revolution, invention, and the emergence of capitalism all led to a great "sifting and sorting" of populations.[6] Peoples once separated by eons of time and vast distances of space were now thrown together through changes in transportation and communication in the name of enterprise. Industrialism itself, through the proliferation of the division of labor, created a world in which the simple organic unity of the agrarian tribe was replaced by the willful unity of specialized function.

Yet this very smashing of the social atom drove people to create wholeness out of diversity. Often cruel and inhuman, the new industrial order operated on a scale that demanded the discovery of purpose beyond narrow conceptions of local meaning. Max Weber saw the "Protestant ethic" as the force behind this purpose; Karl Marx saw it in the historical necessity of controlling productive forces. In any case, technology (invention both social, such as bureaucracy, and nonsocial, such as machines) became the cause and effect of a new "economy of scale." A new order, which changed everything, emerged.

Industrialization and its concomitants—urbanization, technology, population density, and heterogeneity—had an important impact on the development of art as well as science and technology. A key characteristic of industrialization is the creation of large-scale markets. A key characteristic of capitalism is pressure toward the transformation of virtually everything, including music and art, into commodities to be bought and sold in the marketplace. Capitalism also brought about the replacement of noble patronage by middle class or popular audiences. And while the roots of this process go far back into the late medieval period in Europe, these commercial transactions were carried out on an immense scale in the nineteenth century. Society itself was transformed.

In American music the beginnings of what later became the music industry can be traced back to publishing houses that produced sacred song books and instruction books for eighteenth-century singing schools. The profit motive eventually led these publishing firms to expand their offerings beyond psalm books and hymnals to the production of sheet music with broad popular appeal. In short, industrial capitalism linked to a mass market provided the model.[7]

Support for music came more and more to rely on public concerts. Though small in number at first, a cadre of professional musicians grew, depending on public rather than private patronage. This dependence in turn made those who produced music sensitive to the demands of a mass market rather than the tastes of a small elite. Popular culture—music and art produced as a commodity and altered to suit as broad an audience as possible—came of age in the late nineteenth century. It borrowed without shame from both folk and elite sources in the hope of realizing profit. Money itself, intrinsically without value, but valued because of its capacity to command any and every product, became the anchor for the entire system.[8]

Although C. Wright Mills clearly was talking about the limitations of transportation and communication networks when he introduced the concept of "self-balancing" to describe preindustrial America, the same idea applies to music and art. When the idea is applied to music and art, cultural groupings (audiences) become as important as the geographical clusterings. Certain divisions in American music, such as the racial, are obvious. Yet, variation *within* both black and white music cannot be overlooked, nor can certain "crossover" influences. The channeling of African song into a religious context is one example.[9] The influence of plantation life (often sentimentalized) in early American popular song is another, especially in the work of composers such as Stephen Foster.[10] Elements of chance, as well as predictable patterns of interaction, shaped the various combinations of musical form and content leading to the modern era.

American music in the post–Civil War period underwent sweeping changes. The importation of different musical traditions from Africa and Europe, together with the growth of a native entertainment industry, generated a volatile atmosphere for musical production.[11] Changes in the size, composition, and distribution of the population of the United States and the development of new transportation and communication technologies meant that the potential for a mixing-together of musical elements reached a state of "critical mass." The ensuing musical chain reaction took place in big cities, which provided the opportunities for important developments.

Modern cities, then, are, among other things, a consequence of (1) the rapid growth of specialization of activity (the division of labor) and (2) the technology that makes such specialization pay off in increased productive capacity. The modern city is, first and foremost, a marketplace. Goods, services, and ideas are traded for other goods, services, and ideas. The city is not only a place of struggle but also the place of opportunity, of upward mobility, for those equipped to compete in its markets. The city *is* an exchange market in its very essence.[12]

Modern city life often creates a sense of disjunction and uprootedness, and prompts a search for meaning. Members of modern urban societies are forced to accept solidarity despite dissimilarities. City dwellers must learn—often painfully—to seek commonality.

JAZZ AND CITIES: AN IDENTITY

Jazz symbolically fused many of the contradictions of modern society within itself. Jazz is a metaphor for urban existence. Jazz was created by an outcast minority, yet it appealed (albeit in modified form) beyond that minority. Jazz embodied the dynamic tension at the very core of modern life, the tension between the individual "particularized" creator (the soloist) and the group (the ensemble), with its simultaneous demands for improvisation on the one hand and discipline and coordination on the other. While its most important inspiration, the blues, was rural in origin, jazz was—and is—city music. Moreover, jazz shares with the modern city a most important characteristic: both are based on exchange. The canons of jazz[13] permit it to encompass an enormous range of musical traditions; by its very essence it transforms diversity into a commonality of form and feeling.

An expanded music market allowed increasingly sophisticated musicians to present their music as a commodity to be exchanged with a larger audience for fame and fortune. That larger audience ranged from a small segment who saw the new music as an emergent art form to the drinkers and dancers who saw it simply as happy, bouncy music. Jazz players served these and many other clienteles.[14] Social forces, external to jazz, ground against the imminent, internal needs of jazz just as it was developing. In fact, jazz as a child of the new order uniquely represents both its own development as an art and, at the same time, reflects the eclectic coming-of-age of all of America.

As jazz emerged, it pulled together blues and popular American song structures, military and marching band cadences, and piano and dance band styles into an integrated whole that made sense musically in its own terms. As Gunther Schuller correctly points out, the earliest jazz was based on melodic embellishment and therefore was within the American tradition of melodic emphasis.[15] Jazz was surely shaped as much by its audiences as it was by its players. Those audiences were "tune-oriented." Schuller says, "The music played depended almost entirely on for whom it was played."[16] The market for music controlled, muted, and transformed jazz into an element of popular entertainment and culture. As a primarily instrumental music, moreover, jazz was less threatening than, say, the vocal blues (or, much later, rock lyrics) to conventional white and middle-class black values.[17]

THE SOCIAL ORIGINS OF JAZZ

Jazz players came from all over but made their reputations in cities. Jazz, as we have come to know it from recordings and from lore and legend, came out of certain big cities such as New Orleans, Kansas City, Chicago, and New York. Other cities—Detroit, Indianapolis, Newark—produced important jazz players, but whether the very best jazz musicians made it to the jazz capitals, or whether they were recorded, is a moot point. The focus of jazz history must be on what was, not on what could or should have been. Much, if not most, of the best jazz occurs in night clubs, jam sessions, and in other "live" contexts. The only jazz we can retrieve and judge is that recorded by mechanical or electronic means. The story of jazz became the story of recorded jazz.

The big city provided an anchor for jazz because it had a population large enough and diverse enough to support new musical forms. Throughout history, cities have been centers of the arts, especially artistic innovation. The patterns of entertainment circuits and the mass market model established in the latter part of the nineteenth century vitalized all Afro-American music, including the blues, insofar as it transformed it into a universalistic (that is, widely accepted) and sophisticated city music. It was also necessary for each jazz capital to have a substantial black population receptive to a jazz elite. Black audiences provided a "home base" for budding jazz players.[18]

The large American city, no longer contained by self-balanced localism, in the early twentieth century came to dominate beyond its surrounding area. Smaller cities and towns came within big city influence both economically and culturally. As the United States became a national society, it also became a nation of larger regions. Regions themselves, however, became less and less local and more interlocked. Such interlocking, moreover, was not a neat and easily understood process. In retrospect, it is possible to see how certain urban centers rose to preeminence. Some had the advantage of being deep-water ports; others were near areas rich in natural resources. For jazz, the key urban centers in its development were the big cities of New Orleans, Chicago, Kansas City, and New York.

Each major American jazz center was also a regional urban center. New York, and later, Chicago were superdominant major centers for entire sections of the country. It is easy to understand how they grew into the main centers of jazz. New Orleans, the most cosmopolitan of American cities until well into the twentieth century, was also a superdominant regional city, and, after New York, America's largest port. There the most direct amalgamation of Afro-American and Euro-American subcultures occurred. Kansas City represented a special case as a jazz center; its eventual development into a "wide open" town encouraged a nonstop entertainment industry to flourish. Kansas City was also the gateway to the Southwest territory, a particularly fertile area for blues-based music.[19] Other cities produced important jazz, but New York, Chicago, New Orleans, and Kansas City are the keys to jazz history.

JAZZ CIRCUITS

The distribution networks for musical and other entertainment in nineteenth- and early twentieth-century America involved a series of overlapping circuits. Thomas Hennessey has argued that by 1924 there were only four major jazz circuits in America (called territories) and that until well into the 1930s musicians found employment within one or another of them.[20] While these "worlds" mingled at the top, they were quite distinct and independent. Since most entertainment was "live," there was a demand for it, especially for dancing. Hennessey maintains that the territories were arranged into a loose status hierarchy, a "pecking order," with Chicago and New York at the top—the emergence, in other words, of two "superdominants." Many of the best musicians from other territories would move up into the Chicago and New York circuits. Like baseball's minor leagues, the other circuits provided a training ground for major jazz players. At the same time, players moving into the major circuits would bring with them regional specialties such as boogie-woogie or Southwest blues "licks" that often became incorporated into the major-league style. The hegemony of New York and Chicago, of course, was confirmed by the centering of the mass media and especially the recording industry in those two cities. (West Coast dominance came much later.)

Both New Orleans and Kansas City lost their position of preeminence when the recording and radio industries gained control over popular musical entertainment. Chicago and New York, and finally New York alone, accounted for most jazz output. Specialization and the growth of a national hierarchy of urban dominance—abetted by radio—affected jazz, as it did many other areas of American life and culture.[21] A great deal of jazzlike music came to be perceived as part of a style understood to be *the* jazz style. This style might change, but at any given time, the media-based style of jazz predominated over and controlled other variations.

An apparent paradox seems to emerge concerning the origins of jazz. Jazz is big-city music, yet many of the most important early jazz players learned the style and served apprenticeships in so-called territory bands. These bands played in small towns and traveled extensively in all parts of the country. They represented an earlier pre-radio form of mass entertainment and persisted well into the radio era. The key to the apparent paradox can be found in several factors: (1) style-setting occurred in urban, not rural, areas; (2) local status hierarchies emerged with the most prestigious players and bands located in major cities; (3) a national hierarchy finally emerged, which subsumed the local status groupings.[22] Big money and national exposure were reserved for those who were recorded and played in big city—i.e., New York and Chicago—clubs and dance halls.

THE INDUSTRIAL MODEL

The recording industry, like other large industries in the United States, follows the model of monopolistic capitalism.[23] At first there is diversified competition from a variety of producers for consumers. This was the case for jazz recordings in the 1920s. Consumers respond in the aggregate, giving the edge to certain producers who are giving the people what they want, or, through financial control and control of raw materials (musical talent in this case), one or more producers corner the market and drive out competition. This happened in popular music in the United States in the 1930s. The giants, such as CBS (Columbia Records) and NBC (RCA) in recording and broadcasting, can then control the tastes of their consumers by limiting output.[24]

While powerful producers do everything they can to keep their consumers under control, innovation does occur, usually through small independent producers. Ironically, even this independence may aid the giants, since the smaller producers take the highest risks and can often be bought out relatively cheaply or their stars signed to contracts by big companies, should their product catch on. Rock and roll in the 1950s provides an example of this latter process.[25] Sometimes, however, the innovation may even occur within the oligopoly, especially by those who are diversified or who are losing their share of the market. In short, if the outsiders cut far enough into the marginal profits of the inside giants, the insiders either co-opt innovators by incorporating them or their stars into their own production, or they squeeze out the innovative competitor.

When this model is applied to, say, the American automobile industry, the process is clear. When, however, cultural production becomes the matter at hand, certain cautions are in order. In the first place, consumer investment may be quite small—the purchase of a single record. Also, the product is not created in quite the same way. While some recording stars may be "manufactured" by the recording industry in the manner of the Hollywood star system, very often the raw material of the recording industry comes out of various specialized and demographically specific sectors of the record-buying public, i.e., the phenomenon of market segmentation. The jazz record market is small but steady and, like the "classical" market, keeps innovative options open for alert record producers.

Given the historical context in which jazz emerged, one must marvel at the vitality, integrity, and artfulness of the best of it. The real paradox, however, may be that the very origins and tumultuous context in which jazz finds itself are what gives it vitality. Henry Pleasants has explained the paradox in *The Agony of Modern Music* by suggesting that what we have labeled here as the external dynamic of jazz is more a part of "real" jazz than some Platonic notion of jazz essence stripped of social context, sorrowful and cruel as that context may have been.

> Thus the jazz accomplishment is simply defined. It has taken music away from the composers and given it back to musicians and their public. The simplicity sought by serious composers through intellectual and technical experimentation has been achieved by practicing musicians guided by popular taste. Because of popular guidance their product is culturally valid. Because of the absence of popular guidance, the accomplishment of the serious composers is not.
>
> This is obviously something the serious composer cannot admit, even to himself. But the fascination good jazz has for him indicates a strain of social susceptibility seldom apparent in his own compositions. Not even a man so dedicated as the composer to the concept of the composer's absolute social autonomy can be entirely immune to the trends of his own time.
>
> He is fated to go on writing sonatas, symphonies, and operas as long as society as a whole continues to believe that these old forms and the symphony orchestra have a monopoly on respectability and cultural superiority. And there we leave him, apparently unaware—if not notably blissfully—that jazz is modern music—and that nothing else is.[26]

Pleasants' polemical argument could, of course, be extended to other musics with "popular guidance," such as folk music and some manifestations of rock and roll. One could also question the presence of much popular guidance in some jazz. If one, however, accepts a definition of jazz as an art form that extends and recreates popular music (often popular music from earlier eras), the essential question about the interpenetration of jazz and society becomes a socio-political one.

The transformation of both jazz and society was shaped by the emergence of pluralism as the dominant ideological spirit of industrial America. Lost in the often sterile debate over whether Americans are melted, melting, or unmeltable is the fact that some art forms such as jazz (as well as some population segments) are capable of both conformity and uniqueness.

Robert Palmer has recently suggested that the concept of pluralism is equally important in understanding American pop music.

> Closer examination reveals that pop has always been pluralistic—the rock and roll years of the late 50s were also good years for romantic adult pop, and when the Beatles were setting trends in the late 60s, a number of less-renowned stylists were laying the groundwork for today's musical radicalism.[27]

Jazz survives and is vital because it represents an approach to life as well as music. Jazz is a way of playing music, just as democracy based on pluralism is a way of settling the problem of social order. As a method, an approach, rather than a foreclosed paradigm, jazz appeals because it liberates and transforms the commonplace into art. Pluralism and jazz represent the survival of the parts within the whole: the hard work of forging an organic unity out of mechanistic disparity.

NOTES

1. Charles Nanry, *The Jazz Text* (New York: D. van Nostrand, 1979), p. 244.

2. Neil Leonard, *Jazz and The White Americans: The Acceptance of a New Art Form* (Chicago: The University of Chicago Press, 1962); Jonathan Kamin, "Parallels in the Social Reactions to Jazz and Rock," *Journal of Jazz Studies* 2, no. 1 (December 1974), pp. 95-125.

3. Irving Louis Horowitz and Charles Nanry, "Ideologies and Theories about American Jazz," *Journal of Jazz Studies* 2, no. 2, (June 1975): pp. 24-41. For an empirical test of the clustering of pop elements from an audience point of view see: Morris B. Holbrook and Joel Huber, "The Spatial Representation of Responses Toward Jazz: Applications of Consumer Esthetics to Mapping the Market for music," *Journal of Jazz Studies* 5, no. 2 (Spring/Summer 1979), pp. 3-22.

4. Irving Louis Horowitz, "Authenticity and Originality in Jazz: Toward a Paradigm in the Sociology of Music," *Journal of Jazz Studies* 1, no. 1 (October 1973), pp. 57-64.

5. C. Wright Mills, *White Collar* (New York: Oxford University Press, 1953).

6. Harold L. Wilensky and Charles N. Lebeaux, *Industrial Society and Social Welfare* (New York: Russell Sage, 1958).

7. Gilbert Chase, *America's Music* (New York: McGraw-Hill, 1966); Wilfrid Mellers, *Music in a New Foundland* (New York: Knopf, 1967). For a discussion of shifts to the mass market in the nineteenth century see: David Ewen, *The Life and Death of Tin Pan Alley* (New York: Funk and Wagnalls, 1964).

8. Stephen R. Couch, "Class, Politics, and Symphony Orchestras," *Society* 14 (November 1976), pp. 24-29.

9. Eileen Southern, *The Music of Black Americans: A History* (New York: Norton, 1971); Chase, *America's Music,* pp. 230-41.

10. Ewen, *Tin Pan Alley,* pp. 15-64.

11. Ibid.

12. Max Weber, *The City* (New York: The Free Press, 1968).

13. Nanry, *The Jazz Text,* pp. 13-19.

14. Ibid., pp. 20-59.

15. Ibid., pp. 11-12.

16. Gunther Schuller, *Early Jazz: Its Roots and Musical Development* (New York: Oxford University Press, 1968) p. 128.

17. Leonard, *Jazz and The White Americans;* Morroe Berger, "Jazz: Resistance to the Diffusion of a Culture Pattern, *Journal of Negro History* 32 (October 1947), pp. 461-94; Kamin, "Parallels in Jazz and Rock."

18. Harry A. Reed, "The Black Bar in the Making of a Jazz Musician: Bird, Mingus, and Stan Hope," *Journal of Jazz Studies* 5, no. 2 (Spring/Summer, 1979), pp. 76-90.

19. Nanry, *The Jazz Text,* pp. 131-135.

20. Thomas J. Hennessey, "From Jazz to Swing," (Ph.D. diss., Northwestern University, 1973).

21. Nanry, *The Jazz Text,* pp. 126-131.

22. Ibid., pp. 84-88.

23. Ibid., pp. 21-27.

24. Richard A. Peterson and David G. Berger, "Cycles in Symbol Production: The Case of Popular Music," *American Sociological Review* 40, no. 1 (February, 1975), pp. 158-73; R. Serge Denisoff, *Solid Gold: The Popular Record Industry* (New Brunswick, N.J.: Transaction, 1975).

25. Charlie Gillet, *The Sound of the City: The Rise of Rock and Roll* (New York: Sunrise Books, 1970).

26. Henry Pleasants, *The Agony of Modern Music* (New York: Simon and Schuster, 1955), pp. 176-7.

27. Robert Palmer, "Rock and Roll Revisited," *New York Times,* August 24, 1980, p. D21.

MORROE BERGER
(1917-1981)

Characteristically, Morroe Berger was among the very first contributors to the *Journal of Jazz Studies*—his "Fats Waller: The Outside Insider" was the lead article of the first issue. Professor Berger was also a charter member of the *Journal's* editorial board.

For Berger, jazz was an early and abiding love. He did his master's thesis on this subject at Columbia in 1947, and his frequently cited essay "Jazz: Resistance to the Diffusion of a Culture Pattern," first published in the *Journal of Negro History,* was culled from that thesis. It was one of the first genuinely perceptive pieces on the music by an inside outsider.

Berger wanted to do his doctoral dissertation on jazz, but his department chairman did not consider it a fitting topic. Years later, Berger was vastly amused when this same social scientist, while attending a conference in New Orleans, squired a friend of Berger's on a tour of the city during which the cultural significance of jazz was a constant theme.

Changing his dissertation topic was no handicap for Berger, whose interests already ranged widely. A native New Yorker, he graduated from City College in the illustrious class of 1940, but unlike many of his contemporaries, he never became an ideologist. The academic specialty he settled on was the contemporary Near and Middle East, and he became one of America's foremost experts in that field, serving as director of the Near Eastern Studies Program at Princeton and consultant and advisor to many important organizations and the U.S. government. He had a special interest in Egypt, and his two books about that country were based on first-hand research.

In 1975, he was able to combine jazz with his involvement in things Islamic. He persuaded the State Department, which was planning to send him on a lecture tour of the Middle East, to allow him to bring along a jazz group led by Benny Carter, with whom he had first become personally acquainted in 1968.

The warm friendship that grew between these two distinguished and civilized men, both mature in years when they first met, was a unique and productive one. In addition to the tour, there were collaborations at Princeton, where Carter was a visiting professor for several semesters, and where he was awarded an honorary doctorate of humanities in 1974. And some eight years ago, Berger began work on a biographical study of Carter. Completed in 1980, it is a monumental work, painstakingly researched and documented, and infused with the wide-ranging intelligence and profound scholarship of its author. (The task of seeing it through the publishing process now rests with his son and close collaborator, Edward, to whom he bequeathed his love for jazz and concern for scholarly integrity.)

In his most recently published book, *Real and Imagined Worlds: The Novel and Social Science,* a brilliant but unfashionably sane and balanced study, Morroe Berger wrote: "Many scholars and intellectuals find it impossible to hold two separate ideas on one theme at the same time." This was a problem Berger never had—one reason why he was a great teacher.

In this age of overspecialization, Morroe Berger was one of the few true heirs to the humanistic tradition, as a scholar and as a man. He cared.

—**Dan Morgenstern**

BOOK REVIEWS

Ragtime: A Musical and Cultural History
By Edward A. Berlin. 1980. 248 pp.
Berkeley: University of California Press. $16.95.

This cogent, closely reasoned book is a major contribution to the study and understanding of ragtime and popular music. It would not be an exaggeration to claim that it sets new standards for ragtime scholarship, since, unlike most previous efforts in this field, it is based on meticulous (and meticulously documented) research, interpreted with a keen grasp of the music itself and its historical, cultural, social, and esthetic contexts.

Step by step, Berlin strips away the layers of mythology and romanticism that have beclouded our view of this seminal and fascinating American music, and best of all, in so doing makes his subject more rather than less interesting and opens new doors for future investigations.

Among the book's key contributions is the restoration of a proper perspective on ragtime. Since the advent of the "ragtime revival," we have come to think of the music mainly in terms of the achievements of Scott Joplin and so-called classic ragtime, and of the genre itself as primarily pianistic-instrumental. Without in any way slighting the significance of Joplin et al., however, Berlin makes it crystal clear that, from the perspective of the ragtime era itself, the music was thought of primarily as vocal, and seen as part of general popular music.

By placing classic ragtime (which he redefines on the basis of musical principles, in the process arriving at the clearest and most coherent definitions of the various ragtime styles and proving some of them to be nonexistent) in its historical context, and giving due credit and consideration to the much-maligned "commercial" output, as well as to so-called novelty rags, Berlin not so incidentally is able to show that, far from being the creation of a few isolated and uncommonly gifted individuals who failed to achieve the recognition due them, ragtime represented, "despite considerable opposition, the first widespread acceptance of a black cultural influence into the mainstream of American life." And further, that "the importance of ragtime transcends any individual work, composer or group."

Like the literature of jazz, the literature of ragtime has tended to focus on individuals and key works, at the expense of seeing the music whole. Conceivably, a better case for this approach could be made for jazz, its obvious shortcomings notwithstanding. But ragtime places no premium on improvisation and can be studied on the basis of notated, published music. It is on such evidence, copiously exemplified in the text, that Berlin bases his brilliant analysis of ragtime style and its sources. This section of the book alone makes it invaluable. In the space of 100-odd pages, Berlin demonstrates the relationship of ragtime to the march, the cakewalk, black character pieces and "patrols," coon songs, Caribbean dances, and other earlier forms, and then goes on to illustrate the development of a "cohesive" style and its characteristics, and the subsequent gradual "erosion of a distinctive style."

Surrounding this centerpiece are an examination of the perceptions of the music during its own time, and a succinct summary of the book's conclusions from an historical perspective.

The opening section presents a wealth of contemporary comments drawn from a wide variety of sources. Each chapter is scrupulously footnoted; not a single quotation is without attribution. (These annotations are a goldmine of clues to further reading and will prove immensely helpful to students and scholars of ragtime in years to come.) Berlin shows that attitudes toward ragtime varied widely; some early comments are surprisingly perceptive and sympathetic. Berlin's methodology here is similar to that of Neil Leonard in *Jazz and the White Americans,* but a considerably less one-sided picture emerges.

Berlin is eminently fair to earlier writers on the subject. Thus, he gives all due credit to Blesh and Janis, but also takes issue with "their personal, intuitive and non-technical approach," and the book's "confusing, frequently impenetrable entanglement of fact, speculation, and pure fiction."

Such weaknesses Berlin could never be accused of. His book is a model of intelligent, clear scholarship, and though it grew out of a dissertation (at the City University of New York), it is free of academic obscurantism and redundancy. Indeed, the manner in which Berlin has separated his footnotes from the body of the text makes the book eminently readable, which is, alas, not always the case with scholarly works.

There is a most useful "Location Index for Piano Rags in Selected Anthologies" (Berlin's diligent research has also uncovered many interesting rags not represented in these collections); a considerable bibliography, handily divided into two periods (1886-1929 and 1930-1975); and an excellent index showing musical examples in boldface type. There are also some interesting reproductions of rare sheet music covers.

An indispensable book. In his preface, Berlin expresses the hope that his efforts "will help remove ragtime studies from the domain of vague intuition and romantic fantasy, and direct it toward a path of greater critical scrutiny." If approached with the same lack of prejudice and preconceptions and the same regard for facts exhibited by its author, *Ragtime* can't fail to realize these objectives, and one can only hope that it will be read and pondered by scholars and students of jazz as well.

By the way, it is a pleasure—in this age of shoddy book production—to encounter a book so handsomely presented and so free of typographical errors. *Ragtime* deserves nothing less.

—**Dan Morgenstern**

Blues Who's Who: A Biographical Dictionary of Blues Singers
By Sheldon Harris. 1979. 775 pp.
New Rochelle, New York: Arlington House. $35.00.
Softcover: New York: Da Capo Press. $16.95.

This truly monumental tome (it is of a heft unequalled in the history of American vernacular musics) is the result of 18 years of diligent research by a dedicated amateur blues scholar (who incidentally was Marshall Stearns's key associate in the operation of the Institute of Jazz Studies during its first 12 years).

The book contains 571 detailed biographies; 450 photographs, many never seen before; separate indexes of films, theatrical and television shows, and radio programs in which artists listed in the book have appeared; a listing of blues periodicals in print and another of record companies specializing in this music; a listing of nearly 7,000 songs written by the biographees, alphabetical by title; and a 75-page index of names and places appearing in the text. This impressive reference apparatus will be of great use to researchers.

Another nice feature of the book is that all pseudonyms have been cross-referenced; this is especially important in the blues field.

Harris has defined the term blues singer rather broadly. There can be no quarrel with his inclusion of "songsters" such as Mance Lipscomb and "Mississippi" John Hurt, who after all were part and parcel of the tradition that spawned the blues. He is to be commended for including also such blues-singing jazz instrumentalists as Hot Lips Page, Clyde Bernhardt, and Louis Jordan (and many other artists whom the blues traditionalist might pigeonhole as jazz or rhythm-and-blues), for these, too, partook of the blues mainstream and helped to keep it alive.

But this reviewer is less sanguine about such singers as Jean Kittrell, Natalie Lamb, and Pug Horton—not to mention Bonnie Raitt, Woody Guthrie, and Richie Havens—whose connection with the blues would seem more tenuous. However, I much prefer broad boundaries to narrow ones, and it is handy for the generalist to have data on such figures available, especially since their inclusion does not seem to have displaced others with a more legitimate claim.

Indeed, it is a wonder for just how many hitherto totally obscure performers Harris has managed to dig up at least basic data, or even photographs. Harris states that his notebooks eventually contained information on more than 1500 singers, but he decided to eliminate those for whom not enough data could be found to make the "entries factually meaningful and keep the book within bounds."

These criteria have been adhered to. Each entry contains at least a minimum of essential data. In terms of facts on births and deaths, Harris has uncovered an amazing amount of information, and he scrupulously indicates approximated and/or unconfirmed dates and places. He is also very good on personal data such as family relationships, and under this heading includes comments on name similarities ("not to be confused with," etc.) which are most useful.

However, Harris does have a tendency to offer almost too much information in what he calls the "biographical" section. Here we are confronted with sometimes interminable listings of every known engagement or other work credit, interspersed with really significant facts such as education, key associations, major tours, accidents and illnesses, etc. Moreover, the raw career data are listed in a somewhat cumbersome manner. Harris seems enamored of the word "frequent" and uses it so frequently that I estimate its elimination would have saved several dozen pages.

(One feels apologetic about such quibbling, because Harris does give us so much information that hitherto has been either unknown or almost impossible to get at in any comprehensive form, and for that he deserves all possible praise. Such faults as the book has are mainly editing responsibilities, and it's a pity that Arlington House was unable to serve Harris better in this respect—but then, they did publish the book.)

This is followed by a listing of major songs composed by the artist; books (including folios and song collections); honors and awards; influences ("by" and "on"); quotations (from a variety of printed sources, some authoritative, others less so; apparently Harris felt a need for including opinions, since he expresses none of his own); and references to further reading, but unfortunately not to recordings (though every known recording date, with reference to original labels, is included in the "biographical" segment).

Thus we are presented with a wealth of detail, and while some work is required to get at the most significant facts, especially in the case of a long and well-documented career, the large page size and type-face and the clean layout make the digging a bit easier.

The copious photographs, many of them of half- or full-page size and all well-reproduced, greatly enhance the book's appearance and make it a joy to browse in, quite aside from their historical and documentary value. These remarkable faces have a lot to tell us about the blues and add a dimension of life to the necessarily dry recitation of dates and facts.

Because his approach is so all-inclusive, Harris's facts also tell us a lot about the blues and its enormous impact on American and world music and its many and varied sources and tributaries. The representation of contemporary blues artists is excellent, and I was unable to find significant omissions in any area.

This work does for the blues what Feather and Chilton have done for jazz. It will be an essential tool for anyone with a serious interest in this music, now and for years to come. It represents an immense amount of hard work, done without benefit of grants, tenure, or sabbaticals. While it won't make Sheldon Harris rich, it will make him justly famous. All of us are indebted to him.

—Dan Morgenstern

Jazz
By Dean Tudor and Nancy Tudor. 1979. 302 pp.
Littleton, Colorado: Libraries Unlimited. $18.50.

One of four volumes in the series *American Popular Music on Elpee* (sic!)—the others are on Black Music, Grass Roots Music, and Contemporary Popular Music—this book claims (and at first glance appears) to be a buying guide to recordings in the jazz field for librarians and individual collectors.

The Tudors, librarians who have done valuable work in the reference field, might have provided a commendable service if they had confined themselves to guiding the reader through the confusing plethora of recorded jazz materials. Instead, they decided to become *experts*. As they describe it in the introduction, they employed the method of citation analysis over an 11-year period, "which revealed that certain artists and tunes keep appearing; hence, any important record is so by virtue of its historical worth, influence, best-selling nature, and trend setting." The authors "studied about 60 popular music periodicals (containing) over 50,000 relevant reviews and over 10,000 articles." The period surveyed was 1965-76. They also "read more than 2,000 books on popular music, some dating from the 1920s, and . . . actually listened to 14,000-plus long playing albums" in their research for the series.

That such a heavy dosage of raw data should cause indigestion is not surprising, and the results, at least as far as jazz is concerned, are indeed far from perfectly formed. The book is a hodgepodge of second-hand opinions, many of them exceedingly flatulent, presented in an authoritative tone instantly deflated by wayward syntax and confused and confusing use of musical terminology. The book is a disaster, but the Tudors are professional librarians, and the well-organized and seemingly knowledgable surface appearance of their work unfortunately makes it capable of causing mischief.

Lest these remarks be considered intemperate, let me cite chapter and verse:

"It was a different world fifty, forty, thirty years ago; of course, the artists of a prior generation seem funny-strange today. Let us hope the future will still remain kind." (From "What This Book is All About and How to Use It.")

"We have no idea what 'early jazz' sounded like, for no recordings exist from [before the ODJB]. Various black bands had been asked to record their music, but the leaders declined because they felt that their styles and techniques would be stolen by others. The ODJB felt no such concern, for the Dixieland variant of New Orleans music was essentially of a smooth ensemble texture with no soloists and nothing to steal. . . . Oral histories have revealed—in words—the style of some early jazzmen such as Buddy Bolden, Louis Armstrong and Jelly Roll Morton; and other performers have commented on how they arrived at their respective styles, so that it must be assumed that earlier jazzmen sounded something like the late ones." (From "Jazz Music, an Introduction.")

A little knowledge is a dangerous thing. The meat of the book, however, is in the 300-words-or-less evaluations of the approximately 1,300 LPs recommended by the Tudors. These are presented more or less chronologically, according to tried and true historical principles: Ragtime (preceded by a section on anthologies); Geographic Origins and Stylings; Mainstream Swing and Big Bands; Bop; Cool; Modern; and Diverse Themes. Each section (and the many sub-sections) are divided into segments headed "Innovators" and "Standards." Let's see what an almost random sampling yields:

On Armstrong: "He made several significant contributions to the vocabulary of jazz. . . . His affectations—rips, tears, vibratos, half-valve effects, bent notes up and down, etc.—were (and still are) difficult to duplicate." Some "important selections" include "Gilt Bucket Blues" and "Square Me" (the latter no doubt dedicated to the authors).

On Bechet: "On the clarinet, he fashioned definitive trios before Goodman even thought of them, such as 'Blues in Thirds' . . . where there was early counterpoint between the clarinet and the piano." (The record cited was made on Sept. 6, 1940!)

More on Armstrong, from a later section: "Louis was back in his small group element, seeking improvisation, staccato, and legato devices." (This is a complete sentence, with punctuation as given.)

On Art Hodes: ". . . a stride pianist who has recorded for a variety of labels, both large and small, generally featuring a clarinet player."

On Bix Beiderbecke's compositions: "All the music is of a worrisome frame with tempo changes and deep figures, as if Bix really opened his mind through composition." On his playing: "It has often been said, though, that Bix was not so good but that his sidemen were quite poor."

On *Spirituals to Swing:* ". . . the famous [concert] created by John Hammond that lent authenticity to jazz and blues, or rather, legitimatized the music by virtue of its having appeared at Carnegie Hall."

On Benny Carter: "He plays most brass and reed instruments plus piano, excelling on the alto sax. . . . In 1933, he did the arrangements for the marvelous Spike Hughes (q.v.) band." A q.v. yields the correct but contradictory information that Hughes "assembled most of the Benny Carter band and recorded 12 titles with them as arranger-director."

This pair of sentences introduces the entry on McKinney's Cotton Pickers: "This strangely named group was based in Detroit. After Fletcher Henderson, they were very much a favorite of the rare record purchasers." (Inanity aside, it's also incorrect.)

Armstrong again, this time in the 1930s: "He had constant trouble with his lip; he had management problems and personal problems . . . many selections were difficult to record, so several takes were needed."

On Jay McShann: "McShann's band has been characterized as a parallel development to Count Basie, but one with a little more assertiveness and punch."

On Lester Young: "Basically, Young played the jazz phrase in an unhurried manner for the sake of the phrase and for its pure melodic value, without any reference to any systems." And later on: "In some cases, the tune changes dramatically depending on Young's mood and precision."

Chu Berry, we are first told, "was rather poor on slow numbers." Then we read that he recorded "terrific solos" on "Lonesome Nights" and "Ghost of a Chance."

On Bobby Hackett: "Hackett, because of his glamorous looks, was dubbed as another Bix Beiderbecke."

Here is the John Kirby entry, brief enough to be quoted entire: "This sextet, led by bassist John Kirby, was billed as 'the biggest little band in the land.' The material has been commented on as chamber jazz because it didn't seem to swing much (the same charge had been leveled at Ray [sic] Norvo); however, the six members, through the clever arrangements of trumpeter Charlie Shavers, emulated the big band sounds as Clarence Williams did earlier in the 1920s and as Maynard Ferguson was to do in the early 1960s. Kirby's group began in 1937, and diverse personnel over the years included Frankie Newton (trumpet), Russell Procope (alto saxophone solos), Pete Brown (tenor sax), and Buster Bailey (clarinet).''

The modernists fare no better. Here's a tidbit from ''Modern Characteristics'': ''One of the first to work in the modern jazz vein was Lennie Tristano, who influenced Lee Konitz in the formless field as early as 1949.'' Previously, under ''Cool Characteristics,'' we learn that cool jazz ''was simply 'arranged' jazz fostered by Miles Davis in 1949 because he couldn't come to grips with bop.''

This one's for Horace Silver: ''Following Parker's lead, the Jazz Messengers played mainly blues.'' And Ornette Coleman devotees will enjoy this passing reference to Herbie Fields, in the context of the Lips Page jam session recordings: ''Fields is a wildman who knew no restraint, like Coleman two decades later.''

It would be unseemly to continue. In fairness, let me say that there are substantial passages in the book relatively free from howlers, malapropisms, and blithe confusion. It should be clear, however, that the Tudors have merely half-digested the massive amounts of information consumed by them. The result is a well-intentioned but ultimately meaningless cud.

The pity is that the basic selection of records, while not flawless, is quite decent as a whole. If the Tudors had only refrained from the hubris of expertise, the book could be recommended for its stated purpose. But the overlay of frequently mischievous nonsense is so thick as to almost render null and void the potential usefulness of the book as a buyer's guide, in spite of its helpful apparatus for further study, ordering of records, and hints for librarians.

A question must be asked: Would it have been possible for a similarily plotted guide to classical music on records, on a comparable level of incompetence, to find its way into print? The answer is no. Almost certainly, somewhere along the way, a publisher's reader or editor would have become suspicious and done some simple checking. The sad truth is that, in spite of the growing acceptance of jazz as a proper subject for scholarly study (and legitimate library purchases), critical standards in the field remain woefully low, or non-existent.

To put the question another way: Would the Tudors have dared to take a similar autodidactic approach to ''serious'' music, or would some built-in protective mechanism have alerted them before it was too late?

Let us hope that most of the book's users will have no time to read the ''critical'' evaluations and simply employ it as a purchasing guide. But, dear librarians, please keep it in a safe place, out of the reach of the uninitiated. We have enough problems as it is.

—**Dan Morgenstern**

Bibliography of Discographies, vol. 2: Jazz
By Daniel Allen. 1981. 239 pp.
New York: R.R. Bowker. $35.

Several years ago, the late Walter C. Allen noted that many musicologists failed to avail themselves of the extensive discographical literature devoted to black American music. He wrote, ''The academic community may come to recognize discographical research as the dedicated musicological scholarship that it really is'' (*Journal of Jazz Studies,* vol. 1, no. 2, p.

34). In compiling his *Bibliography of Discographies: Jazz,* Allen's son, Daniel, has contributed greatly to this goal, while adhering to the standards of careful scholarship set by his father in the discographical landmark *Hendersonia.*

The younger Allen's work is the second volume in a series of such bibliographies (Volume 1, devoted to discographies of classical music, was compiled by Michael Gray and Gerald Gibson). Volume 2 encompasses "discographies of jazz, blues, ragtime, gospel, and rhythm and blues music published between 1935 and 1980." By citing discographical works from such widely scattered sources as periodicals (many long-defunct), monographs, and relatively obscure privately published materials, Allen has rendered jazz researchers a monumental service.

The book is simple and intelligently arranged. Entries appear under headings which comprise a single alphabetical listing. Most of these headings are individual names; also included are record labels, performing groups, song titles, and other subjects (e.g., Montreux Jazz Festival). Under each heading, discographical works are listed alphabetically by author or title. A numeric code is used to identify the data elements provided by each discography (i.e., inclusion of non-commercial recordings, personnels, matrix numbers, indexes, release dates, take numbers, places and dates of recording, composers, and musicological details). A single index includes authors, distinctive titles, and names of series. Two additional useful lists are provided: small publishers cited and periodicals cited (with addresses).

In practice the bibliography is extremely convenient to use. To locate discographical information on Art Pepper, for example, one looks under the alto saxophonist's name and finds listed two Pepper discographies from the Japanese *Swing Journal* (1973 and 1980), Ernie Edwards's work in the Jazz Discographies Unlimited series, a revised version by Edwards and John C. Irwin, a Pepper discography in the Swedish monthly *Orkester Journalen,* and one by Alun Morgan in the British specialty publication *Discographical Forum.* Also cited are Todd Selbert's discography in Pepper's autobiography *Straight Life,* two "selected" discographies accompanying articles in *Down Beat,* and one in *Different Drummer* magazine.

In a field such as discography, knowledge is highly cumulative, with recent works supposedly incorporating and enlarging upon previous efforts. Allen is aware of this, but includes the earlier works for their historical interest. He scrupulously follows up each entry, listing any subsequently published additions or corrections.

Inevitably, there are omissions. Missing are the excellent limited edition discographies issued by New York radio station WKCR in conjunction with their marathon "festival" broadcasts. Works on Roy Eldridge (1978), Sonny Rollins (1978), Miles Davis (1979), and Louis Armstrong (1980) have appeared in this series.

Such oversights are extremely rare, however, and in no way detract from the book's usefulness. Indeed, Allen's work is a model of organization, comprehensiveness, and detail.

—**Edward Berger**

Jazz Reference and Research Materials: A Bibliography
By Eddie S. Meadows. 1981. 300 pp.
New York: Garland. $25.
(Critical Studies on Black Life and Culture, vol. 22;
Garland Reference Library of the Humanities, vol. 251.)

Meadow's attempt at providing access to the burgeoning jazz literature is a misguided and amateurish effort, bearing all the trappings of scholarship and none of its substance. This is regrettable, because a comprehensive, well-organized, and up-to-date jazz bibliography is sorely needed to replace spotty pioneering works such as Merriam's *A Bibliography of Jazz* and Reisner's *The Literature of Jazz,* selective guides such as Kennington's *The Literature of Jazz* and the more comprehensive, but cumbersome, *International Jazz Bibliography* by Carl Gregor, Duke of Mecklenburg, a revised edition of which will soon be published.

Meadows (an associate professor of music at San Diego State University) merely adds to the confusion. Poor organization, duplication of listings, inconsistency and misspellings limit its usefulness; error-ridden entries, omissions, and incorrect or misleading annotations are more serious shortcomings.

The scope of the book is "to provide a thorough survey of books, articles, and theses and dissertations written on or about specific jazz styles and jazz musicians from the turn of the century through 1978. Those materials considered most significant in and appropriate to the study of jazz subjects and individual jazz artists were the ones selected for inclusion." It contains two sections: "Jazz and its Genres" and "Reference Materials." The first section is subdivided into General, Pre-Swing, Swing, Bop and Modern, with groupings under each for books, articles, and dissertations. The second includes the following sub-categories: Bibliographies-Dictionaries-Encyclopedias, Biographies-Autobiographies, Discographies, Histories-Surveys, Technical Materials, Anthologies-Collections (Recordings), and Jazz Research Libraries. Each section has a separate index which includes authors, subjects, and performers.

One is immediately struck by the overlap between categories. For example, Meadows defines his "General" subdivision of Section I as including "information on jazz analysis and appreciation, criticism, fiction, history, influence, and jazz and the classics. In essence, this category gathers together a range of materials to provide an overall perspective on jazz, its de-velopment, and its significance." How this differs from the "Histories-Surveys" portion of Section II is beyond me. Apparently it is beyond Meadows as well since he repeats some entries in both places. For example, Whitney Balliett's *Sounds of Surprise* (sic) appears as item #3 in Section I—General and #2279 in Section II—Histories-Surveys. For good measure he also throws it into the Modern category of Section I as #1426 (here at least the title is given correctly). This duplication of entries is not an isolated occurrence but commonplace. Thus, although entries are numbered from 1 to 2563, one has no idea how many separate items are really documented. One of the most ubiquitous entries is Leonard Feather's *Encyclopedia of Jazz,* in various editions. The *New Edition of the Encyclopedia of Jazz* is listed a total of five times, with separate numbers. In Section I it appears under General (#24), Pre-Swing (#493), Bop (#1268) and Modern (#1432). Its Pre-Swing entry carries the cryptic justification "includes discussion of Louis Armstrong." In Section II it appears once (#2089).

The *Encyclopedia of Jazz In The Sixties* is close behind with three entries in Section I (one with an incorrect title) and one in Section II.

The *Encyclopedia of Jazz in the Seventies* does not make an appearance until Section II, but to make up for lost time, Meadows lists it twice on adjoining pages. It appears as #2091 with one Leonard *B.* Feather as author and a publication date of 1970. On the next page it is assigned #2094 and the author is now (correctly) Leonard *G.* Feather. Here at least the publication date is correct (1976) and the co-author, Ira Gitler, is noted.

Although confusing, this constant repetition is not as baffling as Meadows's inability to adhere to his own admittedly vague subject scheme. Under the General category of Section I, we find works on such broad topics as *Jazz Improvisation for the B-Flat Soprano Trumpet* and Rufus Reid's *The Evolving Bassist: An Aid for the Double Bass and the Four-and-Six String Electric Basses.* Reid's work does reappear later, however, in the more appropriate Technical Materials—All Purpose Improvisational and Jazz Education Materials category.

Other interesting classifications include Red Norvo under Pre-Swing. An article entitled "Bebop? One Long Search for the Right Note Says Louis Armstrong" is also under Pre-Swing, while the similar "Bebop's The Easy Way Out, Claims Louis" is under Bop. In fact, most material on Armstrong appears under Pre-Swing, while his 1936 *Swing That Music* is under Swing, presumably because the title contains that word. Similarly, the term "avant-garde" is sufficient to assign "Henry Allen Is the Most Avant Garde Trumpet Player in New York City" to the Modern category. Furthermore, this article is indexed only under its author, Don Ellis, not under Henry Red Allen.

The Modern category, which Meadows defines as "primarily concerned with the life and music of selected individuals and groups who have achieved jazz fame since the Bop era," includes articles by Rex Stewart on John Kirby and Big Sid Catlett (nos. 1947 and 1949); the latter does not appear under Catlett in the index. Other "modernists" include Zutty Singleton, Jo Jones, Tiny Grimes, and Bill Coleman. Articles on Bunny Berigan are included under both Pre-Swing and Swing, with the former (#836) not indexed under its subject, Berigan.

Meadows has special problems with discographies. Although they are assigned a separate category in Section II, one finds them scattered haphazardly throughout Section I. For example, John R. T. Davies (indexed as "Davis") and Laurie (whom Meadows has as Laurio) Wright's *Morton's Music* rightly appears under Jelly Roll Morton in the list of individual discographies in Section II. Jepsen's *Discography of Jelly Roll Morton,* however, is missing from this category, appearing only under Pre-Swing in Section I. Connor's and Hicks's *B.G. On the Record: A Biodiscography of Benny Goodman* first appears under Biographies (#2164). It reappears a few pages later under Individual Dis-

cographies with a new number (2258), a new title, *B.G. On The Road* (sic) and a new spelling for one of the authors' names. Walter C. Allen's *Hendersonia: The Music of Fletcher Henderson and his Musicians, A Biodiscography* appears in Swing (#909) and Biographies (#2170) but not Discographies. And once again Meadows has revised the title in one entry. Under Sonny Rollins in Individual Discographies we find a Ph.D. dissertation on Rollins entitled *Melodic Improvisation In American Jazz,* which has a three-page discography, but not Jepsen's Sonny Rollins discography.

Meadows has also incorporated some rather peculiar stylistic innovations. It is a common bibliographic convention to disregard initial articles in alphabetical listings of titles. Yet on pp. 9-10, heading the list of General category magazine articles, are ten titles beginning with the indefinite "a" or "an." At first, Meadows mercifully chooses to disregard the initial definite article for alphabetizing, but in the Modern section, entries 1960-1970 all begin with "the."

Other stylistic inconsistencies abound. On p. 52, two pieces from the anthology *Frontiers of Jazz* are cited (#687 and #694). One is entered under the author and the other under the title, with the author's name not even mentioned.

Despite all its sloppiness, the book might have been partially rescued by the inclusion of carefully detailed indexes to counter the poor organization and seemingly random placement of entries. The indexes, however, manage to achieve the same level of whimsy as the main body of the work. That to Section I contains many nebulous subject headings, some so broad that they are practically useless (e.g., Analyses and Interpretations). Others, such as Anthologies and Discographies, lump together two apparently unrelated topics. In his introduction the author offers some explanations for the headings, but these only complicate matters. Critics and Criticism, we are told, identifies "materials with primarily negative views on jazz," while Jazz: Classics lists "items containing primarily negative comments by classical musicians on jazz.''

Far more serious, however, are the errors of omission in the indexes. The publisher's claim that this book includes a ''detailed author, performer, and subject index'' is simply untrue. A significant portion of articles on individual musicians do not appear under the musician's name in either index. A random check of those articles in Section I clearly devoted to single artists reveals that close to half the artists named do not appear in the index. These omissions occur in all of the Section I subcategories. Some examples: from Pre-Swing: ''Don Ewell Goes Back To New Orleans Rags'' (#607) and ''Albert Nicholas! From New Orleans to Paris'' (#659); from Swing: ''Jimmy Lunceford and His Orchestra'' (#1195) and ''Harry Carney: Boss Baritone'' (#1202), which somehow becomes ''Boss Boutano'' here; from Bop: ''The Billy Eckstine Band'' (#1302) and ''The Legendary Joe Albany'' (#1398); from Modern: ''John Lewis: Success With Integrity'' (#1645) and ''Gene Ammons: Here To Stay'' (#1833). Not one of the artists mentioned in these titles appears anywhere in the index.

Those who did gain entry to the indexes are not home free. An article on alto saxophonist Willie Smith (#1251) is listed under pianist Willie ''The Lion'' Smith. Jan Evensmo appears as ''Evansmo,'' Clare Fischer as ''Fisher,'' Sadik Hakim as ''Radik,'' Bobby Jaspar as ''Jasper,'' Humphrey Lyttleton as ''N. Lyttleton,'' David A. Jasen as ''Jansen,'' Ray Bauduc as ''Bauduc,'' and Arif Mardin as ''Madin.'' Vladimir Simosko's name appears correctly in the index to Section II, but as Somosko in the index to Section I. Elsewhere he turns up as Simasko. Some authors are listed twice in one index under slightly different names (e.g. Dick Hadlock, Richard Hadlock). Some names appear differently in the two indexes: B. Rust, Brian A.L. Rust; Winthrop Sargent, Winthrop Sargeant; W. Dodds, Baby Dodds; Alan Merriam, Alan P. Merriam (incidentally, Merriam's

''Jazz Community,'' entry no. 1784, does not appear under either variant).

Misspelling is not confined to the indexes, but is one of the few consistent features of the book. The interesting cast of characters includes vocalist Better Carter, Cannonbass Adderley, Paul Whitman, Roy Draper, Kaisel Marshall, Jessy Stacy, Paul Gonzales, Red Nicholas, Freddie Gofe, and Sonny Greene (former Ellington drummer).

The Technical Materials portion of Section II avoids some of the inconsistencies and irrelevancies of the rest of the work. It is intelligently arranged, grouping musical instructional aids by instrumental families. Yet even here there are redundancies and glaring omissions from the index. For example, items #2499-2500 are method books for bass by Ron Carter, but he does not appear in the index.

To this point we have concentrated on organizational and stylistic difficulties at the expense of content. From the author's vague statement of scope it is hard to establish the criteria by which he chose items for inclusion. In many cases he seems to have arbitrarily listed brief articles on an artist while ignoring more comprehensive studies. Among longer works, the more glaring oversights include Mercer Ellington's book on his father, Chris Albertson's on Bessie Smith, Howard Waters's *Jack Teagarden's Music,* W.E. Timner's Ellington discography, Jan Evensmo's individual ''solography'' series, and the primary discographical sources on John Coltrane: David Wild's *The Recordings of John Coltrane* and Brian Davis's *John Coltrane Discography.* These omissions are hard to fathom given some of the peculiar items which *are* included. For example, one finds the *International Who's Who, 1965-66* listed as entry #499 under Pre-Swing with the all-purpose justification ''includes information on Louis Armstrong.'' So do the *Encyclopedia Britannica,* the *World Book,* and countless other general reference works.

Meadows does not discuss his annotation policy, but he seems to use short notes to identify the subject of articles when that subject is not evident from the title. Thus, "Mellow Mc-Duff" (#1838) is scrupulously labeled "concerns Jack McDuff." "For Louis Armstrong at 70" (#902) bears the somewhat superfluous annotation: "the impact of Louis Armstrong on jazz." Yet such enigmatic titles as "In Walked Ray" (#1737), "In His Own Right" (#1835), "Caught In The Act" (#1977), and "My Best On Wax" (#782) are devoid of explanation.

Annotations for longer works vary from unclear and misleading to completely incorrect. In the first category we find Chilton's *Who's Who of Jazz* described as containing "biographical information on over one thousand American jazz musicians before 1920." Does this mean musicians who lived and died before 1920? Or information up to 1920 on musicians who may have lived beyond that point? (What Chilton's book actually contains is information on musicians *born* before 1920.)

Of the misleading variety: Meadows concludes his discussion of Frank Tirro's *Jazz: A History* with "examples are drawn from the jazz collection at the Smithsonian." This is an oblique reference to the *Smithsonian Collection of Classic Jazz*, a widely circulated record set, not an archival collection. Readers may also be interested to learn that *Jazz Records, 1897-1942*, entry #2223 (the 1970 edition of Brian Rust's work, from which Meadows has for some reason removed the author's name), includes recordings "up to the Petrillo band" (quite a hot combo in its day).

Factual errors include a reference to Fats Waller, James P. Johnson, Fletcher Henderson, and Don Redman as "Chicago musicians" (#2101), and a summary of Jepsen's *Jazz Records* which concludes, "cross-references are good, but the index is limited" (there is no index). We are also told that a discography of Sidney Bechet (#2250) "covers Bechet's entire career and includes recordings . . . from 1921 to 1964." Apparently this work covers somewhat more than Bechet's "entire career," which presumably ended with his death in 1959.

Some of the opinions expressed by Meadows will also raise a few eyebrows. For example, he correctly warns us about the dangers of Tirro's *Jazz: A History* but uses the phrase "painstaking research" in his evaluation of Ross Russell's fantasies about Charlie Parker, *Bird Lives!*

We have barely scratched the surface in our assessment of this work, which will no doubt be well received by librarians and educators unfamiliar with the field. Readers will have plenty of time for a more detailed evaluation; the publisher notes that *Jazz Reference and Research Materials* is printed on acid-free paper and, unfortunately, will be with us for about 250 years.

—**Edward Berger**

Two other recent works have entered the field of jazz bibliography:

Bibliography of Black Music. By Dominique-René De Lerma. 1981. Vol. 1: Reference Materials (124 pp.); vol. 2: Afro-American Idioms (220 pp.). The Greenwood Encyclopedia of Black Music. Westport, Conn.: Greenwood Press.

Jazz Bibliographie: International Literature on Jazz, Blues, Spirituals, Gospel and Ragtime Music. By Bernhard Hefele. 1981. 368 pp. Munich: K.G. Saur.

Reviews of these works will appear in the next volume of *ARJS*.

THOMAS G. EVERETT

ADDENDA:
MORE CURRENT ENGLISH-LANGUAGE
JAZZ PERIODICALS

Thomas G. Everett, Director of the Harvard University Band, contributed an article, "An Annotated List of English-Language Jazz Periodicals" to *The Journal of Jazz Studies,* vol. 3, no. 2, pp. 47-57. As a continuing service to jazz scholars, he updated his original list in three subsequent *JJS* addenda, which appeared in vol. 4, no. 1, pp. 110-111; vol. 4, no. 2, pp. 94-97; and vol. 5, no. 2, pp. 99-103. *The Annual Review of Jazz Studies* will continue to publish addenda to his listing in this and future volumes. Readers interested in obtaining back copies of *JJS* containing Mr. Everett's listings should write the editors of *ARJS,* c/o Transaction Books, Rutgers University, New Brunswick, New Jersey 08903.

—*The Editors*

BELL'S NEW MUSIC NEWSLETTER
CHIMES
Bell's New Music Newsletter (JJS, vol. 3, no. 2, p. 48) and *Chimes,* its successor, have discontinued publication.

HONG KONG JAZZ RECORD SOCIETY
  Roger Parry, Secretary
  P.O. Box 10536
  GPO Hong Kong
It is not clear how often this newsletter of the Hong Kong Record Society is printed. It is intended for the enthusiastic "fan," and the issue I reviewed (no. 30) deals with traditional and early jazz artists/records. The newsletter is chatty, enjoyable, and makes references to items of note appearing in other periodicals.

INTERPLAY (monthly, $12 per year)
  Berigan Taylor, Editor
  3905 Piedmont Avenue
  Oakland, California 94611
In a newspaper format, *Interplay* has listings, featured artists, and items on jazz and related music in the Bay Area.

JAZZ AT RONNIE SCOTT'S (monthly, membership approximately $10 per year)
  47 Frith Street
  London W1 V5TE, England
This 12-page magazine has pictures and promotion for bookings at Ronnie Scott's Club but also includes reviews and complete listings of record shops, club dates, concerts, freelance and jazz activities in London. Articles emphasize artists appearing at Scott's.

JAZZ AT THE PIZZA EXPRESS
(monthly, annual membership, approximately $10)
  10 Dean Street
  London W1, England
This periodical promotes the activities of the string of Pizza Express clubs in London, but also includes concert and record reviews, profiles, and listings of jazz activities in London.

JAZZ RAG (monthly, $5 per year)
  J. Henry, B. Scott, Editors
  P.O. Box 1124
  Berkeley, California 94701
Jazz Rag is a four-page publication of recent record views often dealing with the less commercial jazz recordings. The recordings are categorized as modern, traditional, or avant-garde.

JAZZ SPOTLITE NEWS
(African-American Classical Music/Jazz;
bimonthly, $10 per year/$15 for two years)
   Jon Saunders, Editor-in-Chief
   701 Seventh Avenue, Suite 9 West
   New York, New York 10036
Printed in newspaper form, the intent of this
periodical is to report and review happenings
of non-commercial jazz and black musicians' views. The same major concerts or
artists may be reviewed by several writers to
offer more in-depth observation. The paper
includes musician advertisements, editori-
als, individual's overviews and recommended recordings of specific periods/
styles, and features on musicians. Musicians
such as Benny Powell, Frank Foster, and
Larry Ridley are among the contributors.

KLACTO (monthly except July, $7 per
year)
   Mike Bloom, Editor
   916 McCully Street
   Honolulu, Hawaii 96826
Klacto (short for Klactoveesedstene) is Hawaii's jazz newsletter. In a $5^1/_2'' \times 8^1/_2''$ format, *Klacto* is newsy, with record reviews,
interviews and information on local clubs
and performers.

MICROGRAPHY
Correction: In *JJS* vol. 5, no. 2, p. 102, the
listing for this valuable periodical incorrectly
stated that it had originally been published in
Dutch and only recently in English. The author is indebted to Helmut Schwarzer for
noting that *Micrography,* while published in
the Netherlands, has been published in English since its inception in December 1968.

NOT JUST JAZZ (The Uncommon
Denomination; two issues per year, 50¢
per copy)
   Randy Fordyce, Managing Editor
   P.O. Box 326
   New York, New York 10024
Issue no. 1 of *Not Just Jazz* is in a newspaper
format of 8 pages and includes articles by
Harold Danko and Chick Corea. It intends to
be a format of discussion for all the arts.

NYC JAZZ (monthly except August and
January, distributed free at various tourist
and music centers in the greater New York
area)
   Bob Frenay, Jr., Editor
   436 West Broadway
   New York, New York 10012
NYC Jazz is a handy, slick periodical for
anyone interested in jazz clubs and concerts
in New York. Clubs are listed alphabetically
with addresses and phone numbers. A map
of the city, with all jazz clubs indicated, is
very valuable for the visitor to New York.
Although the bulk is advertisements, there
are one or two interviews/articles.

*OUTLOOK: THE CREATIVE MUSIC
QUARTERLY* (four issues per year, with
membership in Creative Music Foundation,
$25).
   Karl Hans Berger, Ingrid Berger, Artistic
   Directors
   P.O. Box 671
   Woodstock, New York 12498
Outlook, in newspaper form, offers brief ar-
ticles, interviews, and concert listings of
new music, especially works associated with
the Creative Music Foundation. Authors in-
clude Karl Berger, John Zorn, and Leo
Smith.

RADIO FREE JAZZ

Radio Free Jazz has changed its name to *Jazz Times*.

THE VICTORY MUSIC FOLK AND JAZZ REVIEW (monthly, $8.00)

Chris Lunn, Editor
Victory Music
Box 36
Tillicum, Tacoma, Washington 98492

The Victory Music Folk and Jazz Review is an underground newspaper dealing with folk-jazz in Washington. The publication contains a very complete monthly calendar of jazz in the area, information and reviews on local clubs, and a great many reviews of recent jazz recordings, as well as short reviews of other publications.

RESEARCH NOTES

As a service to the field of jazz scholarship, *ARJS* will publish brief Research Notes as space permits. Comments from readers augmenting articles published in past volumes, as well as solicitations of assistance in current jazz research projects, will be considered for publication under this rubric.

HUTCHERSON DISCOGRAPHY

For a discography of Bobby Hutcherson, I am seeking private tapes and photographs. All assistance will be appreciated and acknowledged.

Gordon F. X. Allen
156-36 92nd Street
Queens, New York 11414

ELLINGTON BIBLIOGRAPHY

For an annotated bibliography of Duke Ellington, I would appreciate hearing from authors and/or collectors who have information about Ellington material in print. All contributors will be acknowledged.

Lawrence Fried
2050 East 18th Street
Apartment F9
Brooklyn, New York 11229

ALAN P. MERRIAM: AN ADDENDUM

Frank J. Gillis published a bibliography of the writings on jazz of the late Alan P. Merriam in the final issue of *JJS* (vol. 6, no. 1, Spring/Summer 1979, pp 93-95). Mr. Gillis has since identified two additional items that should have been included in the list:

"The African Background: An Answer to Barry Ulanov," *Record Changer* 9 (November 1952): 7-8.

"Jazz and African Studies," in *Down Beat Music 1961* (Chicago: Maher Publications, 1960), p. 42.

Most of the previous issues of the JOURNAL OF JAZZ STUDIES, the predecessor to ANNUAL REVIEW OF JAZZ STUDIES, are available through Transaction Books, Rutgers University, New Brunswick, New Jersey 08903. Volume 6, number 1 of JOURNAL OF JAZZ STUDIES includes a cumulative index to all previous issues.